THE MIPS PROGRAMMER'S HANDBOOK

**Erin Farquhar
and Philip Bunce**

MORGAN KAUFMANN PUBLISHERS
SAN FRANCISCO, CALIFORNIA

Editor   *Bruce M. Spatz*
Design, Project Management
     and Electronic Composition   *Professional Book Center*
Cover Art   *Mary Chenoweth*

MIPS is a trademark of MIPS Computer Systems, Inc.
UNIX is a registered trademark of UNIX System Laboratories, Inc.

Library of Congress **Cataloging-in-Publication Data**
Farquhar, Erin.
   The MIPS programmer's handbook   /   Erin Farquhar and Philip Bunce.
      p.   cm.
   Includes index.
   ISBN 1-55860-297-6
   1. Embedded computer systems—Programming.   2. MIPS1
(Microprocessor)   I. Bunce, Philip.   II. Title.
QA76.6.F375   1994
005.265—dc20

                                                             94-396
                                                             CIP

Printed in the United States of America
04 03 02 01   10 9 8 7 6

Morgan Kaufmann Publishers, Inc.
Editorial Offices
340 Pine St., Sixth Floor
San Francisco, CA 94104

Contents

Preface

Our main purpose in writing this book is to show how to write programs for embedded systems that use the MIPS processor. This includes the R2000 and R3000 designed by MIPS Computer Systems, and all its derivatives.

The MIPS architecture was developed at Stanford University by John Hennessy, together with of a group of graduate students. After completing the project in 1984, he co-founded MIPS Computer Systems, Inc., which was formed to build high-performance UNIX workstations using his new architecture.

The chip is now being manufactured by five licensed vendors. Since its original developement for use in UNIX workstations, it has attracted considerable following in the embedded-systems community and is now used for building such things as laser printers, network controllers, and X terminals. As computer consultants hired to provide software support for developers of MIPS-based embedded systems, we discovered that although there are an adequate number of documents describing the hardware architecture, there was almost nothing available that described how the chip is programmed. It was to meet this need that we decided to write our book. The topics we cover include software conventions, initializing the processor, flushing the caches, and exception handling, using example programs with line-by-line explanations.

The authors gratefully acknowledge the valuable critical help received from the following reviewers: John Hennessy (Stanford University), Charles Price (SGI/MIPS Technology), and David Meyer (Purdue Universiy), Mike Amy (LSI Logic), Phil Bourakis (IDT), Jim Alsup (EPI), and Dominic Sweetman (Algorithmics). Special thanks to Bruce Spatz at Morgan Kaufmann Publishers and Lee and Jennifer Ballentine at Professional Book Center, without whose encouragement we might not have finished this book (at least in this century).

To provide a discussion forum for MIPS programmers, the authors have established an electronically-delivered free newsletter. To subscribe to this newsletter, do one of the following: Send Internet email to maug@carmel.com, subject "info," or call our BBS at 408-626-4068, login "maug," no password. The authors are consultants who can be contacted by writing to 100 Dolores Street, Suite 242, Carmel CA 93923, or by sending email to elf@carmel.com or pjb@carmel.com.

Erin Farquhar
Philip Bunce

1

Introduction

This book explains how to write programs for embedded systems that use the MIPS1 processor. The MIPS1 processor includes the R2000 and R3000 designed by MIPS Computer Systems, and all of the derived processors from the licensed semiconductor vendors. But it does not include the R4000 and R6000 and their derivatives.

The MIPS1 architecture has a number of current implementations, which differ in their hardware support for such things as virtual memory, floating-point operations, and caching schemes. In view of this, we decided that for the purposes of this book we would define a "base architecture" which includes the instructions and registers that are common to most MIPS1 implementations. There is no actual physical implementation of this architecture—all the commercial implementations include various extensions.

Because our book focuses on embedded systems, we decided to exclude the Memory Management Unit (MMU) from the definition of the base architecture. In general, only programmers building "general-purpose" computers (i.e. systems that have dynamically- loaded programs) will use an MMU. The few embedded systems with an MMU usually use a commercial operating system such as UNIX to manage the MMU, and issues having to do with porting UNIX are beyond the scope of this book. However, we did include the floating-point instructions, because they are generated directly by the compiler, whether or not the CPU actually contains a hardware Floating-Point Unit.

We have described the MIPS1 base architecture from the point of view of the assembly- and C-language programmer. The topics covered are those that are relevant to engineers writing system-level programs for MIPS-based embedded systems, and include software conventions, initializing the processor, and exception-handling. We have also provided an instruction set reference, organized as one page per instruction, that describes the instructions available to assembly-language programmers, as opposed to the hardware-level instruction set documented in chip vendors' data books.

We do not intend this book to serve as a complete description of the MIPS1 architecture. We feel that such a purpose is better served by the documentation provided by the individual chip manufacturers and software vendors, especially in view of the fact that the extensions to the base architecture are so varied. Thus we intend this book to be read in conjunction with the documentation supplied by the vendor. However, for those readers without such documentation, the overview of the architecture in Appendix A, together with the instruction reference in Chapter 5, should suffice for an understanding of the example programs.

The example programs used throughout this book were compiled and assembled using the MIPS software tools provided by MIPS Computer Systems, Inc., hosted on a Sun Workstation. The programs were tested on a variety of R3000 single-board computers, all of which had at least two serial ports (using the 2681) and one Megabyte of RAM, occupying physical addresses 0x0000.0000–0x0fffff. After compilation, the object file was blown into PROM, which was plugged into the PROM socket addresses 0x1fc0.0000–0x1fc1.ffff.

In each chapter the program examples are explained line-by-line within the text, and their complete listing is provided at the end of that chapter in the section called "Program Listings." Note that in a sequence of programs, changes from one to the next are marked with side bars.

To permit the example programs to be applicable to all MIPS1 implementations, code that is implementation-dependent has been isolated in the include file machine.h (shown in Appendix D).

The reader who is unfamiliar with the MIPS architecture should finish reading this chapter and then read Appendix A, followed by Chapter 5, and then Chapters 2 through 4.

The example programs are available via Internet email, and we have provided instructions on obtaining this feature later in the book.

The remaining chapters of this book are organized as follows:

Chapter 2

This chapter discusses the MIPS software conventions, including register names and usage, as well as the conventions for procedure calls and the format of the stack.

Chapter 3

This chapter explains how to initialize the processor in a bare machine environment, including the code necessary to copy initialized data from PROM into random access memory (RAM), and to size and flush the caches.

Chapter 4

This chapter explains how to write exception handlers. We begin with an example that uses a single interrupt source. Subsequent examples add a second interrupt source, show how to implement nested interrupts, and show how to write exception handlers in C. The final example shows a multiple-interrupt system with priorities, using exception handlers written in both C and assembly language. This chapter also gives examples of using the software interrupts and an exception-handling example for unaligned load and store word operations. We also discuss how to calculate interrupt latency.

Chapter 5

This chapter contains descriptions of all the MIPS1 instructions accepted by the assembler, arranged alphabetically by instruction mnemonic. For each instruction we give the syntax, possible exceptions that can be raised, and examples of how the different addressing modes used by the instruction are expanded into sequences of machine instructions by the assembler. We also have included a description of each of the assembler directives used in our example programs.

Appendices

Appendix A provides an overview of the MIPS architecture. For readers who are unfamiliar with the MIPS architecture and who do not have any other MIPS documentation, the material in Appendix A, together with the listing of instructions and assembler directives in Chapter 5, should provide enough background material to understand the example programs.

Appendix B contains a summary of MIPS instructions and the addressing modes permitted for each instruction.

Appendix C contains a program that generates the correct prologue and epilogue for a specified function.

Appendix D lists all the include files used by the example programs.

Appendix E contains the library functions used by the example C programs.

Appendix F lists the semiconductor companies licensed to manufacture the MIPS processor and the software companies that provide MIPS software development tools for the C language.

2

Software Conventions

2.1 INTRODUCTION

This chapter describes the software conventions defined by the MIPS assembler and compiler. These conventions hold for all MIPS assemblers and compilers, and it is important to adhere to them when you are writing assembly-language routines that will be called from C, or if you call C routines from your assembly-language program.

2.2 REGISTER-USAGE CONVENTIONS

The MIPS register names and their usage are shown in Tables 2.1–2.3. Although both the hardware and software names are recognized by the assembler, most programs will use the register names defined in `mips.h`. This file contains the register definitions in the include file `regdef.h`, which is supplied by MIPS Computer Systems, Inc. It also contains the definitions for coprocessors 0 and 1 registers and bit names. `mips.h` is reproduced in Appendix D.

   The assembler preprocesses all files using the standard C preprocessor, and uses this mechanism to implement file inclusion and macro definitions.

   Executable files for the MIPS processor consist of three main sections: `.text`, `.data`, and `.bss`, used to hold code, initialized global data, and uni-

Table 2.1   CPU General-Purpose Register Usage

Hardware Name	Software Name	Name in mips.h	Usage
$0	—	zero	Constant zero
$1	$at	AT	Assembler temp
$2–$3	—	v0–v1	Function return
$4–$7	—	a0–a3	Incoming args
$8–$15	—	t0–t7	Temporaries
$16–$23	—	s0–s7	Saved temporaries
$24–$25	—	t8–t9	Temporaries
$26–$27	$kt0–$kt1	k0–k1	Exception handling
$28	$gp	gp	Global data pointer
$29	$sp	sp	Stack pointer
$30	$fp	s8	Saved temporary
$31	—	ra	Return address

Table 2.2   Coprocessor 0 (System Control Processor) Register Usage

Proper Name	Hardware Name	Name in mips.h	Access
Bad Virtual Address	$8	C0_BADVA	r
Status Register	$12	C0_SR	r/w*
Cause Register	$13	C0_CAUSE	r**
Exception Program Counter Register	$14	C0_EPC	r
Revision Register	$15	C0_PRID	r

* All bits are read/write except the Ts bit, which is read-only.
** All bits are read-only except the Sw bits, which are read/write.

Table 2.3   Coprocessor 1 (Floating-Point) Register Usage

Hardware Name	Name in mips.h	Usage
$f0–$f3	—	Function return
$f4–$f11	—	Temporaries
$f12–$f15	—	Incoming args
$f16–$f19	—	Temporaries
$f20–$f31	—	Saved temporaries

nitialized global data, respectively. To support the use of the Global Data Pointer Register (called gp and described later in this section), two additional sections are defined: .sdata and .sbss. These sections are used for initialized and uninitialized data that will be referenced relative to gp. Separate sections are defined for these references because the gp-referencing mechanism is limited to a 64 kilobyte (64K) area of memory, and thus not all variables in a large program can be placed in these sections. The default for most tool sets is to place all variables of 8 bytes or fewer in .sdata or .sbss, although this can usually be overridden to include more of your program's data if space permits. It is also common for compilers to put various kinds of constant data in additional sections. For example, constant data that is read-only is often put in a section called .rdata.

From the point of view of register-usage conventions, there are basically three programming environments: initialization, subroutine, and exception handler.

The initialization environment is the least restricted in that there is no program state to be saved, and all the registers are available for use. In the subroutine environment, register usage is more restricted because the caller's state has to be saved and some of the registers are needed for passing arguments and results. Exception handlers are similar to subroutines, except that their register usage is even more restricted, because almost all the registers may already be in use by the interrupted program. In fact, only k0 and k1 can be used as temporaries, and then only while interrupts are disabled.

When a procedure is called, the first four scalar arguments are passed in a0–a3 and any additional arguments are passed in the stack. Floating-point arguments are passed in $f12–$f14 and in the stack. The register usage for those cases where there is a mixture of scalar and floating-point arguments is shown in Table 2.4.

Table 2.4   Mixed-Argument Register Usage

Argument Type				Location			
ARG1	ARG2	ARG3	ARG4	ARG1	ARG2	ARG3	ARG4
Float	Scalar	Float		$f12	a2	Stack	
Float	Scalar	Scalar		$f12	a2	a3	
Scalar	Scalar	Scalar	Float	a0	a1	a2	Stack
Scalar	Scalar	Float		a0	a1	a2 & a3	
Scalar	Float			a0	a2 & a3		

Scalar values are returned from procedures in v0 and v1. Actually, ints, chars, shorts, longs, and pointers are returned only in v0. Floating-point values are returned in $f0–$f3.

Two types of registers can be used by a function to hold temporary values. The first type is referred to simply as "temporaries." Values in these registers are not preserved across a function call, and these registers do not have to be saved before they are used. The second type are "saved" registers. The values in these registers are preserved across function calls, but to guarantee this they must be saved before they are used and restored before exiting the function.

Registers that can be used by the procedure without being saved are a0–a3, t0–t9, v0 and v1 for scalar values, and $f0–$f19 for floating-point values. Keep in mind when using these registers that they are *not* preserved across calls.

Registers that can be used as temporaries and whose values *are* preserved across calls are s0–s7, and s8 if it has not been allocated for use as the frame pointer; for floating-point values, registers $f20–$f30. These registers must be saved before they are used and then restored before exiting the function.

The Global Data Pointer Register, gp (by convention $28), permits a 64K area of memory-resident data to be accessed with a single instruction. The label _gp is initialized by the linker with a 32-bit base address that, when combined with the 16-bit offset in a load or store instruction, accesses a range of 64K. gp relative addressing is used for data in the .sdata and .sbss sections.

By default, data declared using the .comm or .lcomm directive is linked to the .sbss section if it is 8 bytes or fewer. This maximum size can be changed by using the -G command line option. Suppose your program has an uninitialized data structure of 256 bytes called fred, which you declare as follows:

```
.comm fred,256
```

To cause the assembler to assign fred a gp-relative address, use the -G option:

```
as -o test.o -G 256 test.s
```

To permit gp-relative addressing to be used, the gp register must be initialized with the value of the linker-defined symbol _gp:

```
la      gp,_gp
```

To ensure that a gp-relative variable declared in another module will be referenced in the current module using gp-relative addressing, the variable must be explicitly imported, and its size must be specified:

```
.extern fred,256
```

To select this addressing mode for a load or store instruction, the second instruction operand must be the variable's symbolic name. For example,

```
lw t0,fred
```

2.3 STACK USAGE CONVENTIONS

By convention, the stack grows toward lower addresses in memory. The stack pointer register, sp ($29), points to the lowest stack word address (the "top" of the stack) and items on the stack are referenced as positive word offsets from sp.

All the stack space required by a function (its so-called activation record) must be explicitly allocated at one time, at the beginning of the function, and must be aligned on a doubleword boundary.

Stack space is allocated by subtracting the size of the stack (plus any padding required to maintain its required doubleword alignment) from the stack pointer register. For example, to allocate 24 bytes of stack storage:

```
subu     sp,24          # subtract 24 from register sp
```

The unsigned version of the instruction is used because addresses are unsigned. Because we have allocated 24 bytes of space, the legal references in the current activation record are 0(sp), 4(sp), 8(sp), 12(sp), 16(sp), and 20(sp).

On return from a procedure, the activation record is deallocated by incrementing the stack pointer by the same amount it was decremented when the procedure was called.

```
addu     sp,24          # add 24 to register sp
```

By convention, items are "pushed" on the stack by storing them to positive word offsets from the stack pointer, such as

```
sw       ra,20(sp)      # load ra from sp+20
```

and restored from the stack using a load from an sp-relative address:

```
lw       ra,20(sp)
```

Nonleaf functions (functions that call other functions) must allocate a minimum of 24 bytes of stack space: four words reserved for a0–a3, one word for the return address, and one word of padding to maintain the doubleword alignment. Space must be reserved on the stack for a0–a3 so the called function can save registers a0–a3 in the caller's stack area. Although this convention was originally added to support functions that accept a variable number of arguments, compilers now routinely use this area whenever they need to save registers a0–a3. Note that this means that whenever you allocate a stack area, the stack pointer must be set at least 24 bytes below the top of that area to allow for the possibility that your first function requires this save area.

A function's activation record contains, in the order of ascending memory addresses:

1. Space for a0–a3
2. Arguments passed to called functions (outgoing arguments)
3. Saved floating-point registers on 8-byte boundary (lowest numbered register first)
4. Saved registers (lowest numbered register first)
5. Space for local variables allocated by the function

Figure 2.1 shows the layout of the stack for a procedure func. func is called by main, which passes it five arguments—four in registers and one in the stack. So func has the following stack requirements:

1. A maximum of 7 outgoing arguments
2. Four saved floating-point registers
3. Five saved registers
4. Sixteen words of local variable space

Note that one word of padding is required to doubleword-align the floating-point register save area, and another word of padding is required following the integer-register save area to maintain the doubleword alignment of the stack.

Referring to Figure 2.1, the .frame directive specifies the size of the stack context allocated for the function, so this information is available for source-level debuggers. The user defines a virtual frame pointer, pointing to the lowest addressed word location in the previous activation record (i.e., the previous stack pointer), as shown in Figure 2.1. The frame pointer is "virtual" in the sense that it may or may not have a register allocated for it (usually it doesn't).

The .frame directive is used with three parameters: (1) the register relative to which the frame pointer is defined (by convention sp), (2) the location

Code

```
main:                          func:
     li    t0,5                    .frame  sp,136,ra
     sw    t0,4*4(sp)              subu    sp,34*4
     li    a3,4                    sw      ra,16*4(sp)
     li    a2,3                    sw      s3,15*4(sp)
     li    a1,2                    sw      s2,14*4(sp)
     li    a0,1                    sw      s1,13*4(sp)
     jal   func                    sw      s0,12*4(sp)
     j     ra                      s.d     $f22,10*4(sp)
                                   s.d     $f20,8*4(sp)
                           # incoming args: a0..a3 38*4(sp)..
                           # locals 16 words: 18*4(sp)..
                           # 10 temp registers available [t0..t9]
                           # 5 saved registers available [ra s0..]
                           # 4 saved floating-point registers [f20..]
                           # max 7 outgoing args: a0..a3 4*4(sp)..
```

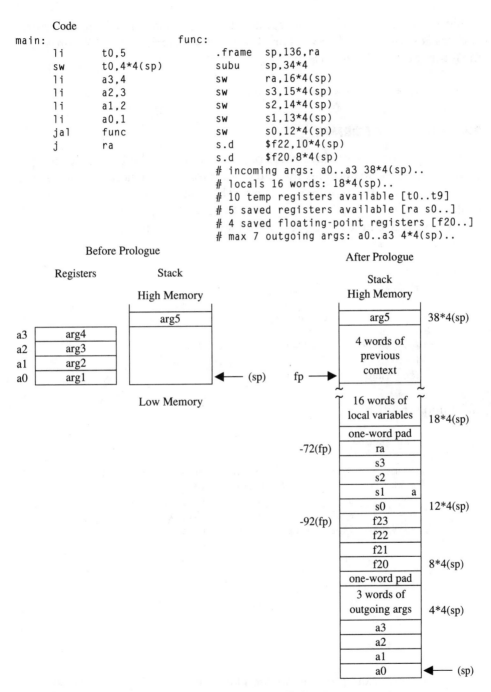

Figure 2.1   Stack Format for Procedure Calls

of the frame pointer relative to sp, and (3) the register in which the return address is saved (usually $31). For example, for a stack size of 24 words and the return address saved in $31:

```
.frame    sp,24,ra
```

2.4 PROCEDURE FORMAT

A procedure consists of three basic parts: a prologue, the body, and an epilogue. The prologue specifies the entry point for the function, allocates stack space, and saves the required registers. The epilogue restores the registers, deallocates the stack, and returns control to the caller.

Here are a simple prologue and epilogue for a leaf function:

```
        .ent func
func:
        ###########################################
        #                                         #
        #              Function body              #
        #                                         #
        ###########################################
        j          ra          # return to caller
        .end func
```

and a nonleaf function:

```
        .ent func
func:
        .frame     sp,24,ra      # declare virtual frame pointer
        .mask      0x80000000,-4 # declare saved register ra
        subu       sp,24         # allocate space for stack
        sw         ra,20(sp)     # save ra on stack
        ###########################################
        #                                         #
        #              Function body              #
        #                                         #
        ###########################################
        lw         ra,20(sp)     # restore ra from stack
        addu       sp,24         # deallocate stack
        j          ra            # return to caller
        .end func
```

In the above examples, the function label func: defines the entry point of the function and is nonoptional. The optional .ent/.end directives are used to inform the assembler of the beginning and end of the function, allowing the disassembler to produce more informative program listings. The .mask directive declares which registers have been saved, allowing the debugger to locate variables that have been saved in the stack. For example, in the statement

```
.mask     0x80000000,-4
```

the first parameter, 0x80000000, is a 32-bit bit mask that specifies which of the general-purpose registers have been saved in the stack. Each mask bit represents one general-purpose register, with bit 0 representing $0, bit 1 representing $1, and so on. Setting the bit means the register is saved in the stack. So with 0x80000000, only $31 is saved. The second parameter, -4, specifies the location of the highest addressed saved register relative to the frame pointer, which is 4 bytes fewer than fp.

For the convenience of the user, a program, genproc, is given in Appendix B. This program generates the correct prologue and epilogue for a specified function.

2.5 PROGRAM LISTINGS

The following example programs illustrate the preceding discussion.

2.5.1 Example 1: A Simple Leaf Function

This function computes the length of a string whose address is passed in a0. The end of the string is indicated by a byte of zero.

```
        .globl f1     # export function f1

        .ent f1       # start of function f1
f1:     # simple leaf function
        .frame sp,0,ra      # frame pointer is sp+0, return address in ra
        # incoming args: a0..a3 & 4*4(sp)..
        # registers available: t0..t9
        # a0 = addr of string
        move    t1,a0       # move contents of a0 into t1
1:      lbu     t0,(a0)     # load unsigned byte pointed to by a0 into t0
        addu    a0,1        # add 1 to a0
        bne     t0,zero,1b  # branch back to 1 if t0!=zero
        subu    v0,a0,t1    # subtract t1 from a0, result in v0
        subu    v0,1        # subtract 1 from v0
        # v0 = length of string
        # return values: v0..v1
        j       ra          # return to caller
        .end f1       # end of function f1
```

2.5.2 Example 2: Leaf Function with Local Array

This function computes the length of a string whose address is passed in a0.
The end of the string is indicated by a byte of zero. Before its length is computed, it is copied into a local array.

```
        .globl f2
        .ent f2
f2:     # leaf function with local array (96 bytes)
        .frame  sp,96,ra
        subu    sp,24*4 /* 24 words = 96 bytes */
        # incoming args: a0..a3 & (4+24)*4(sp)..
        # registers available: t0..t9
        # a0 = addr of string
        # copy string to local array
        addu    a1,sp,0         # addr of local array
1:      lbu     t1,(a0)
        sb      t1,(a1) # store byte from t1 to address pointed to by a1
        addu    a0,1
        addu    a1,1
        bne     t1,zero,1b

        # measure the length
        addu    a0,sp,0         # address of local array
        move    t1,a0
1:      lbu     t0,(a0)
        addu    a0,1
        bne     t0,zero,1b
        subu    v0,a0,t1
        subu    v0,1
        # v0 = length of string
        # return values: v0..v1
        addu    sp,24*4
        j       ra
        .end f2
```

2.5.3 Example 3: Simple Nonleaf Function

In this example, f3 calls f8, passing it two arguments. The first argument is
the value 1, passed in a0, and the second argument is an incoming argument
to f3, passed in a1.

```
        .globl f3
        .ent f3
f3:     # simple nonleaf function
        .mask   0x80000000,-4   # register ra is at fp-4
```

```
        .frame sp,96,ra
        subu    sp,(4+1+1)*4        # min allocation 24 bytes
                                    # a0..a3 ra +1 align
        sw      ra,5*4(sp)
        # incoming args: a0..a3 & (4+(4+1+1))*4(sp)..
        # registers available: t0..t9
        move    a1,a0
        li      a0,1  # load 1 into a0
        jal     f8    # call function f8
        # return values: v0..v1
        lw      ra,5*4(sp)          # load a word from sp+20 into ra
        addu    sp,(4+1+1)*4
        j       ra
        .end f3
```

2.5.4 Example 4: Nonleaf Function
That Saves Three Registers

This function is passed two arguments—the address of an array of pointers to
strings in a0, and the address of a printf format string in a1. For each string
in the array, f1 is called to compute the length, and then printf is called to
print the string itself and its length.

```
        .globl f4
        .ent f4
f4:     # nonleaf function that uses 3 save registers
        .mask   0x80e00000,-4
        .frame sp,32,ra
        subu    sp,(4+4)*4          # a0..a3 ra s0..s2
        sw      ra,8*4(sp)          # store ra on the stack at sp+32
        sw      s2,7*4(sp)
        sw      s1,6*4(sp)
        sw      s0,5*4(sp)
        # incoming args: a0..a3 & (4+(4+4))*4(sp)..
        # registers available: t0..t9 s0..s1
        move    s0,a0
        move    s1,a1
1:      lw      a0,(s0)
        beq     a0,zero,1f
        jal     f1
        move    a0,s1
        lw      a1,(s0)
        move    a2,v0
        jal     printf
        addu    s0,4
        b       1b                  # branch back to 1:
```

```
1:      # no return value
        # return values: v0..v1
        lw      s0,5*4(sp)
        lw      s1,6*4(sp)
        lw      s2,7*4(sp)
        lw      ra,8*4(sp)
        addu    sp,(4+4)*4
        j       ra
        .end f4
```

2.5.5 Example 5: Nonleaf Function That Uses Four Save Registers

This function is passed two arguments—the address of an array of pointers to strings in a0, and the address of a printf format string in a1. Each string in the array is copied to a local array, and then f1 is called to compute the length and printf to print the string itself and its length.

```
        .globl f5
        .ent f5
f5:     # nonleaf function that uses 4 save registers
        # and a 256-byte array
        .mask   0x80f00000,-260
        .frame  sp,296,ra
        subu    sp,(4+5+64+1)*4  # a0..a3 ra s0..s3 256 bytes
+1 align
        sw      ra,9*4(sp)
        sw      s3,8*4(sp)
        sw      s2,7*4(sp)
        sw      s1,6*4(sp)
        sw      s0,5*4(sp)
        # incoming args: a0..a3 & (4+(4+5+64+1))*4(sp)..
        # registers available: t0..t9 s0..s1
        move    s0,a0
        move    s1,a1               # save the format string
2:      lw      a0,(s0)
        beq     a0,zero,2f

        # copy the string
        addu    a2,sp,(10*4)        # addr of local array
1:      lbu     t1,(a0)
        sb      t1,(a2)
        addu    a0,1
        addu    a2,1
        bne     t1,zero,1b
```

```
          # count its length
          addu    a0,sp,(10*4)            # addr of local array
          jal     f1

          move    a0,s1                   # format string
          addu    a1,sp,(10*4)            # addr of local array
          move    a2,v0                   # length
          jal     printf
          addu    s0,4
          b       2b
2:        # no return value
          # return values: v0..v1
          lw      s0,5*4(sp)
          lw      s1,6*4(sp)
          lw      s2,7*4(sp)
          lw      s3,8*4(sp)
          lw      ra,9*4(sp)
          addu    sp,(4+5+64+1)*4
          j       ra
          .end f5
```

2.5.6 Example 6: Simple Floating-Point Leaf Function

This function adds the first and second arguments and returns the result in f0.

```
          .globl f6
          .ent f6
f6:       # simple floating-point leaf function
          .frame sp,0,ra
          # incoming args: $f12 $f14
          # registers available: $f4..$f10 $f16..$f18
          # add.d   $f0,$f12,$f14
          # return values: $f0..$f2
          j       ra
          .end f6
```

3

Initialization

3.1 INTRODUCTION

This chapter describes how to initialize the MIPS processor following reset and how to prepare the processor for execution of a program in cacheable space.

Following reset, all bits in the Status Register are undefined except the Bootstrap Exception Vector (BEV) bit, which is set to 1, and the IEc and KUc bits, which are cleared. This places the processor in kernel mode, with all interrupts disabled, and the General Exception Vector (described in Section 4.1) mapped to the noncacheable, `kseg1` address 0xbfc0.0180 (segments are described in Appendix A, Section A.1). The contents of all other registers, as well as the entries in the cache, are undefined. Execution begins at virtual address 0xbfc00000 (`kseg1`), which is hardmapped to the physical address 0x1fc00000.

Initialization code typically performs the following tasks:

1. Initializes memory
2. Clears the `.bss` and `.sbss` sections
3. Flushes the caches
4. Copies program data from PROM to RAM
5. Initializes the stack pointer and the global data pointer

6. Initializes I/O devices
7. Enables interrupts
8. Switches from noncacheable to cacheable space

The remaining sections of this chapter describe some of the ways these tasks can be accomplished, using two example initialization programs.

3.2 EXAMPLE PROGRAMS

The example programs consist of two modules: an assembler file, asm.s, and a C file, main.c. The code in asm.s initializes the processor following reset and then transfers control to main.c. main.c is a dummy application program that simply prints "Hello world!" repeatedly.

The include file machine.h (reproduced in Appendix D) contains all the definitions and code that are specific to a particular implementation of the MIPS CPU or specific to a particular MIPS-based system. For this chapter, the definitions and code of interest in mips.h are RAMINIT, which initializes memory; INITSIO, which initializes the I/O device; and FLUSH_ICACHE and FLUSH_DCACHE, which flush the two caches.

3.2.1 Example 1: A Simple Initialization

We begin with a very simple initialization, suitable for code that executes in noncacheable space with no support for exceptions. The program is linked for noncacheable space by specifying kseg1 virtual addresses for all the program sections (.text, .data, and .bss):

```
.text start: bfc00000
.data start: a0000000
.bss start: follows data
modules: asm.o, main.o, put2681.o, stdio.o
```

put2681.o is a driver for the 2681 DUART, which is called by stdio.o to output the characters to the screen for "Hello world!" These library files are shown in Appendix E. Note that in the list of object files to be linked, the first file must contain the entry point of the program, in our case, asm.o.

The program begins with a jump to the label init, and then advances the assembler's location counter in the .text section so it is correctly aligned for the beginning of the General Exception Vector.

```
7   reset_exception:
8           j       init
```

```
 9              .align  8

10              .set noreorder
11              nop ; .set reorder
12              .align 7
```

If an exception should occur, the exception handler transfers control to the label _exit, which provides a branch to self (because there is no halt instruction).

```
13  general_exception:
14          j       _exit
```

The program then initializes the RAM, using the macro RAMINIT defined in machine.h.

```
22              RAMINIT
```

For the R3000, the macro RAMINIT is defined as follows:

```
                li t0,SR_BEV
                .set noreorder
                mtc0 t0,CO_SR
                .set reorder
```

Clearing the Status Register is necessary to make sure that PZ, SwC, and IsC bits are zero (refer to Section 3.3.2 for a description of these bits).

The C language requires the .bss section to be cleared prior to the start of the program. This is done using a loop that clears memory starting at the linker-defined symbol _fbss (the first location in .bss) and ending at the symbol end:

```
23           # clear bss
24           la      v0,_fbss
25           la      v1,end
26   1:      sw      $0,0x0(v0)
27           sw      $0,0x4(v0)
28           sw      $0,0x8(v0)
29           sw      $0,0xc(v0)
30           addu    v0,16
31           blt     v0,v1,1b
```

Next the .data section is copied into RAM. This has to be done because C permits the values of variables in the .data section to be modified during execution (of course, the variables have to start in PROM so their initial value is preserved).

For the copy operation, the destination of the copy is from the linker-defined symbol _fdata (the first location in .data) through the symbol edata (the first location after .data). The source of the copy is etext, which is the first location after the .text section (when the PROM is built, the .data section is placed in the PROM immediately following the .text section). Note that with some toolsets, this does not encompass all initialized data, so another symbol or an absolute value (in this case 0xa000.0000) may have to be used in place of the symbol _fdata.

```
32              # copy .data to RAM
33              # src=etext dst=_fdata stop=edata
34              la      t0,etext
35              la      t1,_fdata
36              la      t2,edata
37   1:         lw      t3,(t0)
38              sw      t3,(t1)
39              addu    t0,4
40              addu    t1,4
41              blt     t1,t2,1b
```

The stack size is set to 8K using a preprocessor constant,

```
4   #define STKSIZE 8192
```

and the directive .comm is used to reserve stack space in .bss

```
5              .comm   stack,STKSIZE
```

Because the stack grows toward lower memory addresses, the stack pointer is initialized with the highest address in the reserved space by loading the address of stack+STKSIZE-24 into sp. The additional 24 bytes is to satisfy the minimum stack size requirement for a nonleaf function, as described in Section 2.3.

```
43             la      sp,stack+STKSIZE-24
```

To permit gp-relative addressing to be used, the gp register is initialized with the value in the linker-defined symbol _gp.

```
44             la      gp,_gp
```

The I/O devices are initialized using the preprocessor macro INITSIO, defined in `machine.h`.

```
45              # initialize I/O devices
46              jal     INITSIO
```

Control is then transferred to `main`, using a `jump and link`. If the program should terminate (not usual in a ROM-based system), control will return to the label `_exit`.

```
47              # transfer to main program
48              jal     main
49  _exit:
50              b       _exit
```

3.2.2 Example 2: Initialization That Flushes the Caches

In this example, the C code will execute in cacheable space, which requires flushing the caches and then switching execution from `kseg1` to `kseg0`. Because the code that flushes the caches is processor-specific, we use the macros FLUSH_ICACHE and FLUSH_DCACHE defined in `machine.h`. Discussion of these routines is deferred to Section 3.3.

Because the program will eventually execute in cacheable space, this time we link all the program sections to `kseg0` addresses:

```
.text start: 9fc00000
.data start: 80000000
.bss start: follows data
modules: asm.o, main.o, put2681.o, stdio.o, r3kcflu.o
```

Though the .text section is linked to a `kseg0` address, the program begins executing at the Reset Vector in `kseg1`. You must be careful not to inadvertently access `kseg0` before the caches have been flushed—in this regard, keep in mind that the linker assigns a 32-bit absolute virtual address to all symbolic names, which means the address includes the segment number for which the program was linked. If your program uses a symbolic name as data, by referring to a variable with a fixed address (e.g., a global variable instead of a stack variable), the address's segment number will be the one that was assigned by the linker. For example,

```
la      t0,fred
lw      t0(t0)
```

will use the linker-defined address for fred, which in this case is a `kseg0` address.

Similarly, if a label is put in a register and then used as the target of a jump or branch (a so-called register indirect jump or branch), the segment will change to the segment for which the label was linked. For example,

```
    la      t0,fred
    jal     t0
```

will continue execution at the linker-defined (`kseg0`) symbol for fred.

To avoid kseg0 addresses, OR any 32-bit symbols with K1BASE (defined in `mips.h`). For example,

```
    la      t0,symbol
    or      t0,K1BASE
```

The above technique switches the symbol address to kseg1 because kseg0 and kseg1 are mapped to the same physical addresses. K0BASE is 0x80000000 and K1BASE is 0xa0000000.

Returning to our initialization program, it begins the same way as Example 2: Stack space is reserved in the `.bss` section, space is allocated in the `.text` section for the Exception Vector, RAM is initialized, and the `.bss` section is cleared. But before copying the `.data` section to RAM, we have to flush the caches. This is because the copy routine uses the global symbol `etext`, which will cause the cache to be accessed.

Because the cache flush routines are nonleaf functions, a stack must be allocated before they are called. Stack references are made noncacheable by ORing the stack address with K1BASE.

```
34          la      sp,stack+STKSIZE-24
35          or      sp,K1BASE
```

The global data pointer register is also used by the cache flush routines, so it also has to be initialized with a `kseg1` address.

```
36          la      gp,_gp
37          or      gp,K1BASE
```

Now we call the cache flush routines (discussed in Section 3.3).

```
38          jal     FLUSH_DCACHE
39          jal     FLUSH_ICACHE
```

After the caches have been flushed, the .data section is copied into RAM. Note that data could have been copied to RAM before flushing the caches if the symbol etext had been ORed with K1BASE before being used.

In preparation for switching to cacheable space, sp and gp are restored to their linker-assigned values

```
50          # ok to use kseg0 now, so initialize sp & gp
51          la      sp,stack+STKSIZE-24
52          la      gp,_gp
```

and the I/O devices are initialized:

```
53          # initialize I/O devices
54          jal     INITSIO
```

Now the C program can be called. To force execution to switch to kseg0, the contents of the symbol main are loaded into t0 and a jump indirect on that register is performed:

```
55          # transfer to main program
56          # reg indirect necessary to switch segments
57          la      t0,main
58          jal     t0
```

3.3 FLUSHING THE CACHE

The MIPS1 base architecture supports two variable-size caches, one for instructions and one for data. The caches vary in size from 4K to 256K (in binary multiples), and are direct-mapped—that is, each location in memory may occupy one, and only one, location in the cache. The cache is write-through, which means that all store operations result in data being "written through" to main memory as well as to the cache (unless the cache is "isolated," as explained below).

The caches are organized as a sequence of lines, with each line composed of a *cache tag*, one or more words of contiguous memory locations (instructions or data), and a *Valid bit* for each word in the line.

The cache tag contains the high-order virtual address bits of the entry in the line. It is used by hardware, along with the Valid bit, to determine whether a particular data item is in the cache (a cache "hit") or not (a cache "miss").

The Valid bit is set by hardware when data is written to the cache as the result of a cache miss on a load. Implementations differ as to whether or not stores to memory in cacheable space update the cache and set the Valid bit, and this behavior may be different for partial- versus full-word stores. This bit can be cleared by software (a process called "flushing the cache"), the purpose of which is to ensure that any access to a particular cache item will cause a cache miss, even though the address tag matches.

3.3.1 Flushing the R3000 Cache

The routine that flushes the cache uses 3 bits in the Status Register: the Isolate Cache bit, which prevents writes to locations in the cache from being written through to memory (1 = Cache Isolated); the Swap Cache bit, which selects which cache is accessed (1 = I-Cache, 0 = D-Cache); and the Cache Miss bit, which is set by hardware whenever the cache is isolated and an attempt to read a location in the cache results in a cache miss.

The cache is flushed by first using the Swap Cache bit to select the cache to be flushed, then setting the Isolate Cache bit, and then performing a partial-word write to the line to be flushed, which causes all the Valid bits in the line to be cleared. This process is repeated for each line in the cache.

Our example cache-flush program consists of four functions. There are two main routines: r3k_iflush, which flushes the I-Cache, and r3k_dflush, which flushes the D-Cache. Both call the function size_cache, which returns the size of the cache, and flush_common, which performs the actual cache flush.

We declare two global variables, icache_size and dcache_size, to contain the sizes of the caches, and we put them in the .bss section so they will be initialized to zero.

```
2    .comm    icache_size,4
3    .comm    dcache_size,4
```

The function r3k_iflush allocates space on the stack so the return address register can be saved (this is a nonleaf function).

```
7            subu    sp,24
8            sw      ra,20(sp)
```

Obviously, code that isolates the cache must execute in noncacheable space. So before determining the size of the cache, we have to explictly switch to kseg1 addresses. The objective is to change the PC so the upper 3 bits select kseg1. Because the PC cannot be referenced as a register, the label 1: is inserted just past the end of this piece of code. The address of the label is put in t0 and ORed with K1BASE, and then the program jumps to the address obtained. This jump transfers control to line 17, forcing the PC to kseg1 in the process.

```
11          la      t0,1f
12          li      t1,K1BASE
13          or      t0,t1
14          j       t0
```

The program checks to see whether the appropriate variable is equal to zero. If so, the size of the cache has not yet been determined (i.e., r3k_iflush has not been called before), so the routine cache_size is called. If r3k_iflush has been called before, the variable cache_size will contain the actual size of the cache.

```
16          la      t0,icache_size
17          li      t1,K1BASE
18          or      t0,t1
19          lw      v0,(t0)
```

If icache_size is equal to zero, we call size_cache, which returns the calculated size of the cache in v0. The cache selected is determined by the SwC bit in a0.

```
21          bne     v0,zero,1f
22          li      a0,(SR_ISC|SR_SWC)  # sr bits
23          jal     size_cache
```

If size_cache returns a 0, indicating that it was unable to find a cache, we jump to label 10, which returns to the caller. Otherwise, we use the return value from size_cache to update the variable icache_size, so it will be available to a future call to size_cache.

```
24          # if size == 0, return
25          beq     v0,zero,10f
26          # update size
27          la      t0,icache_size
28          li      t1,K1BASE
29          or      t0,t1
30          sw      v0,(t0)
```

The basic strategy of size_cache is to isolate the cache from main memory, then write a marker (some recognizable pattern) to the first location in the cache, and then consecutively read each possible cache boundary until the marker is read again, indicating the end of the cache (wrap around to the beginning). For the D-Cache, only the Isolate Cache bit is set; for the I-Cache, the Swap Cache bit also has to be set. Before isolating the cache, we have to disable interrupts, because an interrupt occurring when the cache is isolated will not be able to access memory.

```
96              .set noreorder
97              mfc0    t8,C0_SR
98              nop
99              or      t0,a0,t8
100             and     t0,SR_IEC
101             mtc0    t0,C0_SR
```

To handle the unlikely case that the marker is already on one of the cache boundaries, we clear the last address in each of the possible caches.

```
103     lui  v0,0x8000
104     sw   zero,0x1000(v0)          /* (+   4K) */
105     sw   zero,0x2000(v0)          /* (+   8K) */
106     sw   zero,0x4000(v0)          /* (+  16K) */
107     ori  v0,0x8000
108     sw   zero,0(v0)               /* (+  32K) */
109     lui  v0,0x8001
110     sw   zero,0(v0)               /* (+  64K) */
111     lui  v0,0x8002
112     sw   zero,0(v0)               /* (+128K) */
```

Then we write the marker value (0x6d61726b) into the first location in the cache

```
113     lui  a0,0x8000
114     li   a1,0x6d61726b            /* "mark" */
115     sw   a1,0(a0)
```

and load the Cache Miss bit mask into t0.

```
116             li   t0,SR_CM
```

v0, which is the cache-size variable incremented during the search for the marker, is initialized to zero.

```
117             li   v0,0
```

Then we read the first location in the cache

```
118          lw    a2,0(a0)
```

and check the Cache Miss bit (in a0) to see whether a cache miss has occurred.
If the Cache Miss bit is set, indicating the marker is not in the cache, we conclude that something is radically wrong with the operation of the cache and
jump to label 2, which restores the Status Register and returns to the caller.

```
119          mfc0 a3,CO_SR
120          nop
121          and   a3,t0
122          bne   a3,zero,2f           # bra if cache miss
```

If a cache miss hasn't occurred, we check to make sure that the value
read is equal to the marker. If not, again we conclude that the cache is
malfunctioning and branch to label 2.

```
124          bne   a1,a2,2f
```

If the value read is equal to the marker, we set the cache size in v0 to the
minimum possible cache size (4K).

```
126          li    v0,0x1000      /* minimum cache size */
```

Lines 127-137 are the main search loop. Each time through the loop, we
add the current cache size (in v0) to the current address (in a0) and put it in t1:

```
127    1:    addu t1,a0,v0
```

Then we read a word from that address into a2:

```
128          lw    a2,0(t1)
```

We check the Cache Miss bit to make sure no cache miss has occurred
and exit (via 2f) if it has.

```
129          mfc0 a3,CO_SR
130          nop
131          and   a3,t0
132          bne   a3,zero,2f           # bra if cache miss
```

We also check the data to see whether it's equal to the marker. If it is
equal to the marker, we have found the wrap-around point, so we can return
with the size of the cache via 2f.

```
134         beq  a1,a2,2f       /* check data */
```

Each time around the loop, v0 is multiplied by two to get the next possible cache size.

```
135         sll  v0,1
136         j    1b
```

The actual cache-flush operation is performed by flush_common, which is called by both r3k_iflush and r3k_dflush. It is passed two arguments: a0 contains the Status Register bits required to select the cache-flush operation, and a1 contains the value of the variable cache_size.

```
31    1:    li   a0,(SR_ISC|SR_SWC)  # sr bits
32          move a1,v0                # size
33          jal  flush_common

68    flush_common:
69          # a0=sr bits a1=size
```

The Status Register is saved in t8, the nop required for a move from a Coprocessor Register is inserted, and then the required Status Register bits are set. All interrupts are disabled by clearing the Status Register's Current Interrupt Enable bit (interrupts are described in Chapter 3).

```
72          mfc0  t8,CO_SR
73          nop
74          or    t0,a0,t8
75          and   t0,SR_IEC
76          mtc0  t0,CO_SR
```

The cache-flush operation will consist of a store byte of zero to each cache line. So we initialize the variable v0 with the first address in the cache and the variable v1 with the last cache address (by adding cache_size in a1 to K1BASE).

```
77          li    v0,K0BASE
78          addu  v1,v0,a1
```

The Valid bits are cleared by storing a byte to each word in the cache, incrementing by 16 each time around the loop. The loop continues as long as v0 is less than v1. We have unrolled the loop to speed up the flush.

```
80          sb      zero,0x0(v0)
81          sb      zero,0x4(v0)
82          sb      zero,0x8(v0)
83          sb      zero,0xc(v0)
84          addiu   v0,v0,0x10
85          bltu    v0,v1,1b
86          nop
```

The code above assumes that each cache line contains a single memory word, because the store bytes are performed in increments of four. (For implementations that have larger cache lines, the address can be incremented by a larger amount, resulting in a faster cache flush.) After the cache has been flushed, we restore the value of the Status Register and return to the caller.

```
87          mtc0    t8,C0_SR        # restore sr
88          .set reorder
89          j       ra
```

On return from r3k_iflush, we restore the stack frame and return to the caller.

```
34          10:  lw   ra,20(sp)
35               addu sp,24
36               j    ra
```

r3k_dflush is similar to r3k_iflush, except that the variable dcache_size is used instead of icache_size, and only the IsC bit is set in the Status Register contents passed to size_cache and flush_common.

3.3.2 Flushing the LR33000 Cache

The LR33000 family from LSI Logic uses an entirely different technique for flushing the caches. The LR33000 has added a special Coprocessor 0 register, called the Debug and Cache Invalidate Control Register (DCIC). The cache-flush operation makes use of two of the bits in this register, namely, the Instruction Invalidate Enable bit (DCIC_I) and the Data Invalidate Enable bit (DCIC_D).

The cache is flushed by setting either DCIC_I or DCIC_D (never both at the same time) and then performing any store operation (except swc*n*) to an address that occupies any location in the targeted cache line.

Unlike the R3000, the LR33000 family has no way to isolate the cache from memory and thus no way to determine the size of the cache. So when writing a cache-flush routine for the 33000 family, you should have the routine

assume the largest possible cache size. In our example program, we assume an
I-Cache with 512 lines and a D-Cache with 64 lines, each line containing four
words of memory, a cache tag, and four Valid bits.

Our example cache-flush program, r33kcflu.s, consists of two routines:
r33k_iflush, which flushes the I-Cache, and r33k_dflush, which flushes the
D-Cache.

The program begins by saving the Status Register in t7 and then disables
all interrupts by clearing the Status Register's Current Interrupt Enable bit.

```
7        mfc0 t7,CO_SR
8        nop
9        and  t0,t7,SR_IEC
10       mtc0 t0,CO_SR
```

Because r33kcflu.s might be called using a cacheable address, we have
to explictly switch to kseg1 addresses.

```
13       la  t0,1f
14       li  t1,K1BASE
15       or  t0,t1
16       j   t0

17   1:
```

The first (t0) and last (t4) cache addresses to be flushed are computed by
adding K0BASE (the base of the cache) to the number of cache lines minus 1
(because we count from 0) multiplied by 16 (because there are 16 bytes in a
line):

```
17    1:   li   t0,K0BASE
18         addu t4,t0,511*16
```

We save the current DCIC in t8 and set the DCIC_I bit.

```
19        li      t2,DCIC_I

21        mfc0 t8,CO_DCIC
22        nop
23        mtc0 t2,CO_DCIC
```

All the cache lines are invalidated by a sequence of store word instructions to addresses on consecutive four-word boundaries.

```
27    1:    sw    zero,(t0)
28          addu  t0,16
29          bne   t4,t0,1b
```

Then DCIC and the Status Register are restored, and the program returns to the caller.

```
34          mtc0 t8,C0_DCIC      # restore DCIC
35          mtc0 t7,C0_SR        # restore SR
```

The function `r33k_dflush` is the basically the same as `r33k_iflush`, except that it flushes the D-Cache instead of the I-Cache.

3.4 PROGRAM LISTINGS

3.4.1 Example 1: A Simple Initialization

============== init/ex1/main.c ==============

```
1   main()
2   {
3   int i;

4   for (i=0;i<10;i++) puts("Hello world!\n");
5   }
```

============== init/ex1/asm.s ==============

```
1   /* startup code, noncacheable, no exceptions */
2   #include <mips.h>
3   #include <machine.h>

4   #define STKSIZE 8192
5           .comm    stack,STKSIZE

6           .text

7   reset_exception:
8           j        init
9           .align  8

10          .set noreorder
11          nop ; .set reorder
12          .align 7
```

```
13   general_exception:
14            j         _exit

15            .globl init
16            .globl _exit
17            .ent init
18   /*
19    * This is the entry point of the entire application
20    */
21   init:
22            RAMINIT

23            # clear bss
24            la        v0,_fbss
25            la        v1,end
26   1:       sw        $0,0x0(v0)
27            sw        $0,0x4(v0)
28            sw        $0,0x8(v0)
29            sw        $0,0xc(v0)
30            addu      v0,16
31            blt       v0,v1,1b

32            # copy .data to RAM
33            # src=etext dst=_fdata stop=edata
34            la        t0,etext
35            la        t1,_fdata
36            la        t2,edata
37   1:       lw        t3,(t0)
38            sw        t3,(t1)
39            addu      t0,4
40            addu      t1,4
41            blt       t1,t2,1b

42            # initialize sp & gp
43            la        sp,stack+STKSIZE-24
44            la        gp,_gp

45            # initialize I/O devices
46            jal       INITSIO

47            # transfer to main program
48            jal       main

49   _exit:
50            b         _exit
51            .end init
```

3.4.2 Example 2: Initialization That Flushes the Cache

============== init/ex2/main.c ==============

```
1   main()
2   {
3   int i;

4   for (i=0;i<10;i++) puts("Hello world!\n");
5   }
```

============== init/ex2/asm.s ==============

```
1   /* startup code, cacheable, no exceptions */
2   #include <mips.h>
3   #include <machine.h>

4   #define STKSIZE 8192
5           .comm   stack,STKSIZE

6           .text

7   reset_exception:
8           j       init
9           .align  8

10          .set noreorder
11          nop ; .set reorder
12          .align 7
13  general_exception:
14          j       _exit

15          .globl init
16          .globl _exit
17          .ent init
18  /*
19   * This is the entry point of the entire application
20   */
21  init:
22          RAMINIT

23          # clear bss
24          la      v0,_fbss
25          la      v1,end
26  1:      sw      $0,0x0(v0)
27          sw      $0,0x4(v0)
28          sw      $0,0x8(v0)
29          sw      $0,0xc(v0)
```

```
30            addu    v0,16
31            blt     v0,v1,1b

32            # flush the caches
33            # first set up a Kseg1 sp & gp
34            la      sp,stack+STKSIZE-24
35            or      sp,K1BASE
36            la      gp,_gp
37            or      gp,K1BASE
38            jal     FLUSH_DCACHE
39            jal     FLUSH_ICACHE

40            # copy .data to RAM
41            # src=etext dst=_fdata stop=edata
42            la      t0,etext
43            la      t1,_fdata
44            la      t2,edata
45    1:      lw      t3,(t0)
46            sw      t3,(t1)
47            addu    t0,4
48            addu    t1,4
49            blt     t1,t2,1b

50            # ok to use kseg0 now, so initialize sp & gp
51            la      sp,stack+STKSIZE-24
52            la      gp,_gp

53            # initialize I/O devices
54            jal     INITSIO

55            # transfer to main program
56            # reg indirect necessary to switch segments
57            la      t0,main
58            jal     t0
59    _exit:
60            b       _exit
61            .end init
```

3.4.3 Example 3: R3000 Cache Flush

============= lib/r3kcflu.s =============

```
1      #include <mips.h>

2      .comm   icache_size,4
3      .comm   dcache_size,4
```

```
4                 .globl  r3k_iflush
5                 .ent    r3k_iflush
6       r3k_iflush:
7                 subu    sp,24
8                 sw      ra,20(sp)
9
10                # make me uncacheable
11                la      t0,1f
12                li      t1,K1BASE
13                or      t0,t1
14                j       t0

15      1:        # get size
16                la      t0,icache_size
17                li      t1,K1BASE
18                or      t0,t1
19                lw      v0,(t0)

20                # if size == 0, call size_cache
21                bne     v0,zero,1f
22                li      a0,(SR_ISC|SR_SWC)      # sr bits
23                jal     size_cache

24                # if size == 0, return
25                beq     v0,zero,10f

26                # update size
27                la      t0,icache_size
28                li      t1,K1BASE
29                or      t0,t1
30                sw      v0,(t0)

31      1:        li      a0,(SR_ISC|SR_SWC)      # sr bits
32                move    a1,v0                   # size

33                jal     flush_common

34      10:       lw      ra,20(sp)
35                addu    sp,24
36                j       ra
37                .end    r3k_iflush

38                .globl  r3k_dflush
39                .ent    r3k_dflush
40      r3k_dflush:
41                subu    sp,24
42                sw      ra,20(sp)
```

```
43              # get size
44              la      t0,dcache_size
45              li      t1,K1BASE
46              or      t0,t1
47              lw      v0,(t0)

48              # if size == 0, call size_cache
49              bne     v0,zero,1f
50              li      a0,SR_ISC        # sr bits
51              jal     size_cache

52              # if size == 0, return
53              beq     v0,zero,10f

54              # update size
55              la      t0,dcache_size
56              li      t1,K1BASE
57              or      t0,t1
58              sw      v0,(t0)

59      1:      li      a0,SR_ISC        # sr bits
60              move    a1,v0            # size

61              jal     flush_common

62      10:     lw      ra,20(sp)
63              addu    sp,24
64              j       ra
65              .end    r3k_dflush

66              .globl flush_common
67              .ent flush_common
68      flush_common:
69              # a0=sr bits a1=size

70              # set selected SR bits and disable ints
71              .set noreorder
72              mfc0    t8,C0_SR
73              nop
74              or      t0,a0,t8
75              and     t0,SR_IEC
76              mtc0    t0,C0_SR

77              li      v0,K0BASE
78              addu    v1,v0,a1
79      1:      # flush loop
80              sb      zero,0x0(v0)
81              sb      zero,0x4(v0)
```

```
82              sb       zero,0x8(v0)
83              sb       zero,0xc(v0)
84              addiu    v0,v0,0x10
85              bltu     v0,v1,1b
86              nop
87              mtc0     t8,C0_SR              # restore sr
88              .set reorder
89              j        ra
90              .end flush_common

91              .globl size_cache
92              .ent size_cache
93      size_cache:
94              # a0=sr bits rtn=size

95              # set selected SR bits and disable ints
96              .set noreorder
97              mfc0     t8,C0_SR
98              nop
99              or       t0,a0,t8
100             and      t0,SR_IEC
101             mtc0     t0,C0_SR

102             /* clear possible cache boundaries */
103             lui      v0,0x8000
104             sw       zero,0x1000(v0)       /* clear KSEG0 (+  4K) */
105             sw       zero,0x2000(v0)       /*              (+  8K) */
106             sw       zero,0x4000(v0)       /*              (+ 16K) */
107             ori      v0,0x8000
108             sw       zero,0(v0)            /*              (+ 32K) */
109             lui      v0,0x8001
110             sw       zero,0(v0)            /*              (+ 64K) */
111             lui      v0,0x8002
112             sw       zero,0(v0)            /*              (+128K) */

113             lui      a0,0x8000             /* set marker */
114             li       a1,0x6d61726b         /* "mark" */
115             sw       a1,0(a0)

116             li       t0,SR_CM              /* cache-miss bit */

117             li       v0,0         /* no cache if we fail next tests */
118             lw       a2,0(a0)
119             mfc0     a3,C0_SR
120             nop
121             and      a3,t0
122             bne      a3,zero,2f            # bra if cache miss
123             nop
```

```
124            bne      a1,a2,2f
125            nop

126            li       v0,0x1000              /* min cache size */

127    1:      addu     t1,a0,v0
128            lw       a2,0(t1)
129            mfc0     a3,C0_SR
130            nop
131            and      a3,t0
132            bne      a3,zero,2f             # bra if cache miss
133            nop
134            beq      a1,a2,2f               /* check data */
135            sll      v0,1
136            j        1b
137            nop

138    2:      mtc0     t8,C0_SR
139            .set reorder
140            j        ra
141            .end size_cache
```

3.4.4 Example 4: R33000 Cache Flush

============ lib/r33kcflu.s ============

```
1      #include "mips.h"

2              .globl r33k_iflush
3              .ent r33k_iflush
4      r33k_iflush:
5              # disable ints
6              .set noreorder
7              mfc0     t7,C0_SR
8              nop
9              and      t0,t7,SR_IEC
10             mtc0     t0,C0_SR
11             .set reorder

12             # switch to Kseg1
13             la       t0,1f
14             li       t1,K1BASE
15             or       t0,t1
16             j        t0

17     1:      li       t0,K0BASE
18             addu     t4,t0,511*16
19             li       t2,DCIC_I
```

```
20              .set noreorder
21              mfc0    t8,C0_DCIC
22              nop
23              mtc0    t2,C0_DCIC
24              nop
25              nop
26              .set reorder

27      1:      sw      zero,(t0)
28              addu    t0,16
29              bne     t4,t0,1b

30              .set noreorder
31              nop
32              nop
33              nop
34              mtc0    t8,C0_DCIC      # restore DCIC
35              mtc0    t7,C0_SR        # restore SR
36              .set reorder
37              j       ra
38              .end r33k_iflush

39              .globl r33k_dflush
40              .ent r33k_dflush
41      r33k_dflush:
42              # disable ints
43              .set noreorder
44              mfc0    t7,C0_SR
45              nop
46              and     t0,t7,SR_IEC
47              mtc0    t0,C0_SR
48              .set reorder

49              # switch to Kseg1
50              la      t0,1f
51              li      t1,K1BASE
52              or      t0,t1
53              j       t0

54      1:      li      t0,K0BASE
55              addu    t4,t0,63*16
56              li      t2,DCIC_D

57              .set noreorder
58              mfc0    t8,C0_DCIC
59              nop
60              mtc0    t2,C0_DCIC
61              nop
```

```
62              nop
63              .set reorder

64      1:      sw      zero,(t0)
65              addu    t0,16
66              bne     t4,t0,1b

67              .set noreorder
68              nop
69              nop
70              nop
71              mtc0    t8,C0_DCIC
72              mtc0    t7,C0_SR      # restore SR
73              .set reorder
74              j       ra
75              .end r33k_dflush
```

4

Exceptions

4.1 INTRODUCTION

In this chapter we explain how to write exception handlers. Fortunately for the programmer, the MIPS exception-handling mechanism is very straightforward and easy to use.

By *exceptions* we mean any conditions that alter the normal sequence of instructions, causing the processor to transfer control to a predefined location in memory. This predefined location is the so-called exception *vector*, which in the MIPS architecture is the start of the actual exception-handler routine (rather than the address of the routine, as with most other architectures). For the base architecture there is a single exception vector, called the General Exception Vector, whose virtual address depends on the setting of the Status Register's Bootstrap Exception Vector (BEV) bit, as shown in Table 4.1 and described later in this chapter.

The MIPS architecture recognizes 17 exceptions: 8 external interrupts (6 hardware interrupts and 2 software interrupts) and 9 program exception conditions (sometimes referred to as "traps"). The type of exception is encoded in the Exception Code (ExcCode) field of the Cause Register, as shown in Table 4.2.

Table 4.1   General-Exception Vector Addresses

	BEV = 1 (Reset State)	BEV = 0
Virtual Address	0xbfc0.0180 (kseg1)	0x8000.0080 (kseg0)
Physical Address	0x1fc0.0180	0x0000.0080

Table 4.2   ExcCode Field in Cause Register

ExcCode Value	Assembler Mnemonic	Exception Type
0	EXC_INT	External interrupt
1	—	Reserved
2	—	Reserved
3	—	Reserved
4	EXC_ADEL	Address error (load or instruction fetch)
5	EXC_ADES	Address error (data store)
6	EXC_IBE	Bus error (instruction fetch)
7	EXC_DBE	Bus error (data load or store)
8	EXC_SYS	Syscall instruction
9	EXC_BP	Breakpoint
10	EXC_RI	Reserved instruction
11	EXC_CPU	Coprocessor unusable
12	EXC_OVF	Arithmetic overflow
13–15		Not used

When an exception occurs, the following events take place:

1. The currently executing instruction is aborted, as well as any subsequent instructions in the pipeline.
2. In the Status Register, the Previous Kernel/User Mode and Previous Interrupt Enable bits are copied into the Old Mode and Old Interrupt Enable bits respectively, and the Current Mode and Current Interrupt Enable bits are copied into the Previous Mode and Previous Interrupt Enable bits.
3. The Current Interrupt Enable bit is cleared, which disables all interrupts.
4. The Current Kernel/User Mode bit is cleared, which places the processor in Kernel Mode.

5. If the instruction executing when the exception occurred is in the delay slot of a branch, the Branch Delay (BD) bit in the Cause Register is set.

6. The Exception Program Counter Register (EPC) is set with the address at which the program can be correctly restarted. If the instruction causing the exception is in the delay slot of a branch (BD = 1), this register is written with the address of the preceding branch or jump instruction. Otherwise, it is written with the address of the instruction that caused the exception or, in the case of an interrupt, with the address of the next instruction to be executed.

7. The Exception Code (ExcCode) field of the Cause Register is written with a number, between 0 and 15, that encodes the type of exception (refer to Table 4.2).

8. If the exception is a Coprocessor Unusable exception, the Cause Register's Coprocessor Error (CE) field is set with the referenced Coprocessor Unit number (00 = coprocessor 0, etc.).

9. If the exception is an Address Error, the address associated with the illegal access is written to the BadVAddr register.

10. The processor then jumps to the General Exception Vector, whose address depends on the setting of the BEV bit: When BEV = 1, the General Exception Vector is mapped to a noncacheable kseg1 address; when BEV = 0, it is mapped to a cacheable kseg0 address (see Table 4.1).

When the exception handler has completed, it uses the address in the EPC register as the return address in a jump, and then executes a Return From Exception (rfe) instruction in the jump's delay slot. The rfe instruction restores the Current and Previous Mode and Interrupt Enable bits to their contents prior to the interrupt, leaving the old bits unchanged.

4.2 EXTERNAL INTERRUPTS

There are eight external interrupts: six hardware interrupts and two software interrupts. (Note that software interrupts are classified as external interrupts even though they are actually signalled internally.)

Hardware interrupts are asynchronous events signalled via the six interrupt pins INT0–INT5. Software interrupts are synchronous and are signalled by setting the interrupt's corresponding Sw bit in the Cause Register.

External interrupts can be disabled individually by clearing the interrupt's corresponding IntMask bit in the Status Register. They can be disabled as a group by clearing the Status Register's Interrupt Enable bit.

When an INT0–INT5 pin is active or the Sw bit is set, the corresponding Interrupt Pending (IP) bit in the Cause Register is set; when the pin is no longer active or the Sw bit is cleared, the IP bit is cleared.

Pending external interrupts (IP=1) are taken when the following conditions are met:

- Instructions in the Access Memory and Write Results stages of the pipeline have finished executing (the instruction in the ALU stage will be aborted and re-executed following the interrupt).
- Interrupts are enabled (IEc = 1).
- The interrupt's Interrupt Mask bit is set (IntMask$n$ = 1).

4.2.1 Hardware Interrupt Examples

The discussion of hardware interrupts centers on a series of six example programs. Each example program consists of three basic parts: initialization code (init), exception-handling code (handler), and test code in C (main). There are two modules for each example: an assembler file, asm.s, and a C file, main.c.

Execution starts at init. init initializes the processor (as described in the previous chapter) and calls main. When an interrupt occurs, control is transferred to handler.

4.2.1.1 Example 1: A Single Interrupt Source

This example shows a simple scheme for handling a single interrupt source. A timer is programmed to generate interrupts two times per second. The count value in the timer is decremented at some predefined rate. When it reaches zero, an interrupt request is asserted on one of the input pins (INT0–INT5). The association of interrupt requests and particular input pins is defined in the macro CLK1_INT in machine.h. The function handler uses the interrupt to increment the memory location ticks, and main prints the value of ticks whenever it is updated.

The preprocessor symbol USER_INTS specifies which interrupts will be enabled, in this case CLK1_INT.

```
4  #define USER_INTS        (CLK1_INT)
```

After the RAM has been initialized and the .bss cleared, init calls copyHandler, which copies the exception-handler code to the general exeption vector address 0x8000.0080 in RAM (BEV=0).

```
35              la      a0,handler
36              la      a1,ehandler
37              li      a2,0x80000080           # general vector
38              jal     copyHandler


85  copyHandler:

89              or      t0,a0,K1BASE
90              or      t1,a1,K1BASE
91      1:      lw      v0,(t0)
92              sw      v0,(a2)
93              addu    t0,4
94              addu    a2,4
95              blt     t0,t1,1b
96              j       ra
```

Notice that the entire procedure handler has been copied to the vector area. You should check to ensure that your handler will fit between the start of the vector area and the beginning of any allocated memory. In this example, 128 bytes are provided for the handler by specifying a .data start address of 0x80000100 to the linker.

Notice also that copyHandler forces the address of the first two arguments to kseg1, so this function can be used before the D-Cache has been flushed.

After flushing the caches, copying the data to RAM, and initializing sp, gp, and the I/O devices, the macro CLK1_INIT is used to initialize clock 1. CLK1_INIT specifies the frequency of interrupts, where the parameter in the macro call specifies the number of milliseconds between interrupts, in this case 500.

```
62              CLK1_INIT(500)
```

Before enabling interrupts, the program checks to make sure the Sw bits in the Cause Register are cleared, to avoid another exception being generated immediately.

```
66              mtc0    zero,C0_CAUSE
```

Next the Status Register is written with a word that has the user-defined Interrupt Mask (IM) bits set and the Interrupt Enable bit set. This operation will also clear BEV, causing the vectors to be accessed with kseg0 addresses.

```
68              # clear BEV and set IM and IEC bits
69              li      t0,(USER_INTS|SR_IEC)
70              .set noreorder
71              mtc0    t0,CO_SR
72              .set reorder
```

Then control is transferred to main using a jump and link indirect, which switches execution to kseg0 as previously explained.

```
75              la      t0,main
76              jal     t0
```

When an interrupt occurs, control is passed to the procedure handler. handler first acknowledges the interrupt, using the macro CLK1_ACK (in machine.h). Note that the interrupt must be acknowledged before control can be returned to the interrupted program, because the return restores the Status Register, which reenables interrupts. Note that because we have only a single interrupt source, we do not have to check the IP or IM bits to identify the exception.

```
105             CLK1_ACK
```

Then the memory location ticks is incremented by loading the word at the address, adding one to it, and storing it back to memory.

```
107             la      k0,ticks
108             lw      k1,(k0)
109             addu    k1,1
110             sw      k1,(k0)
```

To return to the interrupted C program, the value in the EPC Register is read into k0, and the required nop is inserted (the mfc0 instruction requires two cycles), followed by a jump indirect on k0. The rfe in the delay slot restores the Status Register.

```
113             mfc0    k0,CO_EPC
114             nop
115             j       k0
116             rfe
```

Note that in this very simple example, the interrupt handler uses only two registers for temporary variables. The MIPS register-usage conventions reserve k0 and k1 for use by interrupt service routines. These registers can be used by an interrupt service routine without first being saved, so long as interrupts remain disabled. Thus in this example, no additional registers need to be saved before transferring control to handler.

Note also that because the interrupt handler is very short, interrupts can be left disabled without having any negative impact on interrupt latency. As shown in Section 4.4, as long as the interrupt handler is less than 39 cycles, it will never degrade the maximum interrupt latency (39 cycles is the worst-case number of cycles for which a divide instruction can disable interrupts).

4.2.1.2 Example 2: Two Interrupt Sources

Example 2 adds an interrupt source from a second clock and some "director" code that transfers control to the interrupt handler.

The preprocessor symbol USER_INTS specifies which interrupts will be enabled, in this case interrupts from clock 1 and clock 2.

```
4   #define USER_INTS        (CLK1_INT|CLK2_INT)
```

Space is reserved for the two global variables, ticks and ticks2, that are incremented by the exception handlers.

```
7            .comm ticks,4
8            .comm ticks2,4
```

Rather than copying all of handler to the vector address as was done in Example 1, the program uses the function direct to transfer control to handler. We use the same routine to copy direct as in the previous example so the program will not be sensitive to the exact length of the director code, should we want to change it later.

```
37       la     a0,direct
38       la     a1,edirect
39       li     a2,0x80000080        # general vector
40       jal    copyHandler
```

When an interrupt occurs, control is passed to the procedure handler. handler first checks to see whether the exception is an external interrupt by reading the value of the ExcCode field in the Cause Register. The constant EXCMASK selects the contents of the ExcCode field. EXCMASK is defined in mips.h such that when it is ANDed with the contents of the Cause Register, it selects only the contents of the ExcCode field.

```
121             mfc0    k0,CO_CAUSE

125             and     k1,k0,CAUSE_EXCMASK
126             bne     k1,zero,1f
```

If the ExcCode field is not zero, control is passed to the label 1, indicating a spurious interrupt.

If the value of the ExcCode field is zero, the IP bits in the Cause Register are masked by the Status Register's IntMask field. In the code below, k0 contains the Cause Register. By ANDing it with the Status Register (129–131), we select only those interrupt sources that are enabled.

```
129             mfc0    k1,CO_SR
130             nop
131             and     k0,k1
```

Because there are two possible interrupts, handler has to check both CL1_INT and CLK2_INT and then transfer control to either of the two handlers, clock1 or clock2.

```
134             and     k1,k0,CLK1_INT
135             bne     k1,zero,clock1
```

Both interrupt handlers return to the interrupted program in the same way as the previous example.

4.2.1.3 Example 3: Nested Interrupts

The primary difference between this example and Example 2 is that interrupts are enabled within the clock 1 interrupt handler (clock1).

To enable interrupts, either the interrupt has to be acknowledged or the interrupt source has to be disabled (this is true for software interrupts as well). Also, SR and EPC must be saved, and the cause register, as well, if its contents will be required for future reference.

The program defines an "exception frame" by declaring the stack offsets for the registers that will have to be saved before interrupts can be enabled.

```
4    #define E_SR      0
5    #define E_EPC     1
6    #define E_T0      2
7    #define E_T1      3
8    #define E_SIZE    4
```

The clock 1 `handler` first acknowledges the interrupt and then saves the Status Register and the Exception Program Counter, as well as the two scratch registers, `t0` and `t1`, that will be needed for temporary variables by `handler`. The Status and EPC Registers have to be saved because they will be overwritten if an interrupt occurs. The scratch registers have to be saved because the usual interrupt handler scratch registers, `k0` and `k1`, can only be used when interrupts are disabled.

```
152        subu    sp,E_SIZE*4

154        mfc0    k0,C0_EPC
155        nop
156        sw      k0,E_EPC*4(sp)

157        mfc0    k0,C0_SR
158        nop
159        sw      k0,E_SR*4(sp)

161        sw      t0,E_T0*4(sp)
162        sw      t1,E_T1*4(sp)
```

Then we set IEc to enable interrupts, at which point a clock 2 interrupt can be taken.

```
165        or      k0,SR_IEC
166        mtc0    k0,C0_SR
```

Upon completion, `clock1` disables interrupts by restoring the Status Register. This must be done before the other registers are restored. Note that because the EPC Register is not writable, it is not actually "restored," but simply copied into `k0`, which is used as the target of the jump that precedes the `rfe` instruction.

```
180        lw      t0,E_SR*4(sp)
181        nop
182        mtc0    t0,C0_SR

185        lw      t0,E_T0*4(sp)
186        lw      t1,E_T1*4(sp)
187        lw      k0,E_EPC*4(sp)
188        addu    sp,E_SIZE*4

189        b       done
```

```
206   done:

208          j      k0
209          rfe
```

4.2.1.4 Example 4: Interrupt Handler in C

As in the previous example, interrupts are enabled within the clock 1 interrupt handler, but this time the handler body for clock 1 is written in C.

We define symbolic names for the registers that have to be saved before the C handler is called and declare their stack offsets.

```
 4   #define C_SR    0
 5   #define C_EPC   1
 6   #define C_AT    2
 7   #define C_V0    3
 8   #define C_V1    4
 9   #define C_A0    5
10   #define C_A1    6
11   #define C_A2    7
12   #define C_A3    8
13   #define C_T0    9
14   #define C_T1    10
15   #define C_T2    11
16   #define C_T3    12
17   #define C_T4    13
18   #define C_T5    14
19   #define C_T6    15
20   #define C_T7    16
21   #define C_T8    17
22   #define C_T9    18
23   #define C_RA    19
24   #define C_LO    20
25   #define C_HI    21
26   #define C_SIZE  22
```

clock1 must save additional registers required for a call to a C function. The rule for calls to C programs is that you must save any register that can be used by the compiler without first being saved; AT, v0–v1, a0–a3, t0–t7, t8–t9, ra, and HI and LO. Registers s0–s7 and s8 need not be saved, because the compiler will always save them before using them. k0 and k1 do not need to be saved because when interrupts are enabled they will be used by nested interrupt service routines. gp does not need to be saved if all program modules were linked in a single operation, because they will all have the same _gp value. sp does not need to be saved because its value is preserved by the exception handler.

```
169          subu     sp,C_SIZE*4

184          sw       AT,C_AT*4(sp)
185          sw       v0,C_V0*4(sp)
186          sw       v1,C_V1*4(sp)
187          sw       a0,C_A0*4(sp)
188          sw       a1,C_A1*4(sp)
189          sw       a2,C_A2*4(sp)
190          sw       a3,C_A3*4(sp)
191          sw       t0,C_T0*4(sp)
192          sw       t1,C_T1*4(sp)
193          sw       t2,C_T2*4(sp)
194          sw       t3,C_T3*4(sp)
195          sw       t4,C_T4*4(sp)
196          sw       t5,C_T5*4(sp)
197          sw       t6,C_T6*4(sp)
198          sw       t7,C_T7*4(sp)
199          sw       t8,C_T8*4(sp)
200          sw       t9,C_T9*4(sp)
201          sw       ra,C_RA*4(sp)
202          mflo     t0
203          sw       t0,C_LO*4(sp)
204          mfhi     t0
205          sw       t0,C_HI*4(sp)
```

Before the C function is called, space on the stack is allocated for the minimum stack-context size of a nonleaf function.

```
206          subu     sp,24        # allocate min size context
```

Control is transferred to the C interrupt handler using a *jump and link* instruction, which assumes that c_handler is in the same segment as handler.

```
207          jal      c_handler    # call C handler
```

c_handler increments the memory location ticks.

```
35  c_handler()
36  {
37  ticks++;
38  }
```

On return, the allocated stack context is restored.

```
208           addu    sp,24              # deallocate
```

All saved registers are restored except t0 ($8), which will be needed as a
temporary register when disabling interrupts.

```
209           lw      AT,C_AT*4(sp)
210           lw      v0,C_V0*4(sp)
211           lw      v1,C_V1*4(sp)
212           lw      a0,C_A0*4(sp)
213           lw      a1,C_A1*4(sp)
214           lw      a2,C_A2*4(sp)
215           lw      a3,C_A3*4(sp)
216           # t0 is restored later
217           lw      t1,C_T1*4(sp)
218           lw      t2,C_T2*4(sp)
219           lw      t3,C_T3*4(sp)
220           lw      t4,C_T4*4(sp)
221           lw      t5,C_T5*4(sp)
222           lw      t6,C_T6*4(sp)
223           lw      t7,C_T7*4(sp)
224           lw      t8,C_T8*4(sp)
225           lw      t9,C_T9*4(sp)
226           lw      ra,C_RA*4(sp)
227           lw      t0,C_LO*4(sp)
228           mtlo    t0
229           lw      t0,C_HI*4(sp)
230           mthi    t0
```

To disable interrupts, the saved Status Register contents are copied from
the stack into the Status Register. This requires the use of t0 as a temporary
register, as neither k0 nor k1 can be used because interrupts are not actually
disabled until the completion of the mtc0 instruction.

```
233           lw      t0,C_SR*4(sp)
234           nop
235           mtc0    t0,C0_SR
```

Now t0 can be restored and the stack space deallocated.

```
238           lw      t0,C_T0*4(sp)
239           lw      k0,C_EPC*4(sp)
240           addu    sp,C_SIZE*4

241           b       done
```

To return control to the interrupted program, the saved EPC value is copied either from the stack (if the return is from the C program)

```
239            lw       k0,C_EPC*4(sp)
```

or from C0_EPC (if the return is from the clock 2 handler)

```
255            mfc0     k0,C0_EPC
256            nop
```

followed by the usual jump and rfe.

```
258   done:    # return to interrupted program

260            j        k0
261            rfe
```

4.2.1.5 Example 5: UNIX Time Function Support

This example shows some initialization code in C and the low-level routines that support the UNIX time functions.

The global variables that will be shared by the C program and the assembly language program are declared

```
7   unsigned long _time;
8   int ticks;
```

and the type returned by time is forward declared.

```
9   long time();
```

The C function main calls c_init, which copies the code between the labels direct and edirect to the General Exception Vector at 0x8000.0080 and then flushes the I-Cache.

```
46   d = (unsigned long *) 0x80000080;
47   s = (unsigned long *) direct;
48   while (s < (unsigned long *)edirect) *d++ = *s++;
49   FLUSH_ICACHE;
```

c_init then initializes and enables the two clocks.

```
51  CLK1_INIT(500);

53  CLK2_INIT(100);
```

c_init then calls the assembly-language procedure enableInts, which enables processor interrupts. This portion of the initialization has to be written in assembly language because processor registers (in this case the Status Register) cannot be accessed from C.

```
54  enableInts(CLK1_INT|CLK2_INT);

93  enableInts:
94          .set noreorder
95          mtc0    zero,CO_CAUSE   # make sure sw bits are cleared
96          mfc0    t1,CO_SR
97          nop
98          or      t1,a0           # enable selected ints
99          and     t1,SR_BEV       # clear BEV
100         or      t1,SR_IEC       # overall int enable
101         mtc0    t1,CO_SR        # set those bits
102         .set reorder
103         j       ra
104         .end enableInts
```

On return from c_init, main calls the function time, which returns the number of seconds since the clock was initialized. If this value has changed since the last time it was called, a line is printed containing the current value of seconds and ticks.

```
20          secs = time(0);
21          if (secs != prev) {
22                  printf("\r %d %d  ",secs,ticks);
23                  prev = secs;
24                  }
```

When an interrupt occurs, control is transferred to the General Exception Vector, where the director code jumps to the assembly routine handler (line 126), which performs the usual tests and then transfers control to clock1 or clock2.

The interrupt handler for clock 1 is the same as in Example 4.

The interrupt handler for clock 2 contains low-level routines that update global variables containing information about the current state of clock 2 and that are read by the C function time. This routine implements the UNIX time function.

Two global variables are used: _time and _tenths. Clock 2 is programmed to interrupt ten times per second. _time, declared in C, was previously imported so it could be referenced by the assembly code.

```
26              .extern _time,4
27              .comm   _tenths,4
```

Because very few clock registers provide enough precision to generate a delay of 1 second, the clock register has been programmed for 100 milliseconds and the global variable _tenths is used by software to provide a further division by 10. When _tenths reaches the value 10 (1 second has elapsed), the memory location _time is incremented. This is sufficient to support the UNIX time function because that call is only required to return the number of seconds.

```
237             la      k0,_tenths
238             lw      k1,(k0)
239             addu    k1,1
240             sw      k1,(k0)

241             # overflow?
242             subu    k1,10
243             bne     k1,zero,2f

244             # yes, clr tenths
245             la      k0,_tenths
246             sw      zero,(k0)

247             # update time
248             la      k0,_time
249             lw      k1,(k0)
250             addu    k1,1
251             sw      k1,(k0)
```

4.2.1.6 Example 6: Prioritizing Interrupts

This example shows a general-purpose priority vectoring mechanism, using a Priority Table and a Vector Table, that can be used for both C and assembly-language exception handlers. Also shown are the steps required to enable interrupts of higher priority before passing control to the exception handler.

The Priority Table is used to derive an "interrupt number," from 1–8, designating the highest priority requesting interrupt. The interrupt number is used to generate an interrupt mask and to access an entry in the Vector Table.

In this example, it is assumed that the highest order bit has the highest priority, which means INT5 has the highest priority and SW0 has the lowest.

```
19   unsigned char pri_table[256];
```

The Priority Table is initialized by the function donum.

```
79   donum(addr)
80   unsigned char *addr;
81   {
82   int value,count,n;

83   addr++;
84   value = 1;
85   for (count=1;count <= 128;count <<= 1) {
86           for (n=count;n>0;n-) *addr++ = value;
87           value++;
88           }
89   }
```

The Vector Table has eight entries, where each entry is a 4-byte pointer to a user-defined interrupt handler. The interrupt number is used as an index into the Vector Table to select the correct interrupt handler.

```
17   typedef int Func();
18   Func *vect_table[8];
```

The addresses of the handlers for clocks 1 and 2 are entered in the Vector Table entries 2 and 3, the clocks are initialized, and then processor interrupts are enabled using the assembler procedure enableInts.

For Vector Table entry 3, the address of clk1 is ORed with 1 in order to set the least significant bit, which is used to indicate that the function clk1 is written in assembler. The additional type casting is necessary to persuade the compiler to permit a logical OR with a function address.

```
67   vect_table[CLK1_INTNUM] = clock1;
68   CLK1_INIT(500);

69   /* connect and initialize clock2 */
70   vect_table[CLK2_INTNUM] = (Func *)(((unsigned long)clock2)|1);
71   CLK2_INIT(100);

72   enableInts(CLK1_INT|CLK2_INT);
```

We define symbolic names for the registers that need to be saved before we can enable interrupts.

```
 5  #define E_SR      0
 6  #define E_EPC     1
 7  #define E_AT      2
 8  #define E_RA      3
 9  #define E_SIZE    4          /* must be even, doubleword aligned */
```

We also define symbolic names for the additional registers that need to be saved when we call the C handler.

```
11  #define C_V0      0
12  #define C_V1      1
13  #define C_A0      2
14  #define C_A1      3
15  #define C_A2      4
16  #define C_A3      5
17  #define C_T0      6
18  #define C_T1      7
19  #define C_T2      8
20  #define C_T3      9
21  #define C_T4      10
22  #define C_T5      11
23  #define C_T6      12
24  #define C_T7      13
25  #define C_T8      14
26  #define C_T9      15
27  #define C_LO      16
28  #define C_HI      17
29  #define C_SIZE    18     /* must be even, doubleword aligned */
```

When an interrupt occurs, handler first checks whether it is a hardware interrupt and then saves just those registers required for interrupts to be enabled. Notice AT and ra are saved, rather than t0 and t1 as in the previous example, because the handlers will be called using a *jump and link* instead of a *branch*. Thus the return address must be saved. AT is saved for use as a temporary to permit use of assembler macros in the handler. Notice also that SR is saved last, so the Interrupt-Mask field is in k1 for the test that follows, and k0 contains the contents of the Cause Register.

```
132        subu    sp,E_SIZE*4      # allocate stack space
133        sw      AT,E_AT*4(sp)    # save AT
134        sw      ra,E_RA*4(sp)    # save RA
```

```
135            .set noreorder
136            mfc0    k1,CO_EPC
137            nop
138            sw      k1,E_EPC*4(sp)   # save EPC
139            mfc0    k1,CO_SR
140            nop
141            sw      k1,E_SR*4(sp)    # save SR
142            mfc0    k0,CO_CAUSE
```

The interrupt pending state of all enabled interrupts is extracted from the Cause Register.

```
146            and     k0,k1            # CAUSE is still in k0
147            and     k0,SR_IMASK
```

Next the program determines the interrupt number of the highest priority interrupt, using either of two methods. The first method uses the Priority Table, and the second uses a bit-shift in a loop. The two methods are selected using an ifdef declaration, such that if the variable TABLE is defined, the table look-up method will be used; otherwise, the bit-shift loop method will be used.

```
149  #ifdef TABLE    /*table look-up method*/

154  #else           /*bit-shift loop method*/

160  #endif
```

Using the Priority Table, the IP and SW fields are shifted into the least significant byte of the register (k0), producing a number between 0 and 255. This is added to the base address of the Priority Table followed by a *load byte unsigned* from that address. This producs an interrupt number between 1 and 8 (corresponding to SW0–INT5). For example, if INT2 and INT4 are both pending, the 80th entry in the table will be accessed, which contains the value 7 (the interrupt number of INT4).

```
149  #ifdef TABLE
150            srl     k0,8             # move sw0 in LS position
151            la      k1,pri_table
152            addu    k0,k1            # compute entry address
153            lbu     ra,(k0)          # get int# from table
```

The second method of determining the highest priority requester uses a loop in which a single-bit mask is shifted one place to the left to test each of the Interrupt Pending bits.

```
154  #else
155          sll    k0,31-16      # move bit 16 into MS position
156          li     ra,9          # initial int#
157  1:      sll    k0,1          # move next bit into MS position
158          subu   ra,1          # next int#
159          bgez   k0,1b         # not found, loop back
```

The D-Cache refill size determines which of the two methods is faster. If the refill size is eight words or more, the loop method will be faster, because it does not require any data access and will execute entirely within the I-Cache. The loop method requires three instructions per interrupt bit; therefore, detecting a pending interrupt on INT0 requires 20 cycles. This method is also more suitable for applications that are sensitive to memory utilization.

Once you have determined the interrupt number of the highest priority interrupt, this number is converted into an interrupt mask, the purpose of which is to enable only those interrupts of higher priority.

```
163          li     k0,-1
164          sll    k0,ra
165          sll    k0,8          # move it into position
166          and    k0,SR_IMASK   # clear other bits
```

Then the mask is loaded into the Status Register. Note that the processor sets the IEc bit before the IM field. Thus, if you attempt to set both in the same mtc0 instruction, interrupts will be enabled for the old Mask value before the new Mask field is loaded (which in most cases would result in recursive interrupts).

```
169          lw     k1,E_SR*4(sp)  # get current SR value
170          and    AT,k1,SR_IMASK # get current IM field
171          and    k0,AT          # qual new mask w/ IM field
172          li     AT,SR_IMASK
173          and    k1,AT          # clear IM field
174          or     k1,k0          # load new mask value
175          .set noreorder
176          mtc0   k1,CO_SR       # update SR
177          nop                   # give it time
178          nop                   # ...
179          or     k1,SR_IEC      # now enable ints
180          mtc0   k1,CO_SR       # update SR
```

Then the interrupt number is used as an index into the Vector Table to access the address of the interrupt's handler.

```
185          la      AT,vect_table    # ignore the warning generated
186                                   # by this line
187          subu    ra,1             # zero based table
188          sll     ra,2             # word-size entries
189          addu    AT,ra            # compute entry addr
190          lw      AT,(AT)          # pick up addr from table
```

To determine whether the interrupt handler is written in assembly language or C, the program checks the lsb of the interrupt handler's address in the Vector Table.

```
192          and     ra,AT,1          # test lsb
```

If it is zero, the handler is assumed to be written in C, and the additional registers will be saved.

```
194          beq     ra,zero,c_isr    # branch if in C
```

If the lsb is 1, the handler is in assembler, so no additional registers will be saved (any additional registers required by the handler will need to be saved and then restored). Before control is transferred, the lsb is cleared because all instruction addresses have to be word-aligned.

```
198          srl     AT,1             # clear lsb
199          sll     AT,1

201          jal     AT               # saves return address in ra
```

The above section transfers control to the handler. The only difference between this handler and the assembler handler in Example 5 is that because interrupts are enabled, k0 and k1 cannot be used. In this case t0 and t1 are used instead (they have to be saved first).

Note that because the handler is called as a subroutine from handler (using jal), transfer of control back to the interrupted program must use a j ra not an rfe instruction.

After the handler has completed, control is transferred back to the label done.

The program restores the Status Register, which disables interrupts. Note that SR must be completely restored, because if there are any differences in the state of SR before and after the interrupt, they will be lost if an interrupted program disables interrupts by clearing IEC.

```
205          lw       AT,E_SR*4(sp)
206          nop
207          mtc0     AT,CO_SR
```

After restoring AT and ra, the saved EPC is restored from the stack into k0, the stack space is deallocated, and control is returned to the interrupted program.

```
211          lw       AT,E_AT*4(sp)
212          lw       ra,E_RA*4(sp)
213          lw       k0,E_EPC*4(sp)
214          addu     sp,E_SIZE*4
215          .set     noreorder
216          j        k0              # return to interrupted program
217          rfe
```

In preparation for calling the C handler, space on the stack for the additional registers that have to be saved is allocated, and then the registers are saved.

```
220          subu     sp,C_SIZE*4     # allocate stack space
221          sw       v0,C_V0*4(sp)
222          sw       v1,C_V1*4(sp)
223          sw       a0,C_A0*4(sp)
224          sw       a1,C_A1*4(sp)
225          sw       a2,C_A2*4(sp)
226          sw       a3,C_A3*4(sp)
227          sw       t0,C_T0*4(sp)
228          sw       t1,C_T1*4(sp)
229          sw       t2,C_T2*4(sp)
230          sw       t3,C_T3*4(sp)
231          sw       t4,C_T4*4(sp)
232          sw       t5,C_T5*4(sp)
233          sw       t6,C_T6*4(sp)
234          sw       t7,C_T7*4(sp)

236          sw       t8,C_T8*4(sp)
237          sw       t9,C_T9*4(sp)

242          mflo     ra
243          sw       ra,C_LO*4(sp)
244          mfhi     ra
245          sw       ra,C_HI*4(sp)
```

Before the C routine is called, the minimum stack size for a nonleaf function is allocated.

```
247            subu     sp,24              # allocate min context
248            jal      AT                 # call C handler
```

When the C handler has completed, the stack context is deallocated,

```
249            addu     sp,24              # deallocate context
```

the saved registers are restored,

```
251            lw       v0,C_V0*4(sp)
252            lw       v1,C_V1*4(sp)
253            lw       a0,C_A0*4(sp)
254            lw       a1,C_A1*4(sp)
255            lw       a2,C_A2*4(sp)
256            lw       a3,C_A3*4(sp)
257            lw       t0,C_T0*4(sp)
258            lw       t1,C_T1*4(sp)
259            lw       t2,C_T2*4(sp)
260            lw       t3,C_T3*4(sp)
261            lw       t4,C_T4*4(sp)
262            lw       t5,C_T5*4(sp)
263            lw       t6,C_T6*4(sp)
264            lw       t7,C_T7*4(sp)
265            lw       t8,C_T8*4(sp)
266            lw       t9,C_T9*4(sp)
267            lw       ra,C_LO*4(sp)
268            mtlo     ra
269            lw       ra,C_HI*4(sp)
270            mthi     ra
```

and their stack area is deallocated.

```
271            addu     sp,C_SIZE*4        # deallocate stack space
```

Then control is transferred to the same done label used by the assembler handler.

```
272            b        done               # branch to code to restore regs
```

4.2.2 Software Interrupts Example

The example program first enables processor interrupts by setting the appropriate bit in the IntMask field and setting IEc.

```
  8  enbint:
  9             .set  noreorder
 10             mfc0     k0,C0_SR
 11             nop
 12             or       k0,(SR_IBIT1|SR_IEC)
 13             mtc0     k0,C0_SR
```

A software interrupt request is generated by calling genint, which sets Sw1.

```
101  genint:
102             .set  noreorder
103             mfc0     k0,C0_CAUSE
104             nop
105             or       k0,a0
106             mtc0     k0,C0_CAUSE
```

When the interrupt is taken, control is transferred to handler. handler first acknowledges the interrupt by clearing Sw1

```
117  handler:
118             .set  noat
119             .set  noreorder
120             # acknowledge the interrupt
121             mfc0     k0,C0_CAUSE
122             nop
123             li       k1,CAUSE_SW1
124             and      k0,k1
125             mtc0     k0,C0_CAUSE
```

and then increments the memory location ticks.

```
126             # increment ticks
127             lw       k1,ticks
128             nop
129             addu     k1,1
130             sw       k1,ticks
```

The program returns to the interrupted program by restoring the address from EPC.

```
131             mfc0     k0,C0_EPC
132             nop
133             j        k0
134             rfe
```

4.3 EXCEPTIONS IN A BRANCH DELAY SLOT

If one of the nine program exception conditions (this does not include external hardware and software interrupts) causes an interrupt to occur, and the BD bit is set (indicating that the instruction occupied the delay slot of a branch), some additional processing is necessary to determine the correct address to which control should be passed on completion of the exception handler. This address depends on whether or not the branch is taken; if it is taken, the address is obtained from the relevant instruction field.

In our example program we use an exception handler, called `handler`, that implements unaligned loads and stores.

When an exception occurs, control is transferred to `handler`, which begins by saving EPC, SR, Cause, and AT.

```
144          subu     sp,E_SIZE*4
145          mfc0     k0,CO_EPC
146          nop
147          sw       k0,E_EPC*4(sp)
148          sw       k0,E_IADDR*4(sp)
149          mfc0     k0,CO_SR
150          nop
151          sw       k0,E_SR*4(sp)
152          mfc0     k0,CO_CAUSE
153          nop
154          sw       k0,E_CAUSE*4(sp)
155          sw       AT,E_AT*4(sp)
```

Then the program checks to see whether the exception is a hardware interrupt (if ExcCode = 0). If so, control is transferred to the label `hwint`, which simply restores EPC and returns to the interrupted program.

```
159          # if (EXCCODE == 0) hwint()
160          and      k1,k0,CAUSE_EXCMASK
161          beq      k1,zero,hwint

275  hwint:
276          lw       k0,E_EPC*4(sp)
277          .set noreorder
278          j        k0
279          rfe
```

If it is not a hardware interrupt, we can immediately enable interrupts by setting the IEc bit in SR.

```
163              lw        k0,E_SR*4(sp)
164              or        k0,SR_IEC
166              mtc0      k0,C0_SR
```

Next, we save some registers for use by the exception handler.

```
169              sw        t0,E_T0*4(sp)
170              sw        t1,E_T1*4(sp)
171              sw        t2,E_T2*4(sp)
172              sw        t3,E_T3*4(sp)
173              sw        t4,E_T4*4(sp)
174              sw        a0,E_A0*4(sp)
175              sw        v0,E_V0*4(sp)
176              sw        v1,E_V1*4(sp)
177              sw        ra,E_RA*4(sp)
```

Then the program checks the saved Cause Register to see whether the Branch Delay bit is set (the current Cause Register cannot be used because interrupts have already been enabled and it could contain anything). If BD is not equal to 1, the program branches to line 204.

```
179              lw        t0,E_CAUSE*4(sp)
180              bgez      t0,1f
```

If the Branch Delay bit is set, the program first obtains the address of the preceding branch instruction by loading the saved EPC from the stack into t0

```
183              lw        t0,E_EPC*4(sp)
```

and then fetching the instruction from the address in t0 and putting it in t4.

```
184              lw        t4,(t0)
```

The address of the instruction that caused the exception is obtained by adding 4 to the EPC value in t0. This address is saved on the stack as IADDR, so it can be used later by the program.

```
186              addu      t0,4
187              sw        t0,E_IADDR*4(sp)
```

Next, in preparation for the branch evaluation that occurs later in the program, some registers have to be saved on the stack. First the contents of the register specified by the RT field of the branch instruction is determined by the macro GETFIELD. It extracts a 5-bit field starting at bit 16 from the branch instruction in t4 and puts it in t1.

```
24   #define getfield(d,s,p,n)              \
25            /* dst, src, posn, size */ \
26            sll     d,s,32-(p+n)    ;\
27            srl     d,32-n                \
```

Next, the contents of the register specified by the RT field is obtained using the table getreg, which contains addresses of subroutines that return the contents of the register specified by the index into the table.

```
30   getreg:  .word gr0,gr1,gr2,gr3,gr4,gr5,gr6,gr7,gr8,gr9,gr10,gr11
31            .word gr12,gr13,gr14,gr15,gr16,gr17,gr18,gr19,gr20,gr21
32            .word gr22,gr23,gr24,gr25,gr26,gr27,gr28,gr29,gr30,gr31
```

The value obtained from this is saved on the stack as RTB.

```
189          getfield(t1,t4,16,5)
190          la      t0,getreg        # base addr of table
191          sll     t1,2             # word-size entries
192          addu    t1,t0            # address of entry
193          lw      t1,(t1)          # get contents
194          jal     t1
195          sw      v0,E_RTB*4(sp)   # save value
```

The RS field of the branch instruction is obtained in the same way.

```
197          getfield(t1,t4,21,5)
198          la      t0,getreg        # base addr of table
199          sll     t1,2             # word-size entries
200          addu    t1,t0            # address of entry
201          lw      t1,(t1)          # get contents
202          jal     t1
203          sw      v0,E_RSB*4(sp)   # save value
```

Then the contents of the registers specified by the RT and RS fields of the exception-causing instruction are saved in the stack as RTI and RSI.

```
208          # save(E_RTI,RT(IADDR))
209          getfield(t1,t4,16,5)
210          la      t0,getreg        # base addr of table
211          sll     t1,2             # word-size entries
```

```
212          addu    t1,t0           # address of entry
213          lw      t1,(t1)         # get contents
214          jal     t1
215          sw      v0,E_RTI*4(sp)  # save value

216          # save(E_RSI,RS(IADDR))
217          getfield(t1,t4,21,5)
218          la      t0,getreg       # base addr of table
219          sll     t1,2            # word-size entries
220          addu    t1,t0           # address of entry
221          lw      t1,(t1)         # get contents
222          jal     t1
223          sw      v0,E_RSI*4(sp)  # save value
```

Next, control is transferred to the appropriate handler for the exception that has occurred. This is done using the ExcCode field from the saved Cause Register as an index into vectable, and then a subroutine jump is performed to the address in the table.

```
226          lw      t1,E_CAUSE*4(sp)
227          and     t1,CAUSE_EXCMASK
228          la      t0,vectable
229          addu    t1,t0
230          lw      t1,(t1)
231          jal     t1
```

If the exception was an unaligned load, control is transferred to the label AdEL_handler. AdEL_handler first obtains the instruction that caused the exception.

```
446          lw      t0,E_IADDR*4(sp)
447          lw      t3,(t0)         # get instr
```

Then it masks the offset field of the instruction, sign-extends it, and adds to it the saved RSI value from the stack (this is the address from which the word needs to be loaded).

```
448          sll     t0,t3,16        # mask out offset part
449          sra     t0,16           # sign-extend
450          lw      t1,E_RSI*4(sp)
451          addu    t1,t0
```

Next, the program determines whether the load instruction is a *load word* (lw), a *load halfword* (lh), or a *load halfword unsigned* (lhu). It checks bit 28 first.

```
454              sll     t0,t3,31-28
455              bgez    t0,1f
```

If it is set, the instruction was an lhu, so the word is fetched using a ulhu instruction, placing the result in v0.

```
457              ulhu    v0,(t1)
```

If bit 28 is not set, then bit 27 is tested.

```
459   1:         sll     t0,t3,31-27
460              bgez    t0,1f
```

If bit 27 is set, the instruction was an lw, so the word is fetched using a ulw instruction, placing the result in v0.

```
462              ulw     v0,(t1)
```

If bit 27 is not set, the instruction was an lh, so a ulh is used to fetch the halfword.

```
465              ulh     v0,(t1)
```

Finally, in order that the main exception handler can place the loaded value in the correct destination register, the required register number is put in v1 (by GETFIELD).

```
467              getfield(v1,t3,16,5)
468              j       ra
```

handler first checks v1 to see whether its value is nonzero. A nonzero value indicates that v0 contains a value that needs to be placed in the register designated by v1. This is done using the table putreg, whose function is similar to that of the table getreg described earlier, except that it puts a value in a register instead of getting a value from a register.

```
236              beq     v1,zero,1f
237              la      t0,putreg
238              sll     v1,2
239              addu    v1,t0
240              lw      v1,(v1)
241              move    a0,v0
```

```
242            jal     v1
243    1:

34  putreg: .word   pr0,pr1,pr2,pr3,pr4,pr5,pr6,pr7,pr8,pr9,pr10,pr11
35          .word   pr12,pr13,pr14,pr15,pr16,pr17,pr18,pr19,pr20,pr21
36          .word   pr22,pr23,pr24,pr25,pr26,pr27,pr28,pr29,pr30,pr31
```

Before returning to the interrupted program, the program checks the most significant bit of the saved Cause register to see whether the Branch Delay bit is set. Before the bit is checked, a default return address of EPC+4 is placed in v0 in case the instruction is not in a Branch-Delay slot.

```
245            lw      v0,E_EPC*4(sp)      # default return address
246            addu    v0,4
247            lw      t0,E_CAUSE*4(sp)
248            bgez    t0,1f
```

If BD is not set, the default address of EPC+4 (in v0) is used. If BD is set, the program has to evaluate the branch to determine whether it will be taken.

```
250            lw      a0,E_EPC*4(sp)
251            jal     evalbra
```

The function evalbra determines the address of the next instruction to be executed, which is the correct address to which control should be transferred on completion of the exception handler. evalbra first loads the branch instruction into t4

```
291            lw      t4,E_EPC*4(sp)
292            lw      t4,(t4)             # get instr
```

and then checks to see whether it is a conditional branch by checking the 6-bit field in the instruction starting at bit 26.

```
294            getfield(t0,t4,26,6)        # 0,2&3=no
295            beq     t0,0,ncond          # bra if not conditional
296            beq     t0,2,ncond          # bra if not conditional
297            beq     t0,3,ncond          # bra if not conditional
```

If this value is 0, 2, or 3, the branch is unconditional and control is transferred to the label ncond (line 238).

If the branch is conditional, the program must determine whether the branch will be taken. This is done by jumping to one of the pieces of code in

lines 316–321, one for each of the possible conditional branch instructions.
These sections of code take one or two arguments in t0 and t1, and control is
transferred to the appropriate routine by indexing into the table bcc_table:

```
39  bcc_table:
40              .word 0,bltz,bgez,0,beq,bne,blez,bgtz
```

So the first section of code in this block generates an index that can be
used to access this table.

```
300             getfield(t2,t4,26,3)
301             bne     t2,1,1f
302             getfield(t0,t4,16,1)
303             bne     t0,1,1f
304             li      t2,2
```

Then this index is used to extract the appropriate table entry.

```
305  1:     # t2=index
306         sll     t2,2            # word-size entries
307         la      t3,bcc_table
308         addu    t2,t3
309         lw      t2,(t2)         # get entry
310         # t2=table entry
```

The register values that are required for the conditional branch evaluation are put in t0 and t1

```
311         lw      t0,E_RSB*4(sp)
312         lw      t1,E_RTB*4(sp)
```

and then control is transferred to the selected routine.

```
315         j       t2              # jump thru bcc table[]
```

If the branch is not taken, control is transferred to the label done. This
was why EPC+4 was put in register v0 prior to the jump to evalbra.

```
314         addu    v0,a0,8         # t = epc+8 (not taken)
```

If the branch is taken, control is transferred to line 322. The target address
of the branch is determined by extracting the least significant 16 bits from the
instruction, sign-extending them, and adding them to EPC+4.

```
322  1:      # t = epc+instr+4
323          getfield(t0,t4,0,16)
324          sll     t0,16              # sign-extend t0
325          sra     t0,16-2            # convert to byte offset
326          addu    t0,a0              # add epc
327          addu    v0,t0,4
328          b       done
```

Control is then transferred to the label done.

```
341  done:   # addr is now in v0
342          j       ra
```

If the branch is nonconditional, the 3-bit instruction field starting at bit 26 is examined to see whether it is a jump register. If this field has a value of 0, it is a jump register instruction and control is transferred to line 339.

```
329  ncond:  # jump reg?
330          getfield(t0,t4,26,3)       # 0=jr
331          beq     t0,zero,1f         # bra if jr
```

If not, then the target address can be determined by taking the 26 least significant bits of the instruction, converting them to a byte address, and merging this address with the current segment number in the PC. Then control is transferred to done.

```
332          # t = seg(epc)+instr
333          getfield(t0,t4,0,26)
334          sll     t0,2               # word address
335          srl     t1,a0,28           # get seg
336          sll     t1,28
337          or      v0,t1,t0           # merge seg and offset
338          b       done
```

For the jump register case, the target address is the saved value RSB.

```
340          lw      v0,E_RSB*4(sp)
```

So at the completion of evalbra, the target address is in v0.

```
341  done:   # addr is now in v0
342          j       ra
343          .end evalbra
```

Control then passes back to line 252. Now that the target address is in v0, all registers can be restored except t0 and v0 (lines 255–262), after which interrupts can be disabled by restoring SR (using t0), and then t0 itself can be restored.

```
264             lw      t0,E_SR*4(sp)
265             .set noreorder
266             mtc0    t0,CO_SR
267             lw      t0,E_T0*4(sp)
```

Finally, before v0 is restored, its value is copied into k0, the stack space is deallocated, and then control is passed back to the interrupted program (lines 268–272).

```
268             move    k0,v0
269             lw      v0,E_V0*4(sp)
270             addu    sp,E_SIZE*4
271             j       k0
272             rfe
```

4.4 INTERRUPT LATENCY

Interrupt latency is the amount of time from the assertion of the Interrupt Request line to the execution of the first instruction of the exception handler. This interval of time consists of two parts:

1. The time from the assertion of the interrupt request until the processor recognizes the interrupt
2. The time taken to transfer control to the first instruction of the exception handler

The worst-case time required for #1 above is obtained by determining which of the following four values is largest:

1. Maximum number of cycles for which your code has interrupts disabled
2. Time for the longest instruction (i.e., *divide*, which can cause interrupts to be ignored for up to 39 cycles if the HI or LO registers are read immediately after the divide instruction)
3. Time to process an I-Cache miss:

$$IMISS = ((IREFILL-1)*NLAT) + 1stLAT$$

4. Time to process a D-Cache miss:

$$DMISS = ((DREFILL-1)*NLAT) + 1stLAT$$

where 1stLAT and NLAT are parameters that specify memory latency: 1stLAT is the number of cycles required to fetch the first word during a block refill from memory, and NLAT is the number of cycles required to fetch each subsequent word of the block; IREFILL and DREFILL are the values specifying the cache block refill size for the I-Cache and D-Cache, respectively

The worst-case time required for #2 in the first list above is two cycles (the number of cycles required by hardware to transfer control to the interrupt handler assuming a cache hit) plus the time required for an I-Cache refill. These two values are added together to calculate the worst-case interrupt latency.

For example, if we assume that the maximum number of cycles in which code has interrupts disabled is 20, that the IREFILL size has been set to 16, and that the DREFILL size is set to 8, then 1stLAT = 3 and NLAT = 2. Using the above formula:

$$IMISS = ((16-1)*2)+3 = 33$$
$$DMISS = ((8-1)*2)+3 = 17$$

Therefore, the largest of the four values is the time for the divide instruction, which is 39 cycles. We then add this value to the transfer time, which is IMISS+2 = 35. This results in a worst-case interrupt latency of 74 cycles.

To take another example, the table look-up method for determining the highest priority interrupt, which we used in Example 6, disables interrupts for 36 instructions. To compute the total number of cycles required to execute those instructions, assuming IREFILL and DREFILL values of 8, 1stLAT = 3, and NLAT = 2, we add the results of the following four calculations:

1. IREFILL miss penalty = 36/8 = 5 refills of 17 cycles each = 85 cycles
2. DREFILL miss penalty = 1 refill of 17 cycles
3. Two back-to-back `store word` penalties = 2*5 = 10 cycles
4. The number of cycles to execute 36 instructions assuming no penalties = 36

This results in a total time of 148 cycles. Thus the largest of the four values in this case is 148 cycles. When we add this value to the transfer time, which is IMISS+2 = 35, the result is a worst-case interrupt latency of 183 cycles, or 7.32 microseconds at 25 MHz.

4.5 PROGRAM LISTINGS

4.5.1 Example 1: A Single Interrupt Source

============== excepts/ex1/main.c ==============

```
1      int ticks;

2
/****************************************************************
3      *  main()
4      */
5      main()
6      {
7      int prev;

8      puts("Example 1 started\n");
9      for (;;) {
10             if (ticks != prev) {
11                     printf("\r %d",ticks);
12                     prev = ticks;
13                     }
14             recurse(60);
15             }
16     }

17     /****************************************************************
18     *  recurse(n)
19     */
20     recurse(n)
21     int n;
22     {
23     if (n == 0) return;
24     recurse(n-1);
25     }
```

============== excepts/ex1/asm.s ==============

```
1      /* startup code, cacheable, with exception support */
2      #include <mips.h>
3      #include <machine.h>

4      #define USER_INTS        (CLK1_INT)
5      #define STKSIZE 8192
6              .comm    stack,STKSIZE
```

```
 7              .text

 8      reset_exception:
 9              j       init
10              .align  8
11              .set noreorder
12              nop
13              .set reorder
14              .align 7

15      general_exception:
16              j       _exit

17      /************************************************************
18      *   init:
19      *       This is the entry point of the entire application
20      */
21              .globl init
22              .globl _exit
23              .ent init
24      init:
25              RAMINIT

26              # clear bss
27              la      v0,_fbss
28              la      v1,end
29      1:      sw      $0,0x0(v0)
30              sw      $0,0x4(v0)
31              sw      $0,0x8(v0)
32              sw      $0,0xc(v0)
33              addu    v0,16
34              blt     v0,v1,1b

35              # copy exception handler to vector locations
36              la      a0,handler
37              la      a1,ehandler
38              li      a2,0x80000080           # general vector
39              jal     copyHandler

40              # flush the caches
41              # first set up a Kseg1 sp & gp
42              la      sp,stack+STKSIZE-24
43              or      sp,K1BASE
44              la      gp,_gp
45              or      gp,K1BASE
46              jal     FLUSH_DCACHE
47              jal     FLUSH_ICACHE
```

```
48              # copy .data to RAM
49              # src=etext dst=_fdata stop=edata
50              la      t0,etext
51              la      t1,_fdata
52              la      t2,edata
53      1:      lw      t3,(t0)
54              sw      t3,(t1)
55              addu    t0,4
56              addu    t1,4
57              blt     t1,t2,1b

58              # ok to use kseg0 now, so initialize sp & gp
59              la      sp,stack+STKSIZE-24
60              la      gp,_gp

61              # initialize I/O devices
62              jal     INITSIO

63              CLK1_INIT(500)

64              # enable interrupts
65              # first make sure sw bits are clear
66              .set noreorder
67              mtc0    zero,C0_CAUSE
68              .set reorder
69              # clear BEV and set IM and IEC bits
70              li      t0,(USER_INTS|SR_IEC)
71              .set noreorder
72              mtc0    t0,C0_SR
73              .set reorder

74              # transfer to main program
75              # reg indirect is necessary to switch segments
76              la      t0,main
77              jal     t0

78      _exit:
79              b       _exit
80              .end init

81      /****************************************************
82      *   copyHandler:
83      */
84              .globl copyHandler
85              .ent copyHandler
86      copyHandler:
87              # a0=src a1=end a2=dst
88              # must not change a0 or a1
```

```
89                # must force a0 & a1 to kseg1
90                or      t0,a0,K1BASE
91                or      t1,a1,K1BASE
92       1:       lw      v0,(t0)
93                sw      v0,(a2)
94                addu    t0,4
95                addu    a2,4
96                blt     t0,t1,1b
97                j       ra
98                .end copyHandler


99       /****************************************************************
100      *  handler:
101      */
102               .globl handler
103               .globl ehandler
104               .ent handler
105      handler:
106               CLK1_ACK

107               # increment ticks
108               la      k0,ticks
109               lw      k1,(k0)
110               addu    k1,1
111               sw      k1,(k0)

112               # return to interrupted program
113               .set noreorder
114               mfc0    k0,C0_EPC
115               nop
116               j       k0
117               rfe
118               .set reorder
119      ehandler:
120               .end handler
121               .set at
```

4.5.2 Example 2: Two Interrupt Sources

=============== excepts/ex2/main.c ===============

```
1        /*
2         * Timer 2 is added to increment the global variable 'ticks2'
3         * ten times per second.
4         */
5        extern int ticks;
6        extern int ticks2;
```

```
7      /*****************************************************************
8      * main()
9      * Start point of entire program.
10     */

11     main()
12     {
13     int prev;

14     puts("Example 2 started\n");
15     for (;;) {
16             if (ticks != prev) {
17                     printf("\r %d %d ",ticks,ticks2);
18                     prev = ticks;
19                     }
20             recurse(60);
21             }
22     }


23     /*****************************************************************
24     *  recurse(n)
25     */
26     recurse(n)
27     int n;
28     {
29     if (n == 0) return;
30     recurse(n-1);
31     }
```

============== excepts/ex2/asm.s ==============

```
1      /* startup code, cacheable, with exception support */
2      #include <mips.h>
3      #include <machine.h>

4      #define USER_INTS (CLK1_INT|CLK2_INT)
5      #define STKSIZE 8192
6              .comm    stack,STKSIZE
7              .comm ticks,4
8              .comm ticks2,4

9              .text

10     reset_exception:
11             j       init
12             .align  8
13             .set noreorder
```

```
14              nop
15              .set reorder
16              .align 7

17      general_exception:
18              j       _exit

19      /*************************************************************
20      *   init:
21      *       This is the entry point of the entire application
22      */
23              .globl init
24              .globl _exit
25              .ent init
26      init:
27              RAMINIT

28              # clear bss
29              la      v0,_fbss
30              la      v1,end
31      1:      sw      $0,0x0(v0)
32              sw      $0,0x4(v0)
33              sw      $0,0x8(v0)
34              sw      $0,0xc(v0)
35              addu    v0,16
36              blt     v0,v1,1b

37              # copy exception handler to vector locations
38              la      a0,direct
39              la      a1,edirect
40              li      a2,0x80000080           # general vector
41              jal     copyHandler

42              # flush the caches
43              # first set up a Kseg1 sp & gp
44              la      sp,stack+STKSIZE-24
45              or      sp,K1BASE
46              la      gp,_gp
47              or      gp,K1BASE
48              jal     FLUSH_DCACHE
49              jal     FLUSH_ICACHE

50              # copy .data to RAM
51              # src=etext dst=_fdata stop=edata
52              la      t0,etext
53              la      t1,_fdata
54              la      t2,edata
```

```
55     1:      lw      t3,(t0)
56             sw      t3,(t1)
57             addu    t0,4
58             addu    t1,4
59             blt     t1,t2,1b
60             # ok to use kseg0 now, so initialize sp & gp
61             la      sp,stack+STKSIZE-24
62             la      gp,_gp

63             # initialize I/O devices
64             jal     INITSIO

65             CLK1_INIT(500)
66             CLK2_INIT(100)

67             # enable interrupts
68             # first make sure sw bits are clear
69             .set noreorder
70             mtc0    zero,C0_CAUSE
71             .set reorder
72             # clear BEV and set IM and IEC bits
73             li      t0,(USER_INTS|SR_IEC)
74             .set noreorder
75             mtc0    t0,C0_SR
76             .set reorder

77             # transfer to main program
78             # reg indirect is necessary to switch segments
79             la      t0,main
80             jal     t0

81     _exit:
82             b       _exit
83             .end init

84     /*************************************************************
85      *  copyHandler:
86      */
87             .globl copyHandler
88             .ent copyHandler
89     copyHandler:
90             # a0=src a1=end a2=dst
91             # must not change a0 or a1
92             # must force a0 & a1 to kseg1
93             or      t0,a0,K1BASE
94             or      t1,a1,K1BASE
95     1:      lw      v0,(t0)
```

```
 96              sw      v0,(a2)
 97              addu    t0,4
 98              addu    a2,4
 99              blt     t0,t1,1b
100              j       ra
101              .end copyHandler

102      /***********************************************************
103      *   direct:
104      */
105              .globl direct
106              .globl edirect
107              .ent direct
108      direct:
109              la      k0,handler      # requires a jump indirect
110              j       k0
111      edirect:
112              .end direct

113      /***********************************************************
114      *   handler:
115      */
116              .globl handler
117              .ent handler
118              .set noat
119      handler:

120              # check to see whether it's for me
121              .set noreorder
122              mfc0    k0,C0_CAUSE
123              nop
124              .set reorder

125              # first see whether EXCCODE=0
126              and     k1,k0,CAUSE_EXCMASK
127              bne     k1,zero,1f

128              # mask IP bits with int mask
129              .set noreorder
130              mfc0    k1,C0_SR
131              nop
132              and     k0,k1
133              .set reorder

134              # now check the CLK1 IP bit
135              and     k1,k0,CLK1_INT
136              bne     k1,zero,clock1
```

```
137              # now check the CLK2 IP bit
138              and      k1,k0,CLK2_INT
139              bne      k1,zero,clock2

140      1:      # spurious interrupt, so if we get here, we are in deep
141              # trouble, try just returning to the interrupted program.
142              b        done

143      clock1:
144              CLK1_ACK

145              ##################################################
146              #                                                #
147              #                Handler body                    #
148              # inc memory
149              la       k0,ticks
150              lw       k1,(k0)
151              addu     k1,1
152              sw       k1,(k0)
153              #                                                #
154              ##################################################

155              b        done

156      clock2:
157              CLK2_ACK

158              ##################################################
159              #                                                #
160              #                Handler body                    #
161              # inc memory
162              la       k0,ticks2
163              lw       k1,(k0)
164              addu     k1,1
165              sw       k1,(k0)
166              #                                                #
167              ##################################################

168              .set noreorder
169      done:   mfc0     k0,C0_EPC
170              nop
171              j        k0
172              rfe
173              .set reorder
174              .end handler
175              .set at
```

4.5.3 Example 3: Nested Interrupts

============ excepts/ex3/main.c ============

```
1     /*
2      * The interrupt handler for clock 1 enables interrupt.
3      */
4     extern int ticks;
5     extern int ticks2;

6     /***********************************************************
7      * main()
8      * Start point of entire program.
9      */
10    main()
11    {
12    int prev;

13    puts("Example 3 started\n");
14    for (;;) {
15            if (ticks != prev) {
16                    printf("\r %d %d ",ticks,ticks2);
17                    prev = ticks;
18                    }
19            recurse(60);
20            }
21    }

22    /***********************************************************
23     *  recurse(n)
24     */
25    recurse(n)
26    int n;
27    {
28    if (n == 0) return;
29    recurse(n-1);
30    }
```

============ excepts/ex3/asm.s ============

```
1     /* startup code, cacheable, with exception support */
2     #include <mips.h>
3     #include <machine.h>

4     #define E_SR    0
5     #define E_EPC   1
6     #define E_TO    2
```

```
7        #define E_T1    3
8        #define E_SIZE  4

9        #define USER_INTS (CLK1_INT|CLK2_INT)
10       #define STKSIZE 8192
11               .comm   stack,STKSIZE
12               .comm ticks,4
13               .comm ticks2,4
14               .text
15       reset_exception:
16               j       init
17               .align  8
18               .set noreorder
19               nop
20               .set reorder
21               .align 7

22       general_exception:
23               j       _exit

24       /****************************************************************
25       *   init:
26       *       This is the entry point of the entire application
27       */
28               .globl init
29               .globl _exit
30               .ent init
31       init:
32               RAMINIT

33               # clear bss
34               la      v0,_fbss
35               la      v1,end
36       1:      sw      $0,0x0(v0)
37               sw      $0,0x4(v0)
38               sw      $0,0x8(v0)
39               sw      $0,0xc(v0)
40               addu    v0,16
41               blt     v0,v1,1b

42               # copy exception handler to vector locations
43               la      a0,direct
44               la      a1,edirect
45               li      a2,0x80000080              # general vector
46               jal     copyHandler

47               # flush the caches
48               # first set up a Kseg1 sp & gp
```

```
49              la      sp,stack+STKSIZE-24
50              or      sp,K1BASE
51              la      gp,_gp
52              or      gp,K1BASE
53              jal     FLUSH_DCACHE
54              jal     FLUSH_ICACHE

55              # copy .data to RAM
56              # src=etext dst=_fdata stop=edata
57              la      t0,etext
58              la      t1,_fdata
59              la      t2,edata
60      1:      lw      t3,(t0)
61              sw      t3,(t1)
62              addu    t0,4
63              addu    t1,4
64              blt     t1,t2,1b

65              # ok to use kseg0 now, so initialize sp & gp
66              la      sp,stack+STKSIZE-24
67              la      gp,_gp

68              # initialize I/O devices
69              jal     INITSIO

70              CLK1_INIT(500)
71              CLK2_INIT(100)

72              # enable interrupts
73              # first make sure sw bits are clear
74              .set noreorder
75              mtc0    zero,C0_CAUSE
76              .set reorder
77              # clear BEV and set IM and IEC bits
78              li      t0,(USER_INTS|SR_IEC)
79              .set noreorder
80              mtc0    t0,C0_SR
81              .set reorder

82              # transfer to main program
83              # reg indirect is necessary to switch segments
84              la      t0,main
85              jal     t0

86      _exit:
87              b       _exit
88              .end init
```

```
89          /**************************************************************
90          *   copyHandler:
91          */
92                  .globl copyHandler
93                  .ent copyHandler
94          copyHandler:
95                  # a0=src a1=end a2=dst
96                  # must not change a0 or a1
97                  # must force a0 & a1 to kseg1
98                  or      t0,a0,K1BASE
99                  or      t1,a1,K1BASE
100         1:      lw      v0,(t0)
101                 sw      v0,(a2)
102                 addu    t0,4
103                 addu    a2,4
104                 blt     t0,t1,1b
105                 j       ra
106                 .end copyHandler


107         /**************************************************************
108         *   direct:
109         */
110                 .globl direct
111                 .globl edirect
112                 .ent direct
113         direct:
114                 la      k0,handler      # requires jump indirect
115                 j       k0
116         edirect:
117                 .end direct


118         /**************************************************************
119         *   handler:
120         */
121                 .globl handler
122                 .ent handler
123                 .set noat
124         handler:

125                 # check to see whether it's for me
126                 .set noreorder
127                 mfc0    k0,CO_CAUSE
128                 nop
129                 .set reorder

130                 # first see whether EXCCODE=0
```

```
131              and      k1,k0,CAUSE_EXCMASK
132              bne      k1,zero,1f

133              # mask IP bits with int mask
134              .set noreorder
135              mfc0     k1,CO_SR
136              nop
137              and      k0,k1
138              .set reorder

139              # now check the CLK1 IP bit
140              and      k1,k0,CLK1_INT
141              bne      k1,zero,clock1

142              # now check the CLK2 IP bit
143              and      k1,k0,CLK2_INT
144              bne      k1,zero,clock2

145     1:       # spurious interrupt, so if we get here, we are in deep
146              # trouble, try just returning to the interrupted program.
147              b        done

148     clock1:
149              CLK1_ACK

150              # allocate some space on the stack and then save EPC,
151              # SR, and a couple of scratch regs (t0 & t1) prior to
152              # enabling ints.
153              subu     sp,E_SIZE*4
154              .set noreorder
155              mfc0     k0,CO_EPC
156              nop
157              sw       k0,E_EPC*4(sp)
158              mfc0     k0,CO_SR
159              nop
160              sw       k0,E_SR*4(sp)
161              .set reorder
162              sw       t0,E_T0*4(sp)
163              sw       t1,E_T1*4(sp)

164              # enable ints
165              .set noreorder
166              or       k0,SR_IEC
167              mtc0     k0,CO_SR
168              .set reorder
```

```
169              ##################################################
170              #                                                #
171              #                  Handler body                  #
172              # inc memory
173              la      t0,ticks
174              lw      t1,(t0)
175              addu    t1,1
176              sw      t1,(t0)
177              #                                                #
178              ##################################################

179              # disable ints (restore SR)
180              .set noreorder
181              lw      t0,E_SR*4(sp)
182              nop
183              mtc0    t0,C0_SR
184              .set reorder

185              # restore EPC and deallocate stack
186              lw      t0,E_T0*4(sp)
187              lw      t1,E_T1*4(sp)
188              lw      k0,E_EPC*4(sp)
189              addu    sp,E_SIZE*4

190              b       done

191      clock2:
192              CLK2_ACK

193              ##################################################
194              #                                                #
195              #                  Handler body                  #
196              # inc memory
197              la      k0,ticks2
198              lw      k1,(k0)
199              addu    k1,1
200              sw      k1,(k0)
201              #                                                #
202              ##################################################
203              .set noreorder
204              mfc0    k0,C0_EPC
205              nop
206              .set reorder

207      done:   # return to interrupted program
208              .set noreorder
209              j       k0
210              rfe
```

```
211            .set reorder
212            .end handler
213            .set at
```

4.5.4 Example 4: Interrupt Handler in C

============ excepts/ex4/main.c ============

```
1    /*
2     * The interrupt handler for clock 1 is written in C.
3     */
4    extern int ticks;
5    extern int ticks2;

6    /************************************************************
7    * main()
8    * Start point of entire program
9    */

10   main()
11   {
12   int prev;

13       puts("Example 4 started\n");
14       for (;;) {
15            if (ticks != prev) {
16                 printf("\r %d %d ",ticks,ticks2);
17                 prev = ticks;
18                 }
19            recurse(60);
20            }
21   }

22   /************************************************************
23   *  recurse(n)
24   */
25   recurse(n)
26   int n;
27   {
28   if (n == 0) return;
29   recurse(n-1);
30   }

31   /************************************************************
32   * c_handler()
33   * Interrupt handler for clock 1
34   */
```

```
35      c_handler()
36      {
37      ticks++;
38      }
```

============== excepts/ex4/asm.s ==============

```
1       /* startup code, cacheable, with exception support */
2       #include <mips.h>
3       #include <machine.h>
4       #define C_SR     0
5       #define C_EPC    1
6       #define C_AT     2
7       #define C_V0     3
8       #define C_V1     4
9       #define C_A0     5
10      #define C_A1     6
11      #define C_A2     7
12      #define C_A3     8
13      #define C_T0     9
14      #define C_T1     10
15      #define C_T2     11
16      #define C_T3     12
17      #define C_T4     13
18      #define C_T5     14
19      #define C_T6     15
20      #define C_T7     16
21      #define C_T8     17
22      #define C_T9     18
23      #define C_RA     19
24      #define C_LO     20
25      #define C_HI     21
26      #define C_SIZE   22

27      #define USER_INTS (CLK1_INT|CLK2_INT)
28      #define STKSIZE 8192
29              .comm   stack,STKSIZE
30              .comm ticks,4
31              .comm ticks2,4

32              .text

33      reset_exception:
34              j       init
35              .align  8
36              .set noreorder
37              nop
38              .set reorder
```

```
39                  .align 7

40          general_exception:
41                  j       _exit

42          /***********************************************************
43          *   init:
44          *       This is the entry point of the entire application
45          */
46                  .globl init
47                  .globl _exit
48                  .ent init
49          init:
50                  RAMINIT

51                  # clear bss
52                  la      v0,_fbss
53                  la      v1,end
54          1:      sw      $0,0x0(v0)
55                  sw      $0,0x4(v0)
56                  sw      $0,0x8(v0)
57                  sw      $0,0xc(v0)
58                  addu    v0,16
59                  blt     v0,v1,1b

60                  # copy exception handler to vector locations
61                  la      a0,direct
62                  la      a1,edirect
63                  li      a2,0x80000080                # general vector
64                  jal     copyHandler

65                  # flush the caches
66                  # first set up a Kseg1 sp & gp
67                  la      sp,stack+STKSIZE-24
68                  or      sp,K1BASE
69                  la      gp,_gp
70                  or      gp,K1BASE
71                  jal     FLUSH_DCACHE
72                  jal     FLUSH_ICACHE

73                  # copy .data to RAM
74                  # src=etext dst=_fdata stop=edata
75                  la      t0,etext
76                  la      t1,_fdata
77                  la      t2,edata
78          1:      lw      t3,(t0)
79                  sw      t3,(t1)
80                  addu    t0,4
```

```
81              addu    t1,4
82              blt     t1,t2,1b

83              # ok to use kseg0 now, so initialize sp & gp
84              la      sp,stack+STKSIZE-24
85              la      gp,_gp

86              # initialize I/O devices
87              jal     INITSIO

88      CLK1_INIT(500)
89      CLK2_INIT(100)

90              # enable interrupts
91              # first make sure sw bits are clear
92              .set noreorder
93              mtc0    zero,C0_CAUSE
94              .set reorder
95              # clear BEV and set IM and IEC bits
96              li      t0,(USER_INTS|SR_IEC)
97              .set noreorder
98              mtc0    t0,C0_SR
99              .set reorder
100             # transfer to main program
101             # reg indirect is necessary to switch segments
102             la      t0,main
103             jal     t0

104     _exit:
105             b       _exit
106             .end init

107     /*************************************************************
108      *  copyHandler:
109      */
110             .globl copyHandler
111             .ent copyHandler
112     copyHandler:
113             # a0=src a1=end a2=dst
114             # must not change a0 or a1
115             # must force a0 & a1 to kseg1
116             or      t0,a0,K1BASE
117             or      t1,a1,K1BASE
118     1:      lw      v0,(t0)
119             sw      v0,(a2)
120             addu    t0,4
121             addu    a2,4
122             blt     t0,t1,1b
```

```
123                 j        ra
124                 .end copyHandler

125        /*************************************************************
126        *  direct:
127        */
128                 .globl direct
129                 .globl edirect
130                 .ent direct
131        direct:
132                 la       k0,handler      # requires jump indirect
133                 j        k0
134        edirect:
135                 .end direct

136        /*************************************************************
137        *  handler:
138        */
139                 .globl handler
140                 .ent handler
141                 .set noat
142        handler:

143                 # check to see whether it's for me
144                 .set noreorder
145                 mfc0     k0,CO_CAUSE
146                 nop
147                 .set reorder

148                 # first see whether EXCCODE=0
149                 and      k1,k0,CAUSE_EXCMASK
150                 bne      k1,zero,1f

151                 # mask IP bits with int mask
152                 .set noreorder
153                 mfc0     k1,CO_SR
154                 nop
155                 and      k0,k1
156                 .set reorder

157                 # now check the CLK1 IP bit
158                 and      k1,k0,CLK1_INT
159                 bne      k1,zero,clock1

160                 # now check the CLK2 IP bit
161                 and      k1,k0,CLK2_INT
162                 bne      k1,zero,clock2
```

```
163     1:      # spurious interrupt, so if we get here, we are in deep
164             # trouble, try just returning to the interrupted program.
165             b       done

166     clock1:
167             CLK1_ACK

168             # allocate some space on the stack and then save EPC,
169             # SR prior to enabling ints.
170             subu    sp,C_SIZE*4
171             .set noreorder
172             mfc0    k0,C0_EPC
173             nop
174             sw      k0,C_EPC*4(sp)
175             mfc0    k0,C0_SR
176             nop
177             sw      k0,C_SR*4(sp)
178             .set reorder

179             # enable ints
180             .set noreorder
181             or      k0,SR_IEC
182             mtc0    k0,C0_SR
183             .set reorder

184             # now save the rest of the registers
185             sw      AT,C_AT*4(sp)
186             sw      v0,C_V0*4(sp)
187             sw      v1,C_V1*4(sp)
188             sw      a0,C_A0*4(sp)
189             sw      a1,C_A1*4(sp)
190             sw      a2,C_A2*4(sp)
191             sw      a3,C_A3*4(sp)
192             sw      t0,C_T0*4(sp)
193             sw      t1,C_T1*4(sp)
194             sw      t2,C_T2*4(sp)
195             sw      t3,C_T3*4(sp)
196             sw      t4,C_T4*4(sp)
197             sw      t5,C_T5*4(sp)
198             sw      t6,C_T6*4(sp)
199             sw      t7,C_T7*4(sp)
200             sw      t8,C_T8*4(sp)
201             sw      t9,C_T9*4(sp)
202             sw      ra,C_RA*4(sp)
203             mflo    t0
204             sw      t0,C_LO*4(sp)
```

```
205            mfhi    t0
206            sw      t0,C_HI*4(sp)

207            subu    sp,24            # allocate min size context
208            jal     c_handler        # call C handler
209            addu    sp,24            # deallocate

210            lw      AT,C_AT*4(sp)
211            lw      v0,C_V0*4(sp)
212            lw      v1,C_V1*4(sp)
213            lw      a0,C_A0*4(sp)
214            lw      a1,C_A1*4(sp)
215            lw      a2,C_A2*4(sp)
216            lw      a3,C_A3*4(sp)
217            # t0 is restored later
218            lw      t1,C_T1*4(sp)
219            lw      t2,C_T2*4(sp)
220            lw      t3,C_T3*4(sp)
221            lw      t4,C_T4*4(sp)
222            lw      t5,C_T5*4(sp)
223            lw      t6,C_T6*4(sp)
224            lw      t7,C_T7*4(sp)
225            lw      t8,C_T8*4(sp)
226            lw      t9,C_T9*4(sp)
227            lw      ra,C_RA*4(sp)
228            lw      t0,C_LO*4(sp)
229            mtlo    t0
230            lw      t0,C_HI*4(sp)
231            mthi    t0

232            # disable ints (restore SR)
233            .set noreorder
234            lw      t0,C_SR*4(sp)
235            nop
236            mtc0    t0,C0_SR
237            .set reorder

238            # restore t0, EPC and deallocate stack
239            lw      t0,C_T0*4(sp)
240            lw      k0,C_EPC*4(sp)
241            addu    sp,C_SIZE*4

242            b       done

243    clock2:
244            CLK2_ACK
```

```
245             #############################################
246             #                                           #
247             #              Handler body                 #
248             # inc memory
249             la     k0,ticks2
250             lw     k1,(k0)
251             addu   k1,1
252             sw     k1,(k0)
253             #                                           #
254             #############################################
255             .set noreorder
256             mfc0   k0,C0_EPC
257             nop
258             .set reorder


259     done:   # return to interrupted program
260             .set noreorder
261             j      k0
262             rfe
263             .set reorder
264             .end handler
265             .set at
```

4.5.5 Example 5: UNIX Time Function Support

============== excepts/ex5/main.c ==============

```
1     #include <mips.h>
2     #include <machine.h>

3     /*
4      * Initialization is written in C. Timer 2 is used to implement
5      * the UNIX function 'time,' which returns the number of seconds.
6      */

7     unsigned long _time;
8     int ticks;

9     long time();

10    /***********************************************************
11     * main()
12     * Start point of entire program.
13     */

14    main()
15    {
```

```
16      long secs,prev;

17      puts("Example 5 started\n");
18      c_init();

19      for (prev=0;;) {
20              secs = time(0);
21              if (secs != prev) {
22                      printf("\r %d %d ",secs,ticks);
23                      prev = secs;
24                      }
25              recurse(60);
26              }
27      }

28      /***********************************************************
29      *   recurse(n)
30      */
31      recurse(n)
32      int n;
33      {
34      if (n == 0) return;
35      recurse(n-1);
36      }

37      /***********************************************************
38      * c_init()
39      * Perform initialization.
40      */

41      c_init()
42      {
43      unsigned long *d,*s;
44      int direct(),edirect();

45      /* copy director code to vector */
46      d = (unsigned long *) 0x80000080;
47      s = (unsigned long *) direct;
48      while (s < (unsigned long *)edirect) *d++ = *s++;
49      FLUSH_ICACHE();

50      /* initialize clock1 */
51      CLK1_INIT(500);

52      /* initialize clock2 */
53      CLK2_INIT(100);

54      enableInts(CLK1_INT|CLK2_INT);
```

```
55      }

56      /**************************************************************
57      * c_handler()
58      * Interrupt handler for clock 1
59      */

60      c_handler()
61      {
62      ticks++;
63      }

64      /**************************************************************
65      * long time(long *tloc)
66      * Return the current time in seconds.
67      */

68      long time(tloc)
69      long *tloc;
70      {
71      unsigned long t;

72      t = _time;
73      if (tloc != 0) *tloc = t;
74      return(t);
75      }

76      /**************************************************************
77      * int stime(long *tp)
78      * Set the current time, specified in seconds.
79      */

80      int stime(tp)
81      long *tp;
82      {
83      _time = *tp;
84      return(0);
85      }
```

============== excepts/ex5/asm.s ==============

```
1       #include <mips.h>
2       #include <machine.h>

3       #define C_SR      0
4       #define C_EPC     1
5       #define C_AT      2
6       #define C_V0      3
```

```
 7      #define C_V1     4
 8      #define C_A0     5
 9      #define C_A1     6
10      #define C_A2     7
11      #define C_A3     8
12      #define C_T0     9
13      #define C_T1    10
14      #define C_T2    11
15      #define C_T3    12
16      #define C_T4    13
17      #define C_T5    14
18      #define C_T6    15
19      #define C_T7    16
20      #define C_T8    17
21      #define C_T9    18
22      #define C_RA    19
23      #define C_LO    20
24      #define C_HI    21
25      #define C_SIZE  22

26              .extern _time,4
27              .comm   _tenths,4

28      #define STKSIZE 8192
29              .comm   stack,STKSIZE

30              .text

31      reset_exception:
32              j       init
33              .align  8
34              .set noreorder
35              nop
36              .set reorder
37              .align 7

38      general_exception:
39              j       _exit

40      /************************************************************
41      *  init:
42      *       This is the entry point of the entire application.
43      */
44              .globl init
45              .globl _exit
46              .ent init
47      init:
48              RAMINIT
```

```
49                  # clear bss
50                  la      v0,_fbss
51                  la      v1,end
52          1:      sw      $0,0x0(v0)
53                  sw      $0,0x4(v0)
54                  sw      $0,0x8(v0)
55                  sw      $0,0xc(v0)
56                  addu    v0,16
57                  blt     v0,v1,1b

58                  # flush the caches
59                  # first set up a Kseg1 sp & gp
60                  la      sp,stack+STKSIZE-24
61                  or      sp,K1BASE
62                  la      gp,_gp
63                  or      gp,K1BASE
64                  jal     FLUSH_DCACHE
65                  jal     FLUSH_ICACHE

66                  # copy .data to RAM
67                  # src=etext dst=_fdata stop=edata
68                  la      t0,etext
69                  la      t1,_fdata
70                  la      t2,edata
71          1:      lw      t3,(t0)
72                  sw      t3,(t1)
73                  addu    t0,4
74                  addu    t1,4
75                  blt     t1,t2,1b

76                  # ok to use kseg0 now, so initialize sp & gp
77                  la      sp,stack+STKSIZE-24
78                  la      gp,_gp

79                  # initialize I/O devices
80                  jal     INITSIO

81                  # transfer to main program
82                  # reg indirect is necessary to switch segments
83                  la      t0,main
84                  jal     t0

85      _exit:
86                  b       _exit
87                  .end init

88          /*************************************************************
```

```
89      * enableInts(bits)
90      * Enable specified interrupts.
91      */
92              .globl enableInts
93              .ent enableInts
94      enableInts:
95              .set noreorder
96              mtc0    zero,CO_CAUSE   # make sure sw bits are cleared
97              mfc0    t1,CO_SR
98              nop
99              or      t1,a0           # enable selected ints
100             and     t1,SR_BEV       # clear BEV
101             or      t1,SR_IEC       # overall int enable
102             mtc0    t1,CO_SR        # set those bits
103             .set reorder
104             j       ra
105             .end enableInts

106     /************************************************************
107     * direct()
108     * Transfer control to handler
109     */

110             .globl direct
111             .globl edirect
112             .ent direct
113             .set noat
114     direct:
115             la      k0,handler      # requires jump indirect
116             j       k0
117     edirect:
118             .set at
119             .end direct

120     /************************************************************
121     * handler:
122     * Main interrupt service routine
123     */

124             .globl handler
125             .ent handler
126             .set noat
127     handler:
128             .set noreorder
129             mfc0    k0,CO_CAUSE
130             nop
131             .set reorder
```

```
132              # first see whether EXCCODE=0
133              and     k1,k0,CAUSE_EXCMASK
134              bne     k1,zero,1f
135
136              # mask IP bits with int mask
137              .set noreorder
138              mfc0    k1,CO_SR
139              nop
140              and     k0,k1
141              .set reorder
142              # now check the CLK1 IP bit
143              and     k1,k0,CLK1_INT
144              bne     k1,zero,clock1
145              # now check the CLK2 IP bit
146              and     k1,k0,CLK2_INT
147              bne     k1,zero,clock2

148      1:      # spurious interrupt, so if we get here, we are in deep
149              # trouble, try just returning to the interrupted program.
150              .set noreorder
151              mfc0    k0,CO_EPC
152              nop
153              .set reorder
154              b       done

155      clock1:
156              CLK1_ACK

157              # allocate some space on the stack and then save EPC
158              # and SR prior to enabling ints.
159              subu    sp,C_SIZE*4
160              .set noreorder
161              mfc0    k0,CO_EPC
162              nop
163              sw      k0,C_EPC*4(sp)
164              mfc0    k0,CO_SR
165              nop
166              sw      k0,C_SR*4(sp)
167              .set reorder

168              # enable ints
169              .set noreorder
170              or      k0,SR_IEC
171              mtc0    k0,CO_SR
172              .set reorder

173              # now save the rest of the registers
```

```
174        sw        AT,C_AT*4(sp)
175        sw        v0,C_V0*4(sp)
176        sw        v1,C_V1*4(sp)
177        sw        a0,C_A0*4(sp)
178        sw        a1,C_A1*4(sp)
179        sw        a2,C_A2*4(sp)
180        sw        a3,C_A3*4(sp)
181        sw        t0,C_T0*4(sp)
182        sw        t1,C_T1*4(sp)
183        sw        t2,C_T2*4(sp)
184        sw        t3,C_T3*4(sp)
185        sw        t4,C_T4*4(sp)
186        sw        t5,C_T5*4(sp)
187        sw        t6,C_T6*4(sp)
188        sw        t7,C_T7*4(sp)
189        sw        t8,C_T8*4(sp)
190        sw        t9,C_T9*4(sp)
191        sw        ra,C_RA*4(sp)
192        mflo      t0
193        sw        t0,C_LO*4(sp)
194        mfhi      t0
195        sw        t0,C_HI*4(sp)

196        subu      sp,24           # allocate min size context
197        jal       c_handler       # call C handler
198        addu      sp,24           # deallocate

199        lw        AT,C_AT*4(sp)
200        lw        v0,C_V0*4(sp)
201        lw        v1,C_V1*4(sp)
202        lw        a0,C_A0*4(sp)
203        lw        a1,C_A1*4(sp)
204        lw        a2,C_A2*4(sp)
205        lw        a3,C_A3*4(sp)
206        # t0 is restored later
207        lw        t1,C_T1*4(sp)
208        lw        t2,C_T2*4(sp)
209        lw        t3,C_T3*4(sp)
210        lw        t4,C_T4*4(sp)
211        lw        t5,C_T5*4(sp)
212        lw        t6,C_T6*4(sp)
213        lw        t7,C_T7*4(sp)
214        lw        t8,C_T8*4(sp)
215        lw        t9,C_T9*4(sp)
216        lw        ra,C_RA*4(sp)
217        lw        t0,C_LO*4(sp)
218        mtlo      t0
219        lw        t0,C_HI*4(sp)
```

```
220          mthi    t0

221          # disable ints (restore SR)
222          .set noreorder
223          lw      t0,C_SR*4(sp)
224          nop
225          mtc0    t0,C0_SR
226          .set reorder

227          # restore t0, EPC and deallocate stack
228          lw      t0,C_T0*4(sp)
229          lw      k0,C_EPC*4(sp)
230          addu    sp,C_SIZE*4

231          b       done

232  clock2:
233          CLK2_ACK

234          ##################################################
235          #                                                #
236          #                   Handler body                 #
237          # inc tenths
238          la      k0,_tenths
239          lw      k1,(k0)
240          addu    k1,1
241          sw      k1,(k0)

242          # overflow?
243          subu    k1,10
244          bne     k1,zero,2f

245          # yes, clr tenths
246          la      k0,_tenths
247          sw      zero,(k0)

248          # update time
249          la      k0,_time
250          lw      k1,(k0)
251          addu    k1,1
252          sw      k1,(k0)

253          #                                                #
254          ##################################################

255  2:      .set noreorder
256          mfc0    k0,C0_EPC
257          nop
```

```
258             .set reorder

259   done:    # return to interrupted program
260             .set noreorder
261             j     k0
262             rfe
263             .set reorder
264             .set at
265             .end handler
```

4.5.6 Example 6: Prioritizing Interrupts

============== excepts/ex6/main.c ==============

```
1     #include <mips.h>
2     #include <machine.h>

3     /*
4      * Control is passed to the appropriate interrupt handler via
5      * a vector table after higher priority interrupts have been
6      * reenabled.
7      *
8      * The vector scheme permits handlers to be written in C or
9      * assembler. An assembler handler is indicated by setting the
10     * least significant bit of the address in the vector table.
11     *
12     * Determination of the highest priority can be made either by
13     * a table look-up or by a bit test within a loop. The table
14     * look-up option is selected by defining the preprocessor
15     * symbol TABLE.
16     */

17    typedef int Func();

18    Func *vect_table[8];
19    unsigned char pri_table[256];
20    unsigned long _time;
21    int ticks;

22    long time();
23    int clock1(),clock2();

24    /************************************************************
25     * main()
26     * The start point of the entire program
27     */

28    main()
```

```
29      {
30      long secs,prev;

31      puts("Example 6 started\n");
32      c_init();

33      for (prev=0;;) {
34              secs = time(0);
35              if (secs != prev) {
36                      printf("\r %d %d ",secs,ticks);
37                      prev = secs;
38                      }
39              recurse(60);
40              }
41      }

42      /************************************************************
43       *  recurse(n)
44       */
45      recurse(n)
46      int n;
47      {
48      if (n == 0) return;
49      recurse(n-1);
50      }

51      /************************************************************
52       * c_init()
53       * Perform initialization
54       */

55      c_init()
56      {
57      unsigned long *d,*s;
58      int direct(),edirect();

59      /* copy director code to vector */
60      d = (unsigned long *) 0x80000080;
61      s = (unsigned long *) direct;
62      while (s < (unsigned long *)edirect) *d++ = *s++;
63      FLUSH_ICACHE();

64      /* build priority table */
65      donum(pri_table);

66      /* connect and initialize clock1 */
67      vect_table[CLK1_INTNUM] = clock1;
```

```
68      CLK1_INIT(500);

69      /* connect and initialize clock2 */
70      vect_table[CLK2_INTNUM] = (Func *)(((unsigned long)clock2)|1);
71      CLK2_INIT(100);

72      enableInts(CLK1_INT|CLK2_INT);
73      }

74      /**************************************************************
75      * donum(addr)
76      * Generate table containing int number.
77      * Int numbers are 1 thru 8, corresponding to sw0 thru int5.
78      */

79      donum(addr)
80      unsigned char *addr;
81      {
82      int value,count,n;

83      addr++;
84      value = 1;
85      for (count=1;count <= 128;count <<= 1) {
86              for (n=count;n>0;n-) *addr++ = value;
87              value++;
88              }
89      }

90      /**************************************************************
91      * clock1()
92      * The interrupt handler for clock 1
93      */

94      clock1()
95      {
96      CLK1_ACK;
97      ticks++;
98      }

99      /**************************************************************
100     * long time(long *tloc)
101     * Return the current time in seconds.
102     */

103     long time(tloc)
104     long *tloc;
105     {
```

```
106      unsigned long t;

107      t = _time;
108      if (tloc != 0) *tloc = t;
109      return(t);
110      }

111      /****************************************************************
112      * int stime(long *tp)
113      * Set the current time, specified in seconds.
114      */

115      int stime(tp)
116      long *tp;
117      {
118      _time = *tp;
119      return(0);
120      }
```

============== excepts/ex6/asm.s ==============

```
1      #include <mips.h>
2      #include <machine.h>

3      /*#define TABLE /* select table method to determine priority */

4      /* registers that are saved for all ints */
5      #define E_SR     0
6      #define E_EPC    1
7      #define E_AT     2
8      #define E_RA     3
9      #define E_SIZE   4        /* must be even, doubleword aligned */
10      /* registers that are saved for C handlers */
11      #define C_V0     0
12      #define C_V1     1
13      #define C_A0     2
14      #define C_A1     3
15      #define C_A2     4
16      #define C_A3     5
17      #define C_T0     6
18      #define C_T1     7
19      #define C_T2     8
20      #define C_T3     9
21      #define C_T4     10
22      #define C_T5     11
23      #define C_T6     12
24      #define C_T7     13
25      #define C_T8     14
```

```
26   #define C_T9    15
27   #define C_LO    16
28   #define C_HI    17
29   #define C_SIZE  18       /* must be even, doubleword aligned */

30            .extern _time,4
31            .comm   _tenths,4

32   #define STKSIZE 8192
33            .comm   stack,STKSIZE

34            .text

35   reset_exception:
36            j       init
37            .align  8
38            .set noreorder
39            nop
40            .set reorder
41            .align 7

42   general_exception:
43            j       _exit

44   /************************************************************
45   *   init:
46   *        This is the entry point of the entire application.
47   */
48            .globl init
49            .globl _exit
50            .ent init
51   init:
52            RAMINIT

53            # clear bss
54            la      v0,_fbss
55            la      v1,end
56   1:       sw      $0,0x0(v0)
57            sw      $0,0x4(v0)
58            sw      $0,0x8(v0)
59            sw      $0,0xc(v0)
60            addu    v0,16
61            blt     v0,v1,1b

62            # flush the caches
63            # first set up a Kseg1 sp & gp
64            la      sp,stack+STKSIZE-24
65            or      sp,K1BASE
```

```
66              la       gp,_gp
67              or       gp,K1BASE
68              jal      FLUSH_DCACHE
69              jal      FLUSH_ICACHE

70              # copy .data to RAM
71              # src=etext dst=_fdata stop=edata
72              la       t0,etext
73              la       t1,_fdata
74              la       t2,edata
75      1:      lw       t3,(t0)
76              sw       t3,(t1)
77              addu     t0,4
78              addu     t1,4
79              blt      t1,t2,1b

80              # ok to use k0seg now, so initialize sp & gp
81              la       sp,stack+STKSIZE-24
82              la       gp,_gp

83              # initialize I/O devices
84              jal      INITSIO

85              # transfer to main program
86              # reg indirect is necessary to switch segments
87              la       t0,main
88              jal      t0

89      _exit:
90              b        _exit
91              .end init

92      /****************************************************************
93      * enableInts(bits)
94      * Enable specified interrupts.
95      */

96              .globl enableInts
97              .ent enableInts
98      enableInts:
99              .set noreorder
100             mtc0     zero,C0_CAUSE   # make sure sw bits are cleared
101             mfc0     t1,C0_SR
102             nop
103             or       t1,a0           # enable selected ints
104             and      t1,SR_BEV       # clear BEV
105             or       t1,SR_IEC       # overall int enable
```

```
106                mtc0    t1,CO_SR        # set those bits
107                .set reorder
108                j       ra
109                .end enableInts

110        /****************************************************************
111        * direct()
112        * Transfer control to handler
113        */

114                .globl direct
115                .globl edirect
116                .ent direct
117                .set noat
118        direct:
119                la      k0,handler      # requires jump indirect
120                j       k0
121        edirect:
122                .set at
123                .end direct

124        /****************************************************************
125        * handler:
126        * Main interrupt service routine
127        */

128                .globl handler
129                .ent handler
130                .set noat
131        handler:
132                # save AT, ra, EPC & SR
133                subu    sp,E_SIZE*4      # allocate stack space
134                sw      AT,E_AT*4(sp)   # save AT
135                sw      ra,E_RA*4(sp)   # save RA
136                .set noreorder
137                mfc0    k1,CO_EPC
138                nop
139                sw      k1,E_EPC*4(sp)  # save EPC
140                mfc0    k1,CO_SR
141                nop
142                sw      k1,E_SR*4(sp)   # save SR
143                mfc0    k0,CO_CAUSE
144                nop
145                .set reorder

146                # compute possible requesters, i.e., those not masked
147                and     k0,k1           # CAUSE is still in k0
```

```
148             and      k0,SR_IMASK

149             # determine highest priority requester
150     #ifdef TABLE
151             srl      k0,8              # move sw0 in LS position
152             la       k1,pri_table
153             addu     k0,k1             # compute entry address
154             lbu      ra,(k0)           # get int# from table
155     #else
156             sll      k0,31-16          # move bit 16 into MS position
157             li       ra,9              # initial int#
158     1:      sll      k0,1              # move next bit into MS position
159             subu     ra,1              # next int#
160             bgez     k0,1b             # not found, loop back
161     #endif
162             # int# of highest priority int (1..8) is now in ra

163             # convert int# to mask
164             li       k0,-1
165             sll      k0,ra
166             sll      k0,8              # move it into position
167             and      k0,SR_IMASK       # clear other bits
168             # mask now in k0

169             # load new mask into SR and enable ints
170             lw       k1,E_SR*4(sp)     # get current SR value
171             and      AT,k1,SR_IMASK    # get current IM field
172             and      k0,AT             # qual new mask w/ IM field
173             li       AT,SR_IMASK
174             and      k1,AT             # clear IM field
175             or       k1,k0             # load new mask value
176     .set noreorder
177             mtc0     k1,C0_SR          # update SR
178             nop                        # give it time
179             nop                        # ...
180             or       k1,SR_IEC         # now enable ints
181             mtc0     k1,C0_SR          # update SR
182             nop
183     .set reorder
184             # ints now enabled

185             # use int# (1..8) in ra to index into vector table
186             la       AT,vect_table     # ignore the warning generated
187                                        # by this line
188             subu     ra,1              # zero-based table
189             sll      ra,2              # word-size entries
190             addu     AT,ra             # compute entry addr
```

```
191            lw       AT,(AT)           # pick up addr from table

192            # determine whether handler is in C or ASM
193            and      ra,AT,1           # test lsb
194            .set noreorder
195            beq      ra,zero,1f        # branch if in C
196            nop                        # nop necessary to stop ASM from
197                                       # putting srl in delay slot
198            .set reorder
199            srl      AT,1              # clear lsb
200            sll      AT,1

201            # transfer control to ASM handler
202            jal      AT                # saves return address in ra
203
204    done:   # restore SR, which disables ints
205            .set noreorder
206            lw       AT,E_SR*4(sp)
207            nop
208            mtc0     AT,C0_SR
209            nop
210            .set reorder

211            # now restore other regs and deallocate stack space
212            lw       AT,E_AT*4(sp)
213            lw       ra,E_RA*4(sp)
214            lw       k0,E_EPC*4(sp)
215            addu     sp,E_SIZE*4
216            .set noreorder
217            j        k0                # return to interrupted program
218            rfe
219            .set reorder

220    1:      # save other registers required for C
221            subu     sp,C_SIZE*4       # allocate stack space
222            sw       v0,C_V0*4(sp)
223            sw       v1,C_V1*4(sp)
224            sw       a0,C_A0*4(sp)
225            sw       a1,C_A1*4(sp)
226            sw       a2,C_A2*4(sp)
227            sw       a3,C_A3*4(sp)
228            sw       t0,C_T0*4(sp)
229            sw       t1,C_T1*4(sp)
230            sw       t2,C_T2*4(sp)
231            sw       t3,C_T3*4(sp)
232            sw       t4,C_T4*4(sp)
233            sw       t5,C_T5*4(sp)
```

```
234              sw        t6,C_T6*4(sp)
235              sw        t7,C_T7*4(sp)
236              # 16..23 (s0..s7) don't need to be saved
237              sw        t8,C_T8*4(sp)
238              sw        t9,C_T9*4(sp)
239              # 26..27 (k0..k1) don't need to be saved
240              # 28 (gp) usually the same for ISR and interrupted prog
241              # 29 (sp) doesn't need to be saved
242              # 30 (s8) doesn't need to be saved
243              mflo      ra
244              sw        ra,C_LO*4(sp)
245              mfhi      ra
246              sw        ra,C_HI*4(sp)

247              # call the C routine
248              subu      sp,24                 # allocate min context
249              jal       AT                    # call C handler
250              addu      sp,24                 # deallocate context

251              # restore the machine state
252              lw        v0,C_V0*4(sp)
253              lw        v1,C_V1*4(sp)
254              lw        a0,C_A0*4(sp)
255              lw        a1,C_A1*4(sp)
256              lw        a2,C_A2*4(sp)
257              lw        a3,C_A3*4(sp)
258              lw        t0,C_T0*4(sp)
259              lw        t1,C_T1*4(sp)
260              lw        t2,C_T2*4(sp)
261              lw        t3,C_T3*4(sp)
262              lw        t4,C_T4*4(sp)
263              lw        t5,C_T5*4(sp)
264              lw        t6,C_T6*4(sp)
265              lw        t7,C_T7*4(sp)
266              lw        t8,C_T8*4(sp)
267              lw        t9,C_T9*4(sp)
268              lw        ra,C_LO*4(sp)
269              mtlo      ra
270              lw        ra,C_HI*4(sp)
271              mthi      ra
272              addu      sp,C_SIZE*4           # deallocate stack space
273              b         done                  # branch to code to restore regs
274                                              # and return to interrupted prog
275              .set at
276              .end handler

277      /***********************************************************
278      * clock2()
```

```
279        * Interrupt handler for clock 2
280        */

281                .globl clock2
282                .ent clock2
283        clock2:
284                # save some regs
285                subu    sp,8              # allocate space to save 2 regs
286                sw      t0,0*4(sp)
287                sw      t1,1*4(sp)

288                CLK2_ACKT

289                ####################################################
290                #                                                  #
291                #                 Handler body                     #

292                # inc tenths
293                la      t0,_tenths
294                lw      t1,(t0)
295                addu    t1,1
296                sw      t1,(t0)

297                # overflow?
298                subu    t1,10
299                bne     t1,zero,2f

300                # yes, clr tenths
301                la      t0,_tenths
302                sw      zero,(t0)
303                # update time
304                la      t0,_time
305                lw      t1,(t0)
306                addu    t1,1
307                sw      t1,(t0)

308                #                                                  #
309                ####################################################

310        2:      # restore regs and deallocate stack space
311                lw      t0,0*4(sp)
312                lw      t1,1*4(sp)
313                addu    sp,8

314                j       ra        # return to dispatcher
315                .end clock2
```

4.5.7 Example 7: Software Interrupts

============== excepts/swint/main.c ==============

```
1     #include <mips.h>
2     #include <machine.h>

3     /*
4      * This is the C driver program for swint.s. It enables interrupts
5      * and then generates SW1 interrupts and prints the count.
6      */

7     int ticks;

8     /************************************************************
9      *   main()
10     */
11    main()
12    {
13    int prev;

14        puts("swint example started\n");
15        c_init();

16        for (prev=0;;) {
17                if (ticks != prev) {
18                        printf("\r %d ",ticks);
19                        prev = ticks;
20                        }
21                recurse(60);
22                genint(CAUSE_SW1);
23                }
24    }

25    /************************************************************
26     *   recurse(n)
27     */
28    recurse(n)
29    int n;
30    {
31    if (n == 0) return;
32    recurse(n-1);
33    }

34    /************************************************************
35     *   c_init()
36     */
37    c_init()
```

```
38          {
39          unsigned long *d,*s;
40          int direct(),edirect();

41          /* copy director code to vector */
42          d = (unsigned long *) 0x80000080;
43          s = (unsigned long *) direct;
44          while (s < (unsigned long *)edirect) *d++ = *s++;
45          FLUSH_ICACHE();

46          enableInts(SR_IBIT1);
47          }
```

============= excepts/swint/asm.s =============

```
 1          #include <mips.h>
 2          #include <machine.h>


 3                  .extern ticks,4

 4          #define STKSIZE 8192
 5                  .comm   stack,STKSIZE

 6                  .text

 7          reset_exception:
 8                  j       init
 9                  .align  8
10                  .set noreorder
11                  nop
12                  .set reorder
13                  .align 7

14          general_exception:
15                  j       _exit

16          /**********************************************************
17          *   init:
18          *       This is the entry point of the entire application.
19          */
20                  .globl init
21                  .globl _exit
22                  .ent init
23          init:
24                  RAMINIT

25                  # clear bss
```

```
26              la      v0,_fbss
27              la      v1,end
28      1:      sw      $0,0x0(v0)
29              sw      $0,0x4(v0)
30              sw      $0,0x8(v0)
31              sw      $0,0xc(v0)
32              addu    v0,16
33              blt     v0,v1,1b

34              # flush the caches
35              # first set up a K1seg sp & gp
36              la      sp,stack+STKSIZE-24
37              or      sp,K1BASE
38              la      gp,_gp
39              or      gp,K1BASE
40              jal     FLUSH_DCACHE
41              jal     FLUSH_ICACHE

42              # copy .data to RAM
43              # src=etext dst=_fdata stop=edata
44              la      t0,etext
45              la      t1,_fdata
46              la      t2,edata
47      1:      lw      t3,(t0)
48              sw      t3,(t1)
49              addu    t0,4
50              addu    t1,4
51              blt     t1,t2,1b

52              # ok to use kseg0 now, so initialize sp & gp
53              la      sp,stack+STKSIZE-24
54              la      gp,_gp

55              # initialize I/O devices
56              jal     INITSIO

57              # transfer to main program
58              # reg indirect is necessary to switch segments
59              la      t0,main
60              jal     t0

61      _exit:
62              b       _exit
63              .end init

64      /****************************************************************
65      * enableInts(bits)
66      * Enable specified interrupts.
```

```
67      */

68              .globl enableInts
69              .ent enableInts
70      enableInts:
71              .set noreorder
72              mtc0    zero,CO_CAUSE    # make sure sw bits are cleared
73              mfc0    t1,CO_SR
74              nop
75              or      t1,a0            # enable selected ints
76              and     t1,SR_BEV        # clear BEV
77              or      t1,SR_IEC        # overall int enable
78              mtc0    t1,CO_SR         # set those bits
79              .set reorder
80              j       ra
81              .end enableInts

82      /************************************************************
83      * direct()
84      * Transfer control to handler
85      */

86              .globl direct
87              .globl edirect
88              .ent direct
89              .set noat
90      direct:
91              la      k0,handler       # requires jump indirect
92              j       k0
93      edirect:
94              .set at
95              .end direct

96      /************************************************************
97      *  genint(intmask)
98      *       Generate an SW interrupt
99      */
100             .globl genint
101             .ent genint
102     genint:
103             .set noreorder
104             mfc0    k0,CO_CAUSE
105             nop
106             or      k0,a0
107             mtc0    k0,CO_CAUSE
108             .set reorder
109             j       ra
```

```
110              .end genint

111       /*********************************************************
112       *   handler:
113       *        Handle an SW1 interrupt. This example increments a global
114       *        variable each time an SW1 exception occurs.
115       */
116              .globl handler
117              .ent handler
118       handler:
119              .set noat
120              .set noreorder
121              # acknowledge the interrupt
122              mfc0    k0,CO_CAUSE
123              nop
124              li      k1,CAUSE_SW1
125              and     k0,k1
126              mtc0    k0,CO_CAUSE

127              # increment ticks
128              lw      k1,ticks
129              nop
130              addu    k1,1
131              sw      k1,ticks

132              mfc0    k0,CO_EPC
133              nop
134              j       k0
135              rfe
136              .set reorder
137              .set at
138              .end handler
```

4.5.8 Example 8: Exceptions in a Branch Delay Slot

=============== excepts/bdslot/main.c ===============

```c
1       #include <machine.h>

2       char msg[] = "ABCDEFGHIJK";

3       extern int AdEL,AdES;
4       int *vectable[] = {0,0,0,0,&AdEL,&AdES,0,0,0,0,0,0,0,0,0,0};

5       main()
6       {
7       int *p,i;
```

```
8      puts("bdslot/AdE example started\n");
9      c_init();

10     p = (int *)(msg+1);
11     i = *p;
12     printf("lw=%x (42434445)\n",i);

13     printf("bne not taken,lw=%x (43444546)\n",dotst1(msg+2,0));
14     printf("bne not taken,lh=%x (4243)\n",dotst2(msg+1,0));
15     printf("bne taken,lw=%x (43444546)\n",dotst1(msg+2,1));
16     printf("bne taken,lh=%x (4243)\n",dotst2(msg+1,1));
17     printf("j, lw=%x (43444546)\n",dotst3(msg+2));
18     printf("jr, lw=%x (43444546)\n",dotst4(msg+2));

19     p = (int *)(msg+1);
20     *p = 0x12345678;
21     i = *p;
22     printf("sw=%x (12345678)\n",i);
23     }

24     /*************************************************************
25      * c_init()
26      * Perform initialization
27      */

28     c_init()
29     {
30     unsigned long *d,*s;
31     int direct(),edirect();

32     /* copy director code to vector */
33     d = (unsigned long *) 0x80000080;
34     s = (unsigned long *) direct;
35     while (s < (unsigned long *)edirect) *d++ = *s++;
36     FLUSH_ICACHE();

37     enableInts(0); /* clear BEV */
38     }
```

============ excepts/bdslot/asm.s ============

```
1      #include <mips.h>
2      #include <machine.h>

3      /* stack offset definitions */
4      #define E_RSI   0
5      #define E_RTI   1
6      #define E_RSB   2
```

```
 7      #define E_RTB    3
 8      #define E_EPC    4
 9      #define E_CAUSE  5
10      #define E_IADDR  6
11      #define E_SR     7
12      #define E_T0     8
13      #define E_T1     9
14      #define E_T2     10
15      #define E_T3     11
16      #define E_T4     12
17      #define E_A0     13
18      #define E_V0     14
19      #define E_V1     15
20      #define E_RA     16
21      #define E_AT     17
22      #define E_SIZE   18                       /* must be even */

23      /* macro for getting a field from a register */
24      #define getfield(d,s,p,n)        \
25              /* dst, src, posn, size */ \
26              sll     d,s,32-(p+n)    ;\
27              srl     d,32-n             \

28              .data
29              /* a table used to get a value from a register */
30      getreg: .word gr0,gr1,gr2,gr3,gr4,gr5,gr6,gr7,gr8,gr9,gr10,gr11
31              .word gr12,gr13,gr14,gr15,gr16,gr17,gr18,gr19,gr20,gr21
32              .word gr22,gr23,gr24,gr25,gr26,gr27,gr28,gr29,gr30,gr31

33              /* a table used to put a value in a register */
34      putreg: .word pr0,pr1,pr2,pr3,pr4,pr5,pr6,pr7,pr8,pr9,pr10,pr11
35              .word pr12,pr13,pr14,pr15,pr16,pr17,pr18,pr19,pr20,pr21
36              .word pr22,pr23,pr24,pr25,pr26,pr27,pr28,pr29,pr30,pr31

37              # a table used in evalbra to assist in conditional branch
38              # evaluation
39      bcc_table:
40              .word 0,bltz,bgez,0,beq,bne,blez,bgtz

41      #define STKSIZE 8192
42              .comm   stack,STKSIZE

43              .text

44      reset_exception:
45              j       init
46              .align  8
47              .set    noreorder
```

```
48              nop
49              .set reorder
50              .align 7

51      general_exception:
52              j       _exit

53      /************************************************************
54      *  init:
55      *       This is the entry point of the entire application.
56      */
57              .globl init
58              .globl _exit
59              .ent init
60      init:
61              RAMINIT

62              # clear bss
63              la      v0,_fbss
64              la      v1,end
65      1:      sw      $0,0x0(v0)
66              sw      $0,0x4(v0)
67              sw      $0,0x8(v0)
68              sw      $0,0xc(v0)
69              addu    v0,16
70              blt     v0,v1,1b

71              # flush the caches
72              # first set up a K1seg sp & gp
73              la      sp,stack+STKSIZE-24
74              or      sp,K1BASE
75              la      gp,_gp
76              or      gp,K1BASE
77              jal     FLUSH_DCACHE
78              jal     FLUSH_ICACHE

79              # copy .data to RAM
80              # src=etext dst=_fdata stop=edata
81              la      t0,etext
82              la      t1,_fdata
83              la      t2,edata
84      1:      lw      t3,(t0)
85              sw      t3,(t1)
86              addu    t0,4
87              addu    t1,4
88              blt     t1,t2,1b

89              # ok to use k0seg now, so initialize sp & gp
```

```
90              la      sp,stack+STKSIZE-24
91              la      gp,_gp

92              # initialize I/O devices
93              jal     INITSIO
94              # transfer to main program
95              # reg indirect is necessary to switch segments
96              la      t0,main
97              jal     t0

98      _exit:
99              b       _exit
100             .end init

101     /****************************************************************
102     * enableInts(bits)
103     * Enable specified interrupts.
104     */

105             .globl enableInts
106             .ent enableInts
107     enableInts:
108             .set noreorder
109             mtc0    zero,C0_CAUSE   # make sure sw bits are cleared
110             mfc0    t1,C0_SR
111             nop
112             or      t1,a0           # enable selected ints
113             and     t1,SR_BEV       # clear BEV
114             or      t1,SR_IEC       # overall int enable
115             mtc0    t1,C0_SR        # set those bits
116             .set reorder
117             j       ra
118             .end enableInts

119     /****************************************************************
120     * direct()
121     * Transfer control to handler
122     */

123             .globl direct
124             .globl edirect
125             .ent direct
126             .set noat
127     direct:
128             la      k0,handler      # requires jump indirect
129             j       k0
130     edirect:
```

```
131             .set at
132             .end direct

133     /*************************************************************
134     *   handler
135     *       Start of exception handler. User-defined handlers are
136     *       called via the table vectable. On return from the user-
137     *       defined handler, if v1 is nonzero, the value in v0 is
138     *       placed in the register specified by v1.
139     */
140             .globl handler
141             .ent handler
142     handler:
143             .set noat
144             .set noreorder
145             subu    sp,E_SIZE*4
146             mfc0    k0,C0_EPC
147             nop
148             sw      k0,E_EPC*4(sp)
149             sw      k0,E_IADDR*4(sp)
150             mfc0    k0,C0_SR
151             nop
152             sw      k0,E_SR*4(sp)
153             mfc0    k0,C0_CAUSE
154             nop
155             sw      k0,E_CAUSE*4(sp)
156             sw      AT,E_AT*4(sp)
157             .set at
158             .set reorder
159             # k0 = CAUSE

160             # if (EXCCODE == 0) hwint()
161             and     k1,k0,CAUSE_EXCMASK
162             beq     k1,zero,hwint

163             # enable ints
164             lw      k0,E_SR*4(sp)
165             or      k0,SR_IEC
166             .set noreorder
167             mtc0    k0,C0_SR
168             .set reorder

169             # save t0....
170             sw      t0,E_T0*4(sp)
171             sw      t1,E_T1*4(sp)
172             sw      t2,E_T2*4(sp)
173             sw      t3,E_T3*4(sp)
```

```
174            sw      t4,E_T4*4(sp)
175            sw      a0,E_A0*4(sp)
176            sw      v0,E_V0*4(sp)
177            sw      v0,E_V1*4(sp)
178            sw      ra,E_RA*4(sp)

179            # if (BD != 1) skip bdslot stuff
180            lw      t0,E_CAUSE*4(sp)
181            bgez    t0,1f

182            # we are in BD slot
183            # get instr -> t4
184            lw      t0,E_EPC*4(sp)
185            lw      t4,(t0)

186            # save(E_IADDR,EPC+4)
187            addu    t0,4
188            sw      t0,E_IADDR*4(sp)

189            # save(E_RTB,RT(EPC))
190            getfield(t1,t4,16,5)
191            la      t0,getreg       # base addr of table
192            sll     t1,2            # word-size entries
193            addu    t1,t0           # address of entry
194            lw      t1,(t1)         # get contents
195            jal     t1
196            sw      v0,E_RTB*4(sp)  # save value

197            # save(E_RSB,RS(EPC))
198            getfield(t1,t4,21,5)
199            la      t0,getreg       # base addr of table
200            sll     t1,2            # word-size entries
201            addu    t1,t0           # address of entry
202            lw      t1,(t1)         # get contents
203            jal     t1
204            sw      v0,E_RSB*4(sp)  # save value

205    1:
206            # get instr -> t4
207            lw      t0,E_IADDR*4(sp)
208            lw      t4,(t0)         # get instr

209            # save(E_RTI,RT(IADDR))
210            getfield(t1,t4,16,5)
211            la      t0,getreg       # base addr of table
212            sll     t1,2            # word-size entries
213            addu    t1,t0           # address of entry
```

```
214             lw      t1,(t1)           # get contents
215             jal     t1
216             sw      v0,E_RTI*4(sp)    # save value

217             # save(E_RSI,RS(IADDR))
218             getfield(t1,t4,21,5)
219             la      t0,getreg         # base addr of table
220             sll     t1,2              # word-size entries
221             addu    t1,t0             # address of entry
222             lw      t1,(t1)           # get contents
223             jal     t1
224             sw      v0,E_RSI*4(sp)    # save value

225             ##############################################################
226             #                    call handler                           #
227             lw      t1,E_CAUSE*4(sp)
228             and     t1,CAUSE_EXCMASK
229             la      t0,vectable
230             addu    t1,t0
231             lw      t1,(t1)
232             jal     t1
233             #                                                            #
234             ##############################################################
235
236             # save result, reg# in v1, value in v0
237             beq     v1,zero,1f
238             la      t0,putreg
239             sll     v1,2
240             addu    v1,t0
241             lw      v1,(v1)
242             move    a0,v0
243             jal     v1
244     1:

245             # if (BD != 1) skip bdslot stuff
246             lw      v0,E_EPC*4(sp)    # default return address
247             addu    v0,4
248             lw      t0,E_CAUSE*4(sp)
249             bgez    t0,1f

250             # evalbra puts new pc in v0
251             lw      a0,E_EPC*4(sp)
252             jal     evalbra
253     1:
254             # restore gp regs
255             .set noat
256             lw      t1,E_T1*4(sp)
```

```
257             lw      t2,E_T2*4(sp)
258             lw      t3,E_T3*4(sp)
259             lw      t4,E_T4*4(sp)
260             lw      a0,E_A0*4(sp)
261             lw      v1,E_V1*4(sp)
262             lw      ra,E_RA*4(sp)
263             lw      AT,E_AT*4(sp)

264             # disable ints & restore SR
265             lw      t0,E_SR*4(sp)
266             .set noreorder
267             mtc0    t0,CO_SR
268             lw      t0,E_T0*4(sp)

269             move    k0,v0
270             lw      v0,E_V0*4(sp)
271             addu    sp,E_SIZE*4
272             j       k0
273             rfe
274             .set at
275             .set reorder

276     hwint:
277             lw      k0,E_EPC*4(sp)
278             .set noreorder
279             j       k0
280             rfe
281             .set reorder
282             .end handler


283     /**************************************************************
284     *  evalbra
285     *       Evaluates a branch instruction and determines the
286     *       address of the next instruction. Expects the EPC in
287     *       a0, returns address of next instruction in v0.
288     */
289             .globl evalbra
290             .ent evalbra
291     evalbra:
292             lw      t4,E_EPC*4(sp)
293             lw      t4,(t4)          # get instr

294             # conditional branch?
295             getfield(t0,t4,26,6)    # 0,2&3=no
296             beq     t0,0,ncond      # bra if not conditional
```

```
297                 beq    t0,2,ncond        # bra if not conditional
298                 beq    t0,3,ncond        # bra if not conditional

299                 # is conditional
300                 # is the branch taken?
301                 getfield(t2,t4,26,3)
302                 bne    t2,1,1f
303                 getfield(t0,t4,16,1)
304                 bne    t0,1,1f
305                 li     t2,2
306         1:      # t2=index
307                 sll    t2,2              # word-size entries
308                 la     t3,bcc_table
309                 addu   t2,t3
310                 lw     t2,(t2)           # get entry
311                 # t2=table entry

312                 lw     t0,E_RSB*4(sp)
313                 lw     t1,E_RTB*4(sp)
314                 # t0=(rs) t1=(rt)

315                 addu   v0,a0,8           # t = epc+8 (not taken)
316                 j      t2                # jump thru bcc table[]

317    beq:         beq    t0,t1,1f ; b    done
318    bne:         bne    t0,t1,1f ; b    done
319    bltz:        bltz   t0,1f    ; b    done
320    bgez:        bgez   t0,1f    ; b    done
321    blez:        blez   t0,1f    ; b    done
322    bgtz:        bgtz   t0,1f    ; b    done

323         1:      # t = epc+instr+4
324                 getfield(t0,t4,0,16)
325                 sll    t0,16             # sign-extend t0
326                 sra    t0,16-2           # convert to byte offset
327                 addu   t0,a0             # add epc
328                 addu   v0,t0,4
329                 b      done

330    ncond:       # jump reg?
331                 getfield(t0,t4,26,3)     # 0=jr
332                 beq    t0,zero,1f        # bra if jr

333                 # t = seg(epc)+instr
334                 getfield(t0,t4,0,26)
335                 sll    t0,2              # word address
```

```
336            srl     t1,a0,28         # get seg
337            sll     t1,28
338            or      v0,t1,t0         # merge seg and offset
339            b       done

340     1:     # t = gpr[rs]
341            lw      v0,E_RSB*4(sp)

342     done:  # addr is now in v0
343            j       ra
344            .end evalbra

345     /***********************************************************
346     *   getrg
347     *       Subroutines that are called via the table getreg in
348     *       order to get a value from a specified register. The value
349     *       is placed in the register v0.
350     */
351            .ent getrg
352            # get contents of register
353     getrg:
354     gr0:    move    v0,$0 ; j        ra
355     gr1:    lw      v0,E_AT*4(sp) ; j        ra
356     gr2:    lw      v0,E_V0*4(sp) ; j        ra
357     gr3:    lw      v0,E_V1*4(sp) ; j        ra
358     gr4:    lw      v0,E_A0*4(sp) ; j        ra
359     gr5:    move    v0,$5 ; j        ra
360     gr6:    move    v0,$6 ; j        ra
361     gr7:    move    v0,$7 ; j        ra
362     gr8:    lw      v0,E_T0*4(sp) ; j        ra
363     gr9:    lw      v0,E_T1*4(sp) ; j        ra
364     gr10:   lw      v0,E_T2*4(sp) ; j        ra
365     gr11:   lw      v0,E_T3*4(sp) ; j        ra
366     gr12:   lw      v0,E_T4*4(sp) ; j        ra
367     gr13:   move    v0,$13 ; j       ra
368     gr14:   move    v0,$14 ; j       ra
369     gr15:   move    v0,$15 ; j       ra
370     gr16:   move    v0,$16 ; j       ra
371     gr17:   move    v0,$17 ; j       ra
372     gr18:   move    v0,$18 ; j       ra
373     gr19:   move    v0,$19 ; j       ra
374     gr20:   move    v0,$20 ; j       ra
375     gr21:   move    v0,$21 ; j       ra
376     gr22:   move    v0,$22 ; j       ra
377     gr23:   move    v0,$23 ; j       ra
378     gr24:   move    v0,$24 ; j       ra
379     gr25:   move    v0,$25 ; j       ra
```

```
380     gr26:   move    v0,$26 ; j         ra
381     gr27:   move    v0,$27 ; j         ra
382     gr28:   move    v0,$28 ; j         ra
383     gr29:   move    v0,$29 ; j         ra
384     gr30:   move    v0,$30 ; j         ra
385     gr31:   lw      v0,E_RA*4(sp) ; j          ra
386             .end getrg
387     /************************************************************
388     *   putrg
389     *       Subroutines that are called via the table putreg in
390     *       order to put a value in a specified register. The value
391     *       to be placed in the register is in a0.
392     */
393             .ent putrg
394             # get contents of register
395     putrg:
396     pr0:    move    $0,a0 ; j          ra
397     pr1:    sw      a0,E_AT*4(sp) ; j          ra
398     pr2:    sw      a0,E_V0*4(sp) ; j          ra
399     pr3:    sw      a0,E_V1*4(sp) ; j          ra
400     pr4:    sw      a0,E_A0*4(sp) ; j          ra
401     pr5:    move    $5,a0 ; j          ra
402     pr6:    move    $6,a0 ; j          ra
403     pr7:    move    $7,a0 ; j          ra
404     pr8:    sw      a0,E_T0*4(sp) ; j          ra
405     pr9:    sw      a0,E_T1*4(sp) ; j          ra
406     pr10:   sw      a0,E_T2*4(sp) ; j          ra
407     pr11:   sw      a0,E_T3*4(sp) ; j          ra
408     pr12:   sw      a0,E_T4*4(sp) ; j          ra
409     pr13:   move    $13,a0 ; j         ra
410     pr14:   move    $14,a0 ; j         ra
411     pr15:   move    $15,a0 ; j         ra
412     pr16:   move    $16,a0 ; j         ra
413     pr17:   move    $17,a0 ; j         ra
414     pr18:   move    $18,a0 ; j         ra
415     pr19:   move    $19,a0 ; j         ra
416     pr20:   move    $20,a0 ; j         ra
417     pr21:   move    $21,a0 ; j         ra
418     pr22:   move    $22,a0 ; j         ra
419     pr23:   move    $23,a0 ; j         ra
420     pr24:   move    $24,a0 ; j         ra
421     pr25:   move    $25,a0 ; j         ra
422     pr26:   move    $26,a0 ; j         ra
423     pr27:   move    $27,a0 ; j         ra
424     pr28:   move    $28,a0 ; j         ra
425     pr29:   move    $29,a0 ; j         ra
426     pr30:   move    $30,a0 ; j         ra
```

```
427   pr31:   sw      a0,E_RA*4(sp) ; j        ra
428           .end putrg


429   /*************************************************************
430   *  AdEL
431   *       Address error on load exception handler. The value is
432   *       placed in v0 and the register number in v1.
433   */
434           .globl AdEL
435           .ent AdEL
436   AdEL:
437           /*
438            * lw  8d 1000 1101
439            * lh  85 1000 0101
440            * lhu 95 1001 0101
441            * if (bit(28) == 1) lhu
442            * else {
443            *      if (bit(27) == 1) lw
444            *      else lh
445            *      }
446            */
447           lw      t0,E_IADDR*4(sp)
448           lw      t3,(t0)         # get instr
449           sll     t0,t3,16        # mask out offset part
450           sra     t0,16           # sign extend
451           lw      t1,E_RSI*4(sp)
452           addu    t1,t0
453           # instr in t3, addr in t1

454           # lh, lhu, or lw?
455           sll     t0,t3,31-28
456           bgez    t0,1f

457           # it was an lhu, so use ulhu
458           ulhu    v0,(t1)
459           b       2f

460   1:      sll     t0,t3,31-27
461           bgez    t0,1f

462           # it was an lw, so use ulw
463           ulw     v0,(t1)
464           b       2f

465   1:      # it was an lh, so use ulh
```

```
466              ulh     v0,(t1)

467     2:       # value in v0, reg in v1
468              getfield(v1,t3,16,5)
469              j       ra
470              .end AdEL


471     /**************************************************************
472     *   AdES
473     *       Address error on store exception handler
474     */
475              .globl AdES
476              .ent AdES
477     AdES:
478              /*
479               * sw ad 1010 1101
480               * sh a5 1010 0101
481               * if (bit(27) == 1) sw
482               * else sh
483               */
484              lw      t0,E_IADDR*4(sp)
485              lw      t3,(t0)          # get instr
486              sll     t0,t3,16         # mask out offset part
487              sra     t0,16            # sign-extend
488              lw      t1,E_RSI*4(sp)
489              addu    t1,t0
490              # instr in t3, addr in t1

491              lw      t2,E_RTI*4(sp)
492              # oper in t2

493              # sh or sw?
494              sll     t0,t3,32-27
495              bgez    t0,1f

496              # it was an sw, so use usw
497              usw     t2,(t1)
498              b       2f

499     1:       # it was an sh, so use ush
500              ush     t2,(t1)

501     2:       li      v1,0             # no reg to load
502              j       ra
503              .end AdES
```

```
504          /****************************************************************
505          *   dotst1
506          *        A test program that has an lw instruction in the delay
507          *        slot of a branch.
508          */
509                  .globl dotst1
510                  .ent dotst1
511          dotst1:
512                  .set noreorder
513                  bne     zero,a1,1f
514                  lw      v0,(a0)
515          1:      j       ra
516                  nop
517                  .set reorder
518                  .end dotst1

519          /****************************************************************
520          *   dotst2
521          *        A test program that has an lh instruction in the delay
522          *        slot of a branch.
523          */
524                  .globl dotst2
525                  .ent dotst2
526          dotst2:
527                  .set noreorder
528                  bne     zero,a1,1f
529                  lh      v0,(a0)
530          1:      j       ra
531                  nop
532                  .set reorder
533                  .end dotst2
534          /****************************************************************
535          *   dotst3
536          *        A test program that has an lw instruction in the delay
537          *        slot of a jump.
538          */
539                  .globl dotst3
540                  .ent dotst3
541          dotst3:
542                  .set noreorder
543                  j       1f
544                  lw      v0,(a0)
545          1:      j       ra
546                  nop
547                  .set reorder
548                  .end dotst3
```

```
549     /**********************************************************
550     *   dotst4
551     *       A test program that has an lw instruction in the delay
552     *       slot of a jr.
553     */
554             .globl dotst4
555             .ent dotst4
556     dotst4:
557             .set noreorder
558             la      t0,1f
559             j       t0
560             lw      v0,(a0)
561     1:      j       ra
562             nop
563             .set reorder
564             .end dotst4
```

The example programs are available via Internet e-mail. To obtain instructions on using this feature, send an empty mail message to mipsbook@carmel.com. Alternatively, you can download the files directly by calling (408) 626-4068 at 300, 1200, 2400 or 9600 baud with 8 data bits, no parity, and 1 stop bit; then use "mipsbook" as your log-in name, and no password is required.

5

Instruction Set Reference

5.1 INTRODUCTION

This chapter contains descriptions of all the MIPS1 instructions arranged alphabetically by instruction mnemonic. The MIPS instruction set consists of both *machine* instructions and *synthetic* instructions. The machine instructions are hardwired; synthetic instructions are expanded into sequences of machine instructions by the assembler.

Not all of the machine instructions are available to the programmer. For example, to jump to an address contained in a register, the user writes j t0. This causes the assembler to generate the machine instruction jr t0, where jr is not an accepted assembler mnemonic.

The instruction mnemonic per se does not always determine whether the instruction is a machine or synthetic instruction. Instead, this is usually determined by the instruction's addressing mode. For example, add t0,1 is a machine instruction, whereas add t0,2000000 is a synthetic instruction that is expanded by the assembler into three machine instructions.

In the "Examples" section at the end of each instruction definition, the assembly-language source statement is shown on the left in bold type, and the machine instructions generated by the assembler for the statement are shown below it and to the right in regular type.

This chapter also includes the assembler directives used in the example programs in preceding chapters. Readers should keep in mind that these are generic descriptions, because individual assemblers have their own particular rules.

5.2 SYNTAX DESCRIPTIONS

The syntax definitions specify an operation to be performed and the operands used in the operation. An instruction operand can be a register (CPU or coprocessor), an immediate value, or a label. An *immediate* value is an address or a data item that can be written as an expression, so long as it contains no relocatable symbols. A *label* is a constant or an expression used as a symbolic name for an address. It can include an expression, so long as the expression contains no more than one relocatable symbol. Instruction operands are listed in Table 5.1.

In the syntax descriptions, instruction operands are separated by commas. Braces enclose two or more items of which one, and only one, must be used, with the items separated from each other by a logical OR sign, | . Parentheses, ( ), indicate that the effective address is computed by adding the contents of the register in parentheses to the optional immediate value that precedes it.

For example, the syntax of the load byte instruction is

```
lb DestGpr,Src{Imm|Imm(Gpr)|Label}
```

This means that the destination can be any general-purpose register (DestGpr), and the source can be an immediate value (Imm), an immediate value added to the contents of any general register (Imm(Gpr)), or a label (Label). As shown in Table 5.1, the immediate values can be 1 to 32 bits in size, and the label can be either a text, data, or short data label. The syntax for all instructions, arranged by type, is shown in Table 5.2.

Table 5.1   Instruction Operands

Operand Prefixes

Src ::= Source
Src2 ::= Second source
Dest ::= Destination

Operand Suffixes

.s := Single-precision floating-point
.d ::= Double-precision floating-point
.w ::= 32-bit signed or unsigned integer

Basic Operand Types

Gpr ::= CPU general register
Fpr ::= Floating-point general register
Fpre ::= Floating-point general register, even
Fpcr ::= Floating-point control register
Cpr ::= Coprocessor general register
Cpcr ::= Coprocessor control register
Imm2 ::= Immediate value, power of 2
Imm16 ::= 16-bit immediate value
Imm10 ::= 10-bit immediate value
Imm25 ::= 25-bit immediate value
Imm32z ::= 32-bit immediate value, lower 16 bits = 0
Imm32 ::= 32-bit immediate value
Immfp ::= Floating-point immediate value
Tlabel::= Text (code) label, address in .text section
Dlabel ::= Data label, address in .data section
Slabel ::= Short data label, address in .sdata section, gp-relative

Derived Operand Types

Label ::= {Tlabel | Dlabel | Slabel}
Imm ::= {Imm2 | Imm16 | Imm10 | Imm32 | Imm32z}
Imm(Gpr) ::= {Imm16(Gpr) | Imm32(Gpr) | Imm32z(Gpr)}

Table 5.2   Summary of Instruction Syntax

Load and Store

`la DestGpr,Src{Imm|Imm(Gpr)|Label}`	Load address
`lb DestGpr,Src{Imm|Imm(Gpr)|Label}`	Load byte
`lbu DestGpr,Src{Imm|Imm(Gpr)|Label}`	Load byte unsigned
`ld DestGpre,Src{Imm|Imm(Gpr)|Label}`	Load double
`lh DestGpr,Src{Imm|Imm(Gpr)|Label}`	Load halfword
`lhu DestGpr,Src{Imm|Imm(Gpr)|Label}`	Load halfword unsigned
`lw DestGpr,Src{Imm|Imm(Gpr)|Label}`	Load word
`lwl DestGpr,Src{Imm|Imm(Gpr)|Label}`	Load word left
`lwr DestGpr,Src{Imm|Imm(Gpr)|Label}`	Load word right
`ulh DestGpr,Src{Imm|Imm(Gpr)|Label}`	Unaligned load halfword
`ulhu DestGpr,Src{Imm|Imm(Gpr)|Label}`	Unaligned load halfword unsigned
`ulw DestGpr,Src{Imm|Imm(Gpr)|Label}`	Unaligned load word
`li DestGpr,Src{Imm}`	Load immediate
`lui DestGpr,Src{Imm16}`	Load upper immediate
`sb SrcGpr,Dest{Imm|Imm(Gpr)|Label}`	Store byte
`sd SrcGpre,Dest{Imm|Imm(Gpr)|Label}`	Store double
`sh SrcGpr,Dest{Imm|Imm(Gpr)|Label}`	Store halfword
`sw SrcGpr,Dest{Imm|Imm(Gpr)|Label}`	Store word
`swl SrcGpr,Dest{Imm|Imm(Gpr)|Label}`	Store word left
`swr SrcGpr,Dest{Imm|Imm(Gpr)|Label}`	Store word right
`ush SrcGpr,Dest{Imm|Imm(Gpr)|Label}`	Unaligned store halfword
`usw SrcGpr,Dest{Imm|Imm(Gpr)|Label}`	Unaligned store word

Computational

`add DestGpr,Src1Gpr,Src2(Gpr|Imm)`	Add (with overflow)
`addu DestGpr,Src1Gpr,Src2(Gpr|Imm)`	Add unsigned
`and DestGpr,Src1Gpr,Src2(Gpr|Imm)`	AND
`div DestGpr,Src1Gpr,Src2(Gpr|Imm)`	Divide (signed)
`divu DestGpr,Src1Gpr,Src2(Gpr|Imm)`	Divide unsigned
`xor DestGpr,Src1Gpr,Src2(Gpr|Imm)`	Exclusive OR
`mul DestGpr,Src1Gpr,Src2(Gpr|Imm)`	Multiply
`mulo DestGpr,Src1Gpr,Src2(Gpr|Imm)`	Multiply (with overflow)

Table 5.2 Summary of Instruction Syntax (*continued*)

`mulou DestGpr,Src1Gpr,Src2(Gpr|Imm)`	Multiply (with overflow) unsigned
`nor DestGpr,Src1Gpr,Src2(Gpr|Imm)`	NOR
`or DestGpr,Src1Gpr,Src2(Gpr|Imm)`	OR
`seq DestGpr,Src1Gpr,Src2(Gpr|Imm)`	Set equal
`sge DestGpr,Src1Gpr,Src2(Gpr|Imm)`	Set on greater-than or equal
`sgeu DestGpr,Src1Gpr,Src2(Gpr|Imm)`	Set on greater-than or equal unsigned
`sgt DestGpr,Src1Gpr,Src2(Gpr|Imm)`	Set on greater-than
`sgtu DestGpr,Src1Gpr,Src2(Gpr|Imm)`	Set on greater-than unsigned
`sle DestGpr,Src1Gpr,Src2(Gpr|Imm)`	Set on less-than or equal
`sleu DestGpr,Src1Gpr,Src2(Gpr|Imm)`	Set on less-than or equal unsigned
`slt DestGpr,Src1Gpr,Src2(Gpr|Imm)`	Set on less-than
`sltu DestGpr,Src1Gpr,Src2(Gpr|Imm)`	Set on less-than unsigned
`sne DestGpr,Src1Gpr,Src2(Gpr|Imm)`	Set on not equal
`sub DestGpr,Src1Gpr,Src2(Gpr|Imm)`	Subtract
`subu DestGpr,Src1Gpr,Src2(Gpr|Imm)`	Subtract unsigned
`rem DestGpr,Src1Gpr,Src2(Gpr|Imm)`	Remainder
`remu DestGpr,Src1Gpr,Src2(Gpr|Imm)`	Remainder unsigned
`rol DestGpr,Src1Gpr,Src2(Gpr|Imm)`	Rotate left
`ror DestGpr,Src1Gpr,Src2(Gpr|Imm)`	Rotate right
`sll DestGpr,Src1Gpr,Src2(Gpr|Imm)`	Shift left logical
`sra DestGpr,Src1Gpr,Src2(Gpr|Imm)`	Shift left logical variable
`srl DestGpr,Src1Gpr,Src2(Gpr|Imm)`	Shift right logical
`abs DestGpr` `    DestGpr,SrcGpr`	Absolute value
`neg DestGpr` `    DestGpr,SrcGpr`	Negate (with overflow)
`negu DestGpr` `    DestGpr,SrcGpr`	Negate (without overflow)
`not DestGpr` `    DestGpr,SrcGpr`	NOT
`move DestGpr,SrcGpr`	Move
`mult Src1Gpr,Src2Gpr`	Multiply
`multu Src1Gpr,Src2Gpr`	Multiply unsigned

Table 5.2 Summary of Instruction Syntax (*continued*)

`teq Src1Gpr,Src2{Gpr|Imm}`	Trap if equal
`tge Src1Gpr,Src2{Gpr|Imm}`	Trap if greater-than or equal
`tgeu Src1Gpr,Src2{Gpr|Imm}`	Trap if greater-than or equal unsigned
`tlt Src1Gpr,Src2{Gpr|Imm}`	Trap if less-than
`tltu Src1Gpr,Src2{Gpr|Imm}`	Trap if less-than unsigned
`tne Src1Gpr,Src2{Gpr|Imm}`	Trap if not equal

Jump and Branch

`j {DestGpr|Imm2|Imm16|Label}`	Jump
`jal {SrcGpr|Imm2|Imm16|Label}` `   DestGpr,SrcGpr`	Jump and link
`beq Src1Gpr,Src2(Gpr|Imm),Label`	Branch on equal
`bge Src1Gpr,Src2(Gpr|Imm),Label`	Branch on greater-than or equal
`bgeu Src1Gpr,Src2(Gpr|Imm),Label`	Branch on greater-than or equal unsigned
`bgt Src1Gpr,Src2(Gpr|Imm),Label`	Branch on greater-than
`bgtu Src1Gpr,Src2(Gpr|Imm),Label`	Branch on greater-than unsigned
`ble Src1Gpr,Src2(Gpr|Imm),Label`	Branch on less-than or equal
`bleu Src1Gpr,Src2(Gpr|Imm),Label`	Branch on less-than or equal unsigned
`blt Src1Gpr,Src2(Gpr|Imm),Label`	Branch on less-than
`bltu Src1Gpr,Src2(Gpr|Imm),Label`	Branch on less-than unsigned
`bne Src1Gpr,Src2(Gpr|Imm),Label`	Branch on not equal
`beqz SrcGpr,Tlabel|Slabel`	Branch on equal zero
`bgez SrcGpr,Tlabel|Slabel`	Branch on greater-than or equal zero
`bgezal SrcGpr,Tlabel|Slabel`	Branch on greater-than or equal zero and link
`bgtz SrcGpr,Tlabel|Slabel`	Branch on greater-than zero
`blez SrcGpr,Tlabel|Slabel`	Branch on less-than to equal zero
`bltz SrcGpr,Tlabel|Slabel`	Branch on less-than zero
`bnez SrcGpr,Tlabel|Slabel`	Branch on not equal zero
`bltzal SrcGpr,Tlabel|Slabel`	Branch on less-than zero and link
`b Tlabel|Slabel`	Branch
`bal Tlabel|Slabel`	Branch and link

Special

`break Imm10`	Break

Table 5.2 Summary of Instruction Syntax (*continued*)

`mfhi DestGpr`	Move from HI
`mflo DestGpr`	Move from LO
`mthi DestGpr`	Move to HI
`mtlo DestGpr`	Move to LO
`nop`	No operation
`rfe`	Restore from exception
`syscall`	System call

Coprocessor Interface

`lwc1 DestFpr,Src{Imm|Imm(Gpr)|Label}`	Load word to coprocessor 1
`lwc2 DestCpr,Src{Imm|Imm(Gpr)|Label}`	Load word to coprocessor 2
`lwc3 DestCpr,Src{Imm|Imm(Gpr)|Label}`	Load word to coprocessor 3
`swc1 SrcFpr,Dest{Imm|Imm(Gpr)|Label}`	Store word from coprocessor 1
`swc2 SrcCpr,{Imm|Imm(Gpr)|Label}`	Store word from coprocessor 2
`swc3 SrcCpr,{Imm|Imm(Gpr)|Label}`	Store word from coprocessor 3
`mfc0 DestGpr,SrcCpr`	Move from coprocessor 0
`mfc1 DestGpr,SrcFpr`	Move from coprocessor 1
`mfc2 DestGpr,SrcCpr`	Move from coprocessor 2
`mfc3 DestGpr,SrcCpr`	Move from coprocessor 3
`mtc0 SrcGpr,DestCpr`	Move to coprocessor 0
`mtc1 SrcGpr,DestFpr`	Move to coprocessor 1
`mtc2 SrcGpr,DestCpr`	Move to coprocessor 2
`mtc3 SrcGpr,DestCpr`	Move to coprocessor 3
`bczf Tlabel`	Branch on coprocessor z false
`bczt Tlabel`	Branch on coprocessor z true
`c0 Imm25`	Coprocessor 0 operation
`c1 Imm25`	Coprocessor 1 operation
`c2 Imm25`	Coprocessor 2 operation
`c3 Imm25`	Coprocessor 3 operation
`ctc1 DestFpcr,SrcGpr`	Move control to coprocessor 1
`ctc2 DestCpcr,SrcGpr`	Move control to coprocessor 2

Table 5.2   Summary of Instruction Syntax (*continued*)

`ctc3 DestCpcr,SrcGpr`	Move control to coprocessor 3
`cfc1 DestGpr,SrcFpcr`	Move control from coprocessor 1
`cfc2 DestGpr,SrcCpcr`	Move control from coprocessor 2
`cfc3 DestGpr,SrcCpcr`	Move control from coprocessor 3

Floating-point Load and Store

`l.s DestFpre,Src{Imm|Imm(Gpr)|Label}`	Load floating-point single
`l.d DestFpre,Src{Imm|Imm(Gpr)|Label}`	Load floating-point double
`li.s DestFpre,SrcImmfp`	Load immediate floating-point single
`li.d DestFpre,SrcImmfp`	Load immediate floating-point double
`s.s SrcFpre,Dest{Imm|Imm(Gpr)|Label}`	Store floating-point single
`s.d SrcFpre,Dest(Imm|Imm(Gpr)|Label}`	Store floating-point double

Floating-point Computational

`abs.s DestFpre,SrcFpre`	Floating-point absolute value single
`abs.d DestFpre,SrcFpre`	Floating-point absolute value double
`neg.s DestFpre,SrcFpre`	Negate floating-point single
`neg.d DestFpre,SrcFpre`	Negate floating-point double
`add.s DestFpre,Src1Fpre,Src2Fpre`	Add floating-point single
`add.d DestFpre,Src1Fpre,Src2Fpre`	Add floating-point double
`div.s DestFpre,Src1Fpre,Src2Fpre`	Divide floating-point single
`div.d DestFpre,Src1Fpre,Src2Fpre`	Divide floating-point double
`mul.s DestFpre,Src1Fpre,Src2Fpre`	Multiply floating-point single
`mul.d DestFpre,Src1Fpre,Src2Fpre`	Multiply floating-point double
`sub.s DestFpre,Src1Fpre,Src2Fpre`	Subtract floating-point single
`sub.d DestFpre,Src1Fpre,Src2Fpre`	Subtract floating-point double
`cvt.d.s DestFpre,SrcFpre`	Convert single floating-point to double floating-point
`cvt.d.w DestFpre,SrcFpre`	Convert fixed-point to double floating-point

Table 5.2   Summary of Instruction Syntax (*continued*)

`cvt.s.d DestFpre,SrcFpre`	Convert double floating-point to single floating-point
`cvt.s.w DestFpre,SrcFpre`	Convert fixed-point to single floating-point
`cvt.w.s DestFpre,SrcFpre`	Convert single floating-point to fixed point
`cvt.w.d DestFpre,SrcFpre`	Convert double floating-point to fixed point
`ceil.w.s DestFpre,SrcFpre,Gpr`	Floating-point ceiling single
`ceil.w.d DestFpre,SrcFpre,Gpr`	Floating-point ceiling double
`ceilu.w.s DestFpre,SrcFpre,Gpr`	Floating-point ceiling unsigned single
`ceilu.w.d DestFpre,SrcFpre,Gpr`	Floating-point ceiling unsigned double
`floor.w.s DestFpre,SrcFpre,Gpr`	Floating-point floor single
`floor.w.d DestFpre,SrcFpre,Gpr`	Floating-point floor double
`flooru.w.s DestFpre,SrcFpre,Gpr`	Floating-point floor unsigned single
`flooru.w.d DestFpre,SrcFpre,Gpr`	Floating-point floor unsigned double
`round.w.s DestFpre,SrcFpre,Gpr`	Floating-point round single
`round.w.d DestFpre,SrcFpre,Gpr`	Floating-point round double
`roundu.w.s DestFpre,SrcFpre,Gpr`	Floating-point round unsigned single
`roundu.w.d DestFpre,SrcFpre,Gpr`	Floating-point round unsigned double
`trunc.w.s DestFpre,SrcFpre,Gpr`	Truncate floating-point single
`trunc.w.d DestFpre,SrcFpre,Gpr`	Truncate floating-point double
`truncu.w.s DestFpre,SrcFpre,Gpr`	Truncate floating-point unsigned single
`truncu.w.d DestFpre,SrcFpre,Gpr`	Truncate floating-point unsigned double

Floating-point Relational

`c.cond.fmt Src1Fpre,Src2Fpre`	Floating-point compare

Floating-point Move

`mov.s DestFpre,SrcFpre`	Move single floating-point
`mov.d DestFpre,SrcFpre`	Move double floating-point

5.3 INSTRUCTION DESCRIPTIONS

abs   ABSOLUTE VALUE

Syntax
```
abs DestGpr
abs DestGpr,SrcGpr
```

Description
Computes the absolute value of the contents of the source register and puts the result in the destination register. Generates an overflow exception if the source operand is the maximum negative value, 0x8000.0000.

Exceptions
Break 6 (overflow)

Example
```
abs t0,t2
            bgez        t2,1f
            add         t0,t2,zero
            sub         t0,zero,t2
        1:
abs t0
            bgez        t0,1f
            nop
            sub         t0,zero,t0
        1:
```

abs.s
abs.d

FLOATING-POINT ABSOLUTE VALUE

Syntax

```
abs.s DestFpre,SrcFpre
abs.d DestFpre,SrcFpre
```

Description

Computes the absolute value of the contents of the floating-point source register(s) and puts the result in the destination floating-point register(s).

Exceptions

Coprocessor unusable
Coprocessor exception trap

Floating-point exceptions

Unimplemented operation
Invalid operation

Examples

```
abs.s $f4,$f8
            abs.s     $f4,$f8
abs.d $f4,$f8
            abs.d     $f4,$f8
```

add   ADD

Syntax
add DestGpr,Src1Gpr,Src2(Gpr|Imm)

Description
Adds Src1 to Src2 and puts the result in the destination register. If Src2 is an immediate value less than 32 bits, it is sign-extended before it is added to Src1. Generates an overflow exception if the addition results in a two's-complement overflow.

Exceptions
Break 6 (overflow)

Examples
```
add t0,t1,t2
                    add         t0,t1,t2
add t0,t1,0x4
                    addi        t0,t1,4
add t0,t1,0x1234
                    addi        t0,t1,4660
add t0,t1,0x12340000
                    lui         at,0x1234
                    add         t0,t1,at
add t0,t1,0x12345678
                    lui         at,0x1234
                    ori         at,at,0x5678
                    add         t0,t1,at
```

add.s
add.d

FLOATING-POINT ADD

Syntax

```
add.s DestFpre,Src1Fpre,Src2Fpre
add.d DestFpre,Src1Fpre,Src2Fpre
```

Description

Adds Src1 to Src2 and puts the result in the destination floating-point register(s).

Exceptions

Coprocessor unusable
Coprocessor exception trap

Floating-point exceptions

Unimplemented operation
Invalid operation
Inexact
Overflow
Underflow

Examples

```
add.s $f4,$f6,$f8
                add.s      $f4,$f6,$f8
add.d $f4,$f6,$f8
                add.d      $f4,$f6,$f8
```

addu   ADD UNSIGNED

Syntax
```
addu DestGpr,Src1Gpr,Src2(Gpr|Imm)
```

Description
Adds Src1 to Src2 and puts the result in the destination register. If Src2 is an immediate value less than 32 bits, it is sign-extended before it is added to Src1.

Exceptions
None

Examples
```
addu t0,t1,t2
                addu        t0,t1,t2
addu t0,t1,0x4
                addiu       t0,t1,4
addu t0,t1,0x1234
                addiu       t0,t1,4660
addu t0,t1,0x12340000
                lui         at,0x1234
                addu        t0,t1,at
addu t0,t1,0x12345678
                lui         at,0x1234
                ori         at,at,0x5678
                addu        t0,t1,at
```

and AND

Syntax

```
and DestGpr,Src1Gpr,Src2(Gpr|Imm)
```

Description

Computes the logical AND of the corresponding bits of Src1 and Src2 and puts the result in the destination register. An immediate value is zero-extended.

Exceptions

None

Examples

```
and t0,t1,t2
                and         t0,t1,t2
and t0,t1,0x4
                andi        t0,t1,0x4
and t0,t1,0x1234
                andi        t0,t1,0x1234
and t0,t1,0x12340000
                lui         at,0x1234
                and         t0,t1,at
and t0,t1,0x12345678
                lui         at,0x1234
                ori         at,at,0x5678
                and         t0,t1,at
```

b   BRANCH

Syntax
```
b Tlabel|Slabel
```

Description
Branches unconditionally to the address specified by the label. The instruction in the delay slot is executed before the branch is taken.

Exceptions
None

Example
```
b main
            beq            zero,zero,main
            nop
```

bal   BRANCH AND LINK

Syntax
```
bal Tlabel|Slabel
```

Description
Branches unconditionally to the address specified by the label and puts the return address in register `ra` ($31). The instruction in the delay slot is executed before the branch is taken.

Exceptions
None

Example
```
bal main
            bgezal      zero,main
            nop
```

bc0f
bc2f
bc3f

BRANCH ON COPROCESSOR 0 FALSE
BRANCH ON COPROCESSOR 2 FALSE
BRANCH ON COPROCESSOR 3 FALSE

Syntax

```
bc0f Tlabel
bc2f Tlabel
bc3f Tlabel
```

Description

Branches to the specified address if the coprocessor condition input pin is false, with a delay of one instruction. The instruction in the delay slot is executed before the branch is taken.

Exceptions

Coprocessor unusable

Example

```
bc0f main
```

```
          bc0f         main
```

bc1f   BRANCH ON COPROCESSOR 1 FALSE

Syntax
```
bc1f Tlabel
```

Description
Branches to the specified address if the Condition bit in the Floating-Point Control/Status Register is zero, with a delay of one instruction. The instruction in the delay slot is executed before the branch is taken.

The Condition bit is set by a previous floating-point compare instruction (e.g., c.eq.s), which also has a delay of one instruction.

Exceptions
Coprocessor unusable

Example
```
bc1t main
            bc1t       main
```

bc0t
bc2t
bc3t

BRANCH ON COPROCESSOR 0 TRUE
BRANCH ON COPROCESSOR 2 TRUE
BRANCH ON COPROCESSOR 3 TRUE

Syntax

```
bc0t Tlabel
bc2t Tlabel
bc3t Tlabel
```

Description

Branches to the specified address if the coprocessor condition input pin is true, with a delay of one instruction. The instruction in the delay slot is executed before the branch is taken.

Exceptions

Coprocessor unusable

Example

```
bc0t main
                bc0t        main
bc2t main
                bc2t        main
bc3t main
                bc3t        main
```

bc1t   BRANCH ON COPROCESSOR 1 TRUE

Syntax
```
bc1t Tlabel
```

Description
Branches to the specified address if the Condition bit in the Floating-Point Control/Status Register is 1, with a delay of one instruction. The instruction in the delay slot is executed before the branch is taken.

The Condition bit is set by a previous floating-point compare instruction (e.g., c.eq.s), which also has a delay of one instruction.

Exceptions
Coprocessor unusable

Example
```
bc1t main
                bc1t        main
c.eq.s $f4,$f6
bc1t main
                c.eq.s      $f4,$f6
                nop
                bc1t        main
```

beq   BRANCH ON EQUAL

Syntax
```
beq Src1Gpr,Src2(Gpr|Imm),Label
```

Description
Branches to the specified label when Src1 is equal to Src2. The instruction in
the delay slot is executed before the branch is taken.

Exceptions
None

Examples
```
beq t0,t2,main
                    beq         t0,t2,main
                    nop
beq t0,0x4,main
                    addiu       at,zero,4
                    beq         t0,at,main
                    nop
beq t0,0x1234,main
                    addiu       at,zero,4660
                    beq         t0,at,main
                    nop
beq t0,0x12340000,main
                    lui         at,0x1234
                    beq         t0,at,main
                    nop
beq t0,0x12345678,main
                    lui         at,0x1234
                    ori         at,at,0x5678
                    beq         t0,at,main
                    nop
```

beqz

BRANCH ON EQUAL TO ZERO

Syntax
```
beqz SrcGpr,Tlabel|Slabel
```

Description
Branches to the specified label when the contents of the source register is equal to zero. The instruction in the delay slot is executed before the branch is taken.

Exceptions
None

Examples
```
beqz t0,main
                beq        t0,zero,main
                nop
```

bge   BRANCH ON GREATER-THAN OR EQUAL

Syntax
```
bge Src1Gpr,Src2(Gpr|Imm),Label
```

Description
Branches to the specified label when Src1 is greater than or equal to Src2. The operands are treated as signed 32-bit values. The instruction in the delay slot is executed before the branch is taken.

Exceptions
None

Examples
```
bge t0,t2,main
                slt        at,t0,t2
                beq        at,zero,main
                nop
bge t0,0x4,main
                slti       at,t0,4
                beq        at,zero,main
                nop
bge t0,0x1234,main
                slti       at,t0,4660
                beq        at,zero,main
                nop
bge t0,0x12340000,main
                lui        at,0x1234
                slt        at,t0,at
                beq        at,zero,main
                nop
bge t0,0x12345678,main
                lui        at,0x1234
                ori        at,at,0x5678
                slt        at,t0,at
                beq        at,zero,main
                nop
```

bgeu   BRANCH ON GREATER-THAN OR EQUAL UNSIGNED

Syntax
```
bgeu Src1Gpr,Src2(Gpr|Imm),Label
```

Description
Branches to the specified label when Src1 is greater than or equal to Src2. The operands are treated as unsigned 32-bit values. The instruction in the delay slot is executed before the branch is taken.

Exceptions
None

Examples
```
bgeu t0,t2,main
                sltu        at,t0,t2
                beq         at,zero,main
                nop
bgeu t0,0x4,main
                sltiu       at,t0,4
                beq         at,zero,main
                nop
bgeu t0,0x1234,main
                sltiu       at,t0,4660
                beq         at,zero,main
                nop
bgeu t0,0x12340000,main
                lui         at,0x1234
                sltu        at,t0,at
                beq         at,zero,main
                nop
bgeu t0,0x12345678,main
                lui         at,0x1234
                ori         at,at,0x5678
                sltu        at,t0,at
                beq         at,zero,main
                nop
```

bgez   BRANCH ON GREATER-THAN OR EQUAL TO ZERO

Syntax
```
bgez SrcGpr,Tlabel|Slabel
```

Description
Branches to the specified label when the contents of the source register, treated as a signed 32-bit value, is greater than or equal to zero. The instruction in the delay slot is executed before the branch is taken.

Exceptions
None

Example
```
bgez t0,main
                bgez        t0,main
                nop
```

bgezal

BRANCH ON GREATER-THAN OR EQUAL TO ZERO AND LINK

Syntax
```
bgezal SrcGpr,Tlabel|Slabel
```

Description
Branches to the specified label when the contents of the source register, treated as a 32-bit value, is greater than or equal to zero. The return address is put in register ra ($31).

Exceptions
None

Example
```
bgezal t0,main
                bgezal      t0,main
                nop
```

bgt   BRANCH ON GREATER-THAN

Syntax
```
bgt Src1Gpr,Src2(Gpr|Imm),Label
```

Description
Branches to the specified label when Src1 is greater than Src2. The operands
are treated as signed 32-bit values. The instruction in the delay slot is executed before the branch is taken.

Exceptions
None

Examples
```
bgt t0,t2,main
                    slt       at,t2,t0
                    bne       at,zero,main
                    nop
bgt t0,0x4,main
                    slti      at,t0,5
                    beq       at,zero,main
                    nop
bgt t0,0x1234,main
                    slti      at,t0,4661
                    beq       at,zero,main
                    nop
bgt t0,0x12340000,main
                    lui       at,0x1234
                    ori       at,at,0x1
                    slt       at,t0,at
                    beq       at,zero,main
                    nop
bgt t0,0x12345678,main
                    lui       at,0x1234
                    ori       at,at,0x5679
                    slt       at,t0,at
                    beq       at,zero,main
                    nop
```

bgtu   BRANCH ON GREATER-THAN UNSIGNED

Syntax
```
bgtu Src1Gpr,Src2(Gpr|Imm),Label
```

Description
Branches to the specified label when Src1 is greater than Src2. The operands are treated as unsigned 32-bit values. The instruction in the delay slot is executed before the branch is taken.

Exceptions
None

Examples
```
bgtu t0,t2,main
                sltu       at,t2,t0
                bne        at,zero,main
                nop
bgtu t0,0x4,main
                sltiu      at,t0,5
                beq        at,zero,main
                nop
bgtu t0,0x1234,main
                sltiu      at,t0,4661
                beq        at,zero,main
                nop
bgtu t0,0x12340000,main
                lui        at,0x1234
                ori        at,at,0x1
                sltu       at,t0,at
                beq        at,zero,main
                nop
bgtu t0,0x12345678,main
                lui        at,0x1234
                ori        at,at,0x5679
                sltu       at,t0,at
                beq        at,zero,main
                nop
```

bgtz   BRANCH ON GREATER-THAN ZERO

Syntax
```
bgtz SrcGpr,Tlabel|Slabel
```

Description
Branches to the specified label when the contents of the source register, treated as a signed 32-bit value, is greater than zero. The instruction in the delay slot is executed before the branch is taken.

Exceptions
None

Example
```
bgtz t0,main
                bgtz        t0,main
                nop
```

ble   BRANCH ON LESS-THAN OR EQUAL

Syntax
```
ble Src1Gpr,Src2(Gpr|Imm),Label
```

Description
Branches to the specified label when Src1 is less than or equal to Src2. The operands are treated as signed 32-bit values. The instruction in the delay slot is executed before the branch is taken.

Exceptions
None

Examples
```
ble t0,t2,main
                slt        at,t2,t0
                beq        at,zero,main
                nop
ble t0,0x4,main
                slti       at,t0,5
                bne        at,zero,main
                nop
ble t0,0x1234,main
                slti       at,t0,4661
                bne        at,zero,main
                nop
ble t0,0x12340000,main
                lui        at,0x1234
                ori        at,at,0x1
                slt        at,t0,at
                bne        at,zero,main
                nop
ble t0,0x12345678,main
                lui        at,0x1234
                ori        at,at,0x5679
                slt        at,t0,at
                bne        at,zero,main
                nop
```

bleu   BRANCH ON LESS-THAN OR EQUAL UNSIGNED

Syntax
```
bleu Src1Gpr,Src2(Gpr|Imm),Label
```

Description
Branches to the specified label when Src1 is less than or equal to Src2. The operands are treated as unsigned 32-bit values. The instruction in the delay slot is executed before the branch is taken.

Exceptions
None

Examples
```
bleu t0,t2,main
                sltu        at,t2,t0
                beq         at,zero,main
                nop
bleu t0,0x4,main
                sltiu       at,t0,5
                bne         at,zero,main
                nop
bleu t0,0x1234,main
                sltiu       at,t0,4661
                bne         at,zero,main
                nop
bleu t0,0x12340000,main
                lui         at,0x1234
                ori         at,at,0x1
                sltu        at,t0,at
                bne         at,zero,main
                nop
bleu t0,0x12345678,main
                lui         at,0x1234
                ori         at,at,0x5679
                sltu        at,t0,at
                bne         at,zero,main
                nop
```

blez   BRANCH ON LESS-THAN OR EQUAL TO ZERO

Syntax

```
blez SrcGpr,Tlabel|Slabel
```

Description

Branches to the specified label when the contents of the source register, treated as a signed 32-bit value, is less-than or equal to zero. The instruction in the delay slot is executed before the branch is taken.

Exceptions

None

Example

```
blez t0,main
              blez      t0,main
              nop
```

blt   BRANCH ON LESS-THAN

Syntax
```
blt Src1Gpr,Src2(Gpr|Imm),Label
```

Description
Branches to the specified label when Src1 is less than Src2. The operands are treated as signed 32-bit values. The instruction in the delay slot is executed before the branch is taken.

Exceptions
None

Examples
```
blt t0,t2,main
                slt         at,t0,t2
                bne         at,zero,main
                nop
blt t0,0x4,main
                slti        at,t0,4
                bne         at,zero,main
                nop
blt t0,0x1234,main
                slti        at,t0,4660
                bne         at,zero,main
                nop
blt t0,0x12340000,main
                lui         at,0x1234
                slt         at,t0,at
                bne         at,zero,main
                nop
blt t0,0x12345678,main
                lui         at,0x1234
                ori         at,at,0x5678
                slt         at,t0,at
                bne         at,zero,main
                nop
```

bltu   BRANCH ON LESS-THAN UNSIGNED

Syntax
```
bltu Src1Gpr,Src2(Gpr|Imm),Label
```

Description
Branches to the specified label when Src1 is less than Src2. The operands are
treated as unsigned 32-bit values. The instruction in the delay slot is executed
before the branch is taken.

Exceptions
None

Examples
```
bltu t0,t2,main
                sltu        at,t0,t2
                bne         at,zero,main
                nop
bltu t0,0x4,main
                sltiu       at,t0,4
                bne         at,zero,main
                nop
bltu t0,0x1234,main
                sltiu       at,t0,4660
                bne         at,zero,main
                nop
bltu t0,0x12340000,main
                lui         at,0x1234
                sltu        at,t0,at
                bne         at,zero,main
                nop
bltu t0,0x12345678,main
                lui         at,0x1234
                ori         at,at,0x5678
                sltu        at,t0,at
                bne         at,zero,main
                nop
```

bltz   BRANCH ON LESS-THAN ZERO

Syntax
```
bltz SrcGpr,Tlabel|Slabel
```

Description
Branches to the specified label when the contents of the source register, treated as a signed 32-bit value, is less-than zero. The instruction in the delay slot is executed before the branch is taken.

Exceptions
None

Example
```
bltz t0,main
            bltz      t0,main
            nop
```

bltzal

BRANCH ON LESS-THAN ZERO AND LINK

Syntax
```
bltzal SrcGpr,Tlabel|Slabel
```

Description
Branches to the specified label when the contents of the source register, treated as a signed 32-bit value, is less-than zero. The return address is put in register ra ($31). The instruction in the delay slot is executed before the branch is taken.

Exceptions
None

Example
```
bltzal t0,main
          bltzal      t0,main
          nop
```

bne   BRANCH ON NOT EQUAL

Syntax
```
bne Src1Gpr,Src2(Gpr|Imm),Label
```

Description
Branches to the specified label when Src1 is not equal to Src2. The instruction
in the delay slot is executed before the branch is taken.

Exceptions
None

Examples
```
bne t0,t2,main
                    bne         t0,t2,main
                    nop
bne t0,0x4,main
                    addiu       at,zero,4
                    bne         t0,at,main
                    nop
bne t0,0x1234,main
                    addiu       at,zero,4660
                    bne         t0,at,main
                    nop
bne t0,0x12340000,main
                    lui         at,0x1234
                    bne         t0,at,main
                    nop
bne t0,0x12345678,main
                    lui         at,0x1234
                    ori         at,at,0x5678
                    bne         t0,at,main
                    nop
```

bnez   BRANCH ON NOT EQUAL TO ZERO

Syntax
```
bnez SrcGpr,Tlabel|Slabel
```

Description
Branches to the specified label when the contents of the source register is not
equal to zero. The instruction in the delay slot is executed before the branch
is taken.

Exceptions
None

Example
```
bnez t0,main
            bne         t0,zero,main
            nop
```

break   BREAKPOINT

Syntax
```
break Imm10
```

Description
Causes a Breakpoint exception. The break codes generated by the compiler are:

```
6 = Overflow
7 = Divide by Zero
8 = Trap on Condition
```

The code field can be used for software parameters, and is accessed by the exception handler by reading the contents of the memory word containing the instruction (via the EPC).

Exceptions
Breakpoint

Example
```
break 6
```
```
                break 6
```

c0	COPROCESSOR 0 OPERATION
c1	COPROCESSOR 1 OPERATION
c2	COPROCESSOR 2 OPERATION
c3	COPROCESSOR 3 OPERATION

Syntax

```
c0 Imm25
c1 Imm25
c2 Imm25
c3 Imm25
```

Description

Performs the coprocessor operation specified by the immediate value.

Exceptions

Coprocessor unusable

Example

```
c1 0x1234
            46001234   c.olt.s $f2,$f0
            00000000   nop
```

c.cond.s
c.cond.d

FLOATING-POINT COMPARE SINGLE
FLOATING-POINT COMPARE DOUBLE

Syntax

```
c.cond.s Src1Fpre,Src2Fpre
c.cond.d Src1Fpre,Src2Fpre
```

Description

Compares Src1 and Src2 according to the condition specified in the instruction and sets the Condition bit in the Floating-Point Control/Status Register to reflect the result of the compare, after a delay of one instruction.

After the one-instruction delay, the Condition bit can be tested using a `bc1t` or `bc1f` instruction.

Condition	True If	Exception If Unordered
eq	Src1=Src2	No
f	never true	No
lt	Src1<Src2	Yes
nge	Src1<Src2 or unordered	Yes
ngl	Src1=Src2 or unordered	Yes
ngle	unordered	Yes
ngt	Src1<=Src2 or unordered	Yes
ole	Src2<=Src2 and ordered	No
olt	Src2<Src1 and ordered	No
seq	Src1=Src2 and ordered	Yes
sf	never true	Yes
un	Src1 or Src2 unordered	No
ueq	Src1=Src2 or unordered	No
ule	Src1<=Src2 or unordered	No
ult	Src1 <Src2 or unordered	No

Note: The result of the compare is unordered if either operand is a NaN.

Exceptions

Coprocessor unusable
Coprocessor exception trap

Floating-point exceptions
Unimplemented operation
Invalid operation

Example
`c.eq.s $f4,$f6`

`c.eq.s $f4,$f6`

ceil.w.s
ceil.w.d

FLOATING-POINT CEILING SINGLE
FLOATING-POINT CEILING DOUBLE

Syntax
```
ceil.w.s DestFpre,SrcFpre,Gpr
ceil.w.d DestFpre,SrcFpre,Gpr
```

Description
Computes the ceiling of the contents of the source floating-point register(s)
and puts the resulting 32-bit signed integer in the destination floating-point
register, using a third, general-purpose register to hold a temporary value.

Exceptions
Coprocessor unusable
Coprocessor exception trap

Floating-point exceptions
Unimplemented operation
Invalid operation

Examples
```
ceil.w.s $f4,$f6,t2
                cfc1        t2,$31
                cfc1        t2,$31
                nop
                ori         at,t2,0x3
                xori        at,at,0x1
                ctc1        at,$31
                nop
                cvt.w.s     $f4,$f6
                ctc1        t2,$31
                nop
                nop
ceil.w.d $f4,$f6,t2
                cfc1        t2,$31
                cfc1        t2,$31
                nop
                ori         at,t2,0x3
                xori        at,at,0x1
                ctc1        at,$31
                nop
```

```
cvt.w.d    $f4,$f6
ctc1       t2,$31
nop
nop
```

ceilu.w.s
ceilu.w.d

FLOATING-POINT CEILING UNSIGNED SINGLE
FLOATING-POINT CEILING UNSIGNED DOUBLE

Syntax

```
ceilu.w.s DestFpre,SrcFpre,Gpr
ceilu.w.d DestFpre,SrcFpre,Gpr
```

Description

Computes the ceiling of the contents of the source floating-point register(s) and puts the resulting 32-bit unsigned integer in the destination floating-point register, using a third, general-purpose register to hold a temporary value.

Exceptions

Coprocessor unusable
Coprocessor exception trap

Floating-point exceptions

Unimplemented operation
Invalid operation

Examples

```
ceilu.w.d $f4,$f6,t2
                cfc1        t2,$31
                cfc1        t2,$31
                nop
                ori         at,t2,0xf83
                xori        at,at,0xf81
                ctc1        at,$31
                nop
                cvt.w.d     $f4,$f6
                ctc1        t2,$31
                nop
                nop
```

cfc1   MOVE CONTROL FROM COPROCESSOR 1
cfc2   MOVE CONTROL FROM COPROCESSOR 2
cfc3   MOVE CONTROL FROM COPROCESSOR 3

Syntax
```
cfc1 DestGpr,SrcFpcr
cfc2 DestGpr,SrcCpcr
cfc3 DestGpr,SrcCpcr
```

Description
Moves the contents of the coprocessor control register to the destination general register.

For coprocessor 1, only control registers 0 (Implementation Revision Register) and 31 (Floating-Point Control/Status Register) are permitted.

Exceptions
Coprocessor unusable

Example
```
cfc1 t0,$31
            cfc1 t0,$31
```

ctc1   MOVE CONTROL TO COPROCESSOR 1
ctc2   MOVE CONTROL TO COPROCESSOR 2
ctc3   MOVE CONTROL TO COPROCESSOR 3

Syntax
```
ctc1 DestFpcr,SrcGpr
ctc2 DestCpcr,SrcGpr
ctc3 DestCpcr,SrcGpr
```

Description
Moves the contents of the general register to the specified coprocessor control register.

For coprocessor 1, only control register 31 (Floating-Point Control/Status Register) is permitted.

Exceptions
Coprocessor unusable

Example
```
ctc1 t0,$31
```

cvt.d.s
cvt.d.w

FLOATING-POINT CONVERT SINGLE TO
DOUBLE FIXED-POINT

Syntax

```
cvt.d.s DestFpre,SrcFpre
cvt.d.w DestFpre,SrcFpre
```

Description

Converts the contents of the floating-point source register to a double-precision floating-point value and puts it in the floating-point destination register(s).

Exceptions

Coprocessor unusable
Coprocessor exception trap

Floating-point exceptions

Unimplemented operation
Invalid operation

Examples

```
cvt.d.s $f4,$f8
                cvt.d.s    $f4,$f8
cvt.d.w $f4,$f8
                cvt.d.w    $f4,$f8
```

cvt.s.d
cvt.s.w

FLOATING-POINT CONVERT DOUBLE TO
SINGLE FIXED-POINT

Syntax
```
cvt.s.d DestFpre,SrcFpre
cvt.s.w DestFpre,SrcFpre
```

Description
Converts the contents of the floating-point source register(s) to a single-precision floating-point value and puts it in the floating-point destination register.

Exceptions
Coprocessor unusable
Coprocessor exception trap

Floating-point exceptions
Unimplemented operation
Invalid operation

Examples
```
cvt.s.d $f4,$f8
                cvt.s.d    $f4,$f8
cvt.s.w $f4,$f8
                cvt.s.w    $f4,$f8
```

cvt.w.s
cvt.w.d

FLOATING-POINT CONVERT SINGLE TO
DOUBLE FIXED-POINT

Syntax
```
cvt.w.s DestFpre,SrcFpre
cvt.w.d DestFpre,SrcFpre
```

Description
Converts the contents of the Floating-Point Source Register(s) to a 32-bit signed integer and puts it in the Floating-Point Destination Register.

Exceptions
Coprocessor unusable
Coprocessor exception trap

Floating-point exceptions
Unimplemented operation
Invalid operation

Examples
```
cvt.w.s $f4,$f8
                cvt.w.s    $f4,$f8
cvt.w.d $f4,$f8
                cvt.w.d    $f4,$f8
```

div   DIVIDE

Syntax
```
div DestGpr,Src1Gpr,Src2(Gpr|Imm)
```

Description
Divides Src1 by Src2 and puts the quotient in the destination register. The operands are treated as signed 32-bit values, and the result is rounded toward zero. A breakpoint exception is generated by divide-by-zero or by the division of the maximum negative number by -1 (overflow).

In this case the name of the macro instruction is the same as the name of the machine instruction. The machine instruction is accessed by specifying register $0 as the destination. The machine instruction puts the quotient in the LO register and the remainder in the HI register. It does not check for divide-by-zero or overflow.

To avoid an interlock or stall, there must be at least 35 cycles between the `div` instruction and a subsequent `mfhi` or `mflo` instruction. If an interlock occurs, interrupts will be ignored until the divide completes. Also, there must be at least two instructions between the `div` instruction and any preceding `mflo` or `mfhi` instruction.

Exceptions
Break 6 (overflow)
Break 7 (divide by zero)

Examples
```
div t0,t1,t2
            div       t1,t2
            mflo      t0
            bne       t2,zero,1f
            nop
            break     7
      1:    addiu     at,zero,-1
            bne       t2,at,1f
            lui       at,0x8000
            bne       t1,at,1f
            nop
            break     6
      1:
```

```
div t0,t1,0x4
                bgez        t1,1f
                add         at,t1,zero
                addiu       at,at,3
          1:    sra         t0,at,2
div t0,t1,0x1234
                addiu       at,zero,4660
                div         t1,at
                mflo        t0
                nop
                nop
div t0,t1,0x12340000
                lui         at,0x1234
                div         t1,at
                mflo        t0
                nop
                nop
div t0,t1,0x12345678
                lui         at,0x1234
                ori         at,at,0x5678
                div         t1,at
                mflo        t0
                nop
                nop div zero,t0,t2
                div         t0,t2
div zero,t0,0x4
                bgez        t0,1f
                add         at,t0,zero
                addiu       at,at,3
          1:    sra         zero,at,2
div zero,t0,0x1234
                addiu       at,zero,4660
                div         t0,at
div zero,t0,0x12340000
                lui         at,0x1234
                div         t0,at
div zero,t0,0x12345678
                lui         at,0x1234
                ori         at,at,0x5678
                div         t0,at
```

div.s
div.d

FLOATING-POINT DIVIDE SINGLE
FLOATING-POINT DIVIDE DOUBLE

Syntax
```
div.s DestFpre,Src1Fpre,Src2Fpre
div.d DestFpre,Src1Fpre,Src2Fpre
```

Description
Divides Src1 by Src2 and puts the result in the floating-point destination register(s).

Exceptions
Coprocessor unusable
Coprocessor exception trap

Floating-point exceptions
Unimplemented operation
Invalid operation
Inexact
Overflow
Divide-by-zero

Examples
```
div.s $f4,$f6,$f8
                nop
                div.s       $f4,$f6,$f8
div.d $f4,$f6,$f8
                nop
                div.d       $f4,$f6,$f8
```

divu   DIVIDE UNSIGNED

Syntax
```
divu DestGpr,Src1Gpr,Src2(Gpr|Imm)
```

Description
Divides Src1 by Src2 and puts the quotient in the destination register. The operands are treated as unsigned 32-bit values, and the result is rounded toward zero. A breakpoint exception is generated by divide-by-zero or by the division of the maximum negative number by -1 (overflow).

In this case the name of the macro instruction is the same as the name of the machine instruction. The machine instruction is accessed by specifying register $0 as the destination. The machine instruction puts the quotient in the LO register and the remainder in the HI register. It does not check for divide-by-zero.

To avoid an interlock or stall, there must be at least 35 cycles between the `divu` instruction and a subsequent `mfhi` or `mflo` instruction. Also, there must be at least two instructions between the `divu` instruction and any preceding `mflo` or `mfhi` instruction.

Exceptions
Break 7 (divide-by-zero)

Examples
```
divu t0,t1,t2
                divu        t1,t2
                mflo        t0
                bne         t2,zero,1f
                nop
                break       7
        1:
divu t0,t1,0x4
                srl         t0,t1,2
divu t0,t1,0x1234
                addiu       at,zero,4660
                divu        t1,at
                mflo        t0
                nop
                nop
```

```
divu t0,t1,0x12340000
                lui             at,0x1234
                divu            t1,at
                mflo            t0
                nop
                nop
divu t0,t1,0x12345678
                lui             at,0x1234
                ori             at,at,0x5678
                divu            t1,at
                mflo            t0
                nop
                nop
divu zero,t0,t2
                divu            t0,t2
divu zero,t0,0x4
                srl             zero,t0,2
divu zero,t0,0x1234
                addiu           at,zero,4660
                divu            t0,at
divu zero,t0,0x12340000
                lui             at,0x1234
                divu            t0,at
divu zero,t0,0x12345678
                lui             at,0x1234
                ori             at,at,0x5678
                divu            t0,at
```

floor.w.s
floor.w.d

FLOATING-POINT FLOOR SINGLE
FLOATING-POINT FLOOR DOUBLE

Syntax
```
floor.w.s DestFpre,SrcFpre,Gpr
floor.w.d DestFpre,SrcFpre,Gpr
```

Description
Computes the floor of the contents of the source floating-point register(s)
and puts the resulting 32-bit signed integer in the destination floating-point
register, using a third, general-purpose register to hold a temporary value.

Exceptions
Coprocessor unusable
Coprocessor exception trap

Floating-point exceptions
Unimplemented operation
Invalid operation

Examples
```
floor.w.s $f4,$f6,t2
                cfc1        t2,$31
                cfc1        t2,$31
                nop
                ori         at,t2,0x3
                xori        at,at,0
                ctc1        at,$31
                nop
                cvt.w.s     $f4,$f6
                ctc1        t2,$31
                nop
                nop
floor.w.d $f4,$f6,t2
                cfc1        t2,$31
                cfc1        t2,$31
                nop
                ori         at,t2,0x3
                xori        at,at,0
                ctc1        at,$31
                nop
```

```
        cvt.w.d     $f4,$f6
        ctc1        t2,$31
        nop
        nop
```

flooru.w.s   FLOATING-POINT FLOOR UNSIGNED SINGLE
flooru.w.d   FLOATING-POINT FLOOR UNSIGNED DOUBLE

Syntax

```
flooru.w.s DestFpre,SrcFpre,Gpr
flooru.w.d DestFpre,SrcFpre,Gpr
```

Description

Computes the floor of the contents of the source floating-point register(s) and puts the resulting 32-bit unsigned integer in the destination floating-point register, using a third, general-purpose register to hold a temporary value.

Exceptions

Coprocessor unusable
Coprocessor exception trap

Floating-point exceptions

Unimplemented operation
Invalid operation

Examples

```
flooru.w.s $f4,$f6,t2
                cfc1        t2,$31
                cfc1        t2,$31
                nop
                ori         at,t2,0xf83
                xori        at,at,0xf80
                ctc1        at,$31
                nop
                cvt.w.s     $f4,$f6
                ctc1        t2,$31
                nop
                nop
flooru.w.d $f4,$f6,t2
                cfc1        t2,$31
                cfc1        t2,$31
                nop
                ori         at,t2,0xf83
                xori        at,at,0xf80
                ctc1        at,$31
                nop
```

```
cvt.w.d     $f4,$f6
ctc1        t2,$31
nop
nop
```

j   JUMP

Syntax
`j {SrcGpr|Imm2|Imm16|Label}`

Description
Unconditionally jumps to the specified location, with a delay of one instruction.

Exceptions
Address error

Examples
```
j t2
                jr          t2
                nop
j 0x4
                j           0x4
                nop
j 0x1234
                j           0x1234
                nop
j main
                j           main
                nop
```

jal   JUMP AND LINK

Syntax
```
jal {SrcGpr|Imm2|Imm16|Label}
jal DestGpr,SrcGpr
```

Description
Jumps to the specified location, with a delay of one instruction, and puts the
return address in a general register. By default, the return address is placed
in register ra ($31). If two registers are specified, the first is used for the
return address and the second contains the target address. The instruction in
the delay slot is executed before the jump is taken.

Exceptions
None

Examples
```
jal t2
                jalr        ra,t2
                nop
jal 0x4
                jal         0x4
                nop
jal 0x1234
                jal         0x1234
                nop
jal main
                jal         main
                nop
```

l.s
l.d

FLOATING-POINT LOAD SINGLE
FLOATING-POINT LOAD DOUBLE

Syntax
```
l.s DestFpre,Src{Imm|Imm(Gpr)|Label}
l.d DestFpre,Src{Imm|Imm(Gpr)|Label}
```

Description
Loads the floating-point value from the address specified by the source into the destination floating-point register(s). For double-precision, this instruction should be used instead of two lwc1 instructions to avoid Endian-specific code.

Exceptions
Coprocessor unusable

Examples
```
l.s $f4,0x4
                lwc1        $f4,4(zero)
                nop
l.s $f4,0x1234
                lwc1        $f4,4660(zero)
                nop
l.s $f4,0x12340000
                lui         at,0x1234
                lwc1        $f4,0(at)
                nop
l.s $f4,0x12345678
                lui         at,0x1234
                lwc1        $f4,22136(at)
                nop
l.s $f4,0x1234(t2)
                lwc1        $f4,4660(t2)
                nop
l.s $f4,0x12340000(t2)
                lui         at,0x1234
                addu        at,at,t2
                lwc1        $f4,0(at)
                nop
l.s $f4,0x12345678(t2)
                lui         at,0x1234
                addu        at,at,t2
```

```
                    lwc1        $f4,22136(at)
                    nop
1.s $f4,main
                    lui         at,0x40
                    lwc1        $f4,432(at)
                    nop
1.s $f4,dat1
                    lwc1        $f4,-30692(gp)
                    nop
1.d $f4,0x4
                    lwc1        $f5,4(zero)
                    lwc1        $f4,8(zero)
                    nop
1.d $f4,0x1234
                    lwc1        $f5,4660(zero)
                    lwc1        $f4,4664(zero)
                    nop
1.d $f4,0x12340000
                    lui         at,0x1234
                    lwc1        $f5,0(at)
                    lwc1        $f4,4(at)
                    nop
1.d $f4,0x12345678
                    lui         at,0x1234
                    lwc1        $f5,22136(at)
                    lwc1        $f4,22140(at)
                    nop
1.d $f4,0x1234(t2)
                    lwc1        $f5,4660(t2)
                    lwc1        $f4,4664(t2)
                    nop
1.d $f4,0x12340000(t2)
                    lui         at,0x1234
                    addu        at,at,t2
                    lwc1        $f5,0(at)
                    lwc1        $f4,4(at)
                    nop
1.d $f4,0x12345678(t2)
                    lui         at,0x1234
                    addu        at,at,t2
                    lwc1        $f5,22136(at)
                    lwc1        $f4,22140(at)
                    nop
1.d $f4,main
                    lui         at,0x40
                    lwc1        $f5,432(at)
                    lwc1        $f4,436(at)
                    nop
```

```
l.d $f4,dat1
                lwc1        $f5,-30692(gp)
                lwc1        $f4,-30688(gp)
                nop
```

la   LOAD ADDRESS

Syntax
```
la DestGpr,Src{Imm|Imm(Gpr)|Label}
```

Description
Loads the specified address into the destination register.

Exceptions
None

Examples
```
la t0,0x4
                addiu        t0,zero,4
la t0,0x1234
                addiu        t0,zero,4660
la t0,0x12340000
                lui          t0,0x1234
                addiu        t0,t0,0
la t0,0x12345678
                lui          t0,0x1234
                addiu        t0,t0,22136
la t0,0x1234(t2)
                addiu        t0,t2,4660
la t0,0x12340000(t2)
                lui          t0,0x1234
                addu         t0,t0,t2
                addiu        t0,t0,0
la t0,0x12345678(t2)
                lui          t0,0x1234
                addu         t0,t0,t2
                addiu        t0,t0,22136
la t0,main
                lui          t0,0x40
                addiu        t0,t0,432
la t0,dat1
                addiu        t0,gp,-30692
```

lb   LOAD BYTE

Syntax
```
lb DestGpr,Src{Imm|Imm(Gpr)|Label}
```

Description
Sign-extends the contents of the byte at the memory location specified by the address and loads it into the destination register, with a delay of one instruction.

Exceptions
Bus error
Address error

Examples
```
lb t0,0x4
                lb        t0,4(zero)
                nop
lb t0,0x1234
                lb        t0,4660(zero)
                nop
lb t0,0x12340000
                lui       t0,0x1234
                lb        t0,0(t0)
                nop
lb t0,0x12345678
                lui       t0,0x1234
                lb        t0,22136(t0)
                nop
lb t0,0x1234(t2)
                lb        t0,4660(t2)
                nop
lb t0,0x12340000(t2)
                lui       t0,0x1234
                addu      t0,t0,t2
                lb        t0,0(t0)
                nop
lb t0,0x12345678(t2)
                lui       t0,0x1234
                addu      t0,t0,t2
                lb        t0,22136(t0)
                nop
```

```
lb t0,main
                lui         t0,0x40
                lb          t0,432(t0)
                nop
lb t0,dat1
                lb          t0,-30692(gp)
                nop
```

lbu   LOAD BYTE UNSIGNED

Syntax
```
lbu DestGpr,Src{Imm|Imm(Gpr)|Label}
```

Description
Zero-extends the contents of the byte at the memory location specified by the address and loads it into the destination register, with a delay of one instruction.

Exceptions
Bus error
Address error

Examples
```
lbu t0,0x4
                lbu         t0,4(zero)
                nop
lbu t0,0x1234
                lbu         t0,4660(zero)
                nop
lbu t0,0x12340000
                lui         t0,0x1234
                lbu         t0,0(t0)
                nop
lbu t0,0x12345678
                lui         t0,0x1234
                lbu         t0,22136(t0)
                nop
lbu t0,0x1234(t2)
                lbu         t0,4660(t2)
                nop
lbu t0,0x12340000(t2)
                lui         t0,0x1234
                addu        t0,t0,t2
                lbu         t0,0(t0)
                nop
lbu t0,0x12345678(t2)
                lui         t0,0x1234
                addu        t0,t0,t2
                lbu         t0,22136(t0)
                nop
```

```
lbu t0,main
                  lui          t0,0x40
                  lbu          t0,432(t0)
                  nop
lbu t0,dat1
                  lbu          t0,-30692(gp)
                  nop
```

ld   LOAD DOUBLE

Syntax
`ld DestGpre,Src{Imm|Imm(Gpr)|Label}`

Description
Loads the contents of the doubleword at the memory location specified by the address and loads it into the even/odd destination register pair, with a delay of one instruction.

For compatibility with future machines, addresses should be doubleword-aligned. This instruction should be used instead of two `lw` instructions in order to avoid Endian-specific code.

Exceptions
Bus error
Address error

Examples
These examples were assembled with Big Endian byte ordering.

```
ld t0,0x4
                lw          t0,4(zero)
                lw          t1,8(zero)
                nop
ld t0,0x1234
                lw          t0,4660(zero)
                lw          t1,4664(zero)
                nop
ld t0,0x12340000
                lui         at,0x1234
                lw          t0,0(at)
                lw          t1,4(at)
                nop
ld t0,0x12345678
                lui         at,0x1234
                lw          t0,22136(at)
                lw          t1,22140(at)
                nop
ld t0,0x1234(t2)
                lw          t0,4660(t2)
                lw          t1,4664(t2)
                nop
```

```
ld t0,0x12340000(t2)
                lui        at,0x1234
                addu       at,at,t2
                lw         t0,0(at)
                lw         t1,4(at)
                nop
ld t0,0x12345678(t2)
                lui        at,0x1234
                addu       at,at,t2
                lw         t0,22136(at)
                lw         t1,22140(at)
                nop
ld t0,main
                lui        at,0x40
                lw         t0,432(at)
                lw         t1,436(at)
                nop
ld t0,dat1
                lw         t0,-30692(gp)
                lw         t1,-30688(gp)
                nop
```

lh   LOAD HALFWORD

Syntax
```
lh DestGpr,Src{Imm|Imm(Gpr)|Label}
```

Description
Sign-extends the contents of the halfword at the memory location specified
by the address and loads it into the destination register, with a delay of one
instruction.

Exceptions
Bus error
Address error

Examples
```
lh t0,0x4
                    lh          t0,4(zero)
                    nop
lh t0,0x1234
                    lh          t0,4660(zero)
                    nop
lh t0,0x12340000
                    lui         t0,0x1234
                    lh          t0,0(t0)
                    nop
lh t0,0x12345678
                    lui         t0,0x1234
                    lh          t0,22136(t0)
                    nop
lh t0,0x1234(t2)
                    lh          t0,4660(t2)
                    nop
lh t0,0x12340000(t2)
                    lui         t0,0x1234
                    addu        t0,t0,t2
                    lh          t0,0(t0)
                    nop
lh t0,0x12345678(t2)
                    lui         t0,0x1234
                    addu        t0,t0,t2
                    lh          t0,22136(t0)
                    nop
```

```
lh t0,main
                lui         t0,0x40
                lh          t0,432(t0)
                nop
lh t0,dat1
                lh          t0,-30692(gp)
                nop
```

lhu   LOAD HALFWORD UNSIGNED

Syntax
```
lhu DestGpr,Src{Imm|Imm(Gpr)|Label}
```

Description
Zero-extends the contents of the halfword at the memory location specified by the address and loads it into the destination register, with a delay of one instruction.

Exceptions
Bus error
Address error

Examples
```
lhu t0,0x4
                    lhu         t0,4(zero)
                    nop
lhu t0,0x1234
                    lhu         t0,4660(zero)
                    nop
lhu t0,0x12340000
                    lui         t0,0x1234
                    lhu         t0,0(t0)
                    nop
lhu t0,0x12345678
                    lui         t0,0x1234
                    lhu         t0,22136(t0)
                    nop
lhu t0,0x1234(t2)
                    lhu         t0,4660(t2)
                    nop
lhu t0,0x12340000(t2)
                    lui         t0,0x1234
                    addu        t0,t0,t2
                    lhu         t0,0(t0)
                    nop
lhu t0,0x12345678(t2)
                    lui         t0,0x1234
                    addu        t0,t0,t2
                    lhu         t0,22136(t0)
                    nop
```

```
lhu t0,main
                lui             t0,0x40
                lhu             t0,432(t0)
                nop
lhu t0,dat1
                lhu             t0,-30692(gp)
                nop
```

li   LOAD IMMEDIATE

Syntax
li DestGpr,Src{Imm16}

Description
Loads the immediate value into the destination register.

Exceptions
None

Examples

```
li t0,0x4
                addiu       t0,zero,4
li t0,0x1234
                addiu       t0,zero,4660
li t0,0x12340000
                lui         t0,0x1234
li t0,0x12345678
                lui         t0,0x1234
                ori         t0,t0,0x5678
```

li.s
li.d

FLOATING-POINT LOAD IMMEDIATE SINGLE
FLOATING-POINT LOAD IMMEDIATE DOUBLE

Syntax

```
li.s DestFpre,SrcImmfp
li.d DestFpre,SrcImmfp
```

Description

Loads the floating-point immediate value into the floating-point destination register(s).

Exceptions

Coprocessor unusable
Bus error
Address error

Examples

```
li.s $f4,2.3
                lwc1          $f4,-32752(gp)
                nop
li.d $f4,2.3
                lwc1          $f5,-32752(gp)
                lwc1          $f4,-32748(gp)
                nop
```

lui   LOAD UPPER IMMEDIATE

Syntax
```
lui DestGpr,Src{Imm16}
```

Description
Loads the immediate value into the most significant 16 bits of the destination register. The least significant 16 bits are set to zero.

Exceptions
None

Examples
```
lui t0,0x4
                lui      t0,0x4
lui t0,0x1234
                lui      t0,0x1234
```

lw   LOAD WORD

Syntax
```
lw DestGpr,Src{Imm|Imm(Gpr)|Label}
```

Description
Sign-extends the contents of the word at the memory location specified by the address and loads it into the destination register, with a delay of one instruction.

Exceptions
Bus error
Address error

Examples
```
lw t0,0x4
                lw          t0,4(zero)
                nop
lw t0,0x1234
                lw          t0,4660(zero)
                nop
lw t0,0x12340000
                lui         t0,0x1234
                lw          t0,0(t0)
                nop
lw t0,0x12345678
                lui         t0,0x1234
                lw          t0,22136(t0)
                nop
lw t0,0x1234(t2)
                lw          t0,4660(t2)
                nop
lw t0,0x12340000(t2)
                lui         t0,0x1234
                addu        t0,t0,t2
                lw          t0,0(t0)
                nop
lw t0,0x12345678(t2)
                lui         t0,0x1234
                addu        t0,t0,t2
                lw          t0,22136(t0)
                nop
```

```
lw t0,main
                lui        t0,0x40
                lw         t0,432(t0)
                nop
lw t0,dat1
                lw         t0,-30692(gp)
                nop
```

lwc1   LOAD WORD TO COPROCESSOR 1

Syntax
lwc1 DestFpr,Src{Imm|Imm(Gpr)|Label}

Description
Loads the word from the address specified by the source into the Destination
Floating-Point Register, with a delay of one instruction.

Exceptions
Bus error
Address error
Coprocessor unusable

Examples
```
lwc1 $f4,0x4
                lwc1        $f4,4(zero)
                nop
lwc1 $f4,0x1234
                lwc1        $f4,4660(zero)
                nop
lwc1 $f4,0x12340000
                lui         at,0x1234
                lwc1        $f4,0(at)
                nop
lwc1 $f4,0x12345678
                lui         at,0x1234
                lwc1        $f4,22136(at)
                nop
lwc1 $f4,0x1234(t2)
                lwc1        $f4,4660(t2)
                nop
lwc1 $f4,0x12340000(t2)
                lui         at,0x1234
                addu        at,at,t2
                lwc1        $f4,0(at)
                nop
lwc1 $f4,0x12345678(t2)
                lui         at,0x1234
                addu        at,at,t2
                lwc1        $f4,22136(at)
                nop
```

```
lwc1 $f4,main
                lui         at,0x40
                lwc1        $f4,432(at)
                nop
lwc1 $f4,dat1
                lwc1        $f4,-30692(gp)
                nop
```

lwc2
lwc2

LOAD WORD TO COPROCESSOR 2
LOAD WORD TO COPROCESSOR 3

Syntax

```
lwc2 DestCpr,Src{Imm|Imm(Gpr)|Label}
lwc3 DestCpr,Src{Imm|Imm(Gpr)|Label}
```

Description

Loads the word from the address specified by the source into the Destination Coprocessor General Register, with a delay of one instruction.

Exceptions

Bus error
Address error
Coprocessor unusable

lwl   LOAD WORD LEFT

Syntax
```
lwl DestGpr,Src{Imm|Imm(Gpr)|Label}
```

Description
Loads a number of bytes from memory to the destination register starting at the specified address. The transfer involves incrementing the address until a word boundary is reached. The bytes are copied into the destination register starting with the left (most significant) byte of the register.

This instruction provides a way to access unaligned data without the overhead of an interrupt service routine. The only address error exception generated by this instruction is the exception caused by a user-mode program attempting to access an address in kernel space.

Note that the contents of the destination register will differ depending on the byte ordering convention: with Big Endian ordering, the first byte loaded will be the most significant byte and with Little Endian it will be the least significant byte, so the destination register contents will differ.

The ulw can be used instead of this instruction in order to avoid Endian-specific code.

Exceptions
Bus error
Address error

Examples
```
lwl t0,0x4
                lwl        t0,4(zero)
                nop
lwl t0,0x1234
                lwl        t0,4660(zero)
                nop
lwl t0,0x12340000
                lui        at,0x1234
                lwl        t0,0(at)
                nop
lwl t0,0x12345678
                lui        at,0x1234
                lwl        t0,22136(at)
                nop
```

```
lwl t0,0x1234(t2)
                    lwl        t0,4660(t2)
                    nop
lwl t0,0x12340000(t2)
                    lui        at,0x1234
                    addu       at,at,t2
                    lwl        t0,0(at)
                    nop
lwl t0,0x12345678(t2)
                    lui        at,0x1234
                    addu       at,at,t2
                    lwl        t0,22136(at)
                    nop
lwl t0,main
                    lui        at,0x40
                    lwl        t0,432(at)
                    nop
lwl t0,dat1
                    lwl        t0,-30692(gp)
                    nop
```

Big Endian

```
lwl t0,0(t1) lwr t0,3(t1)
                    lwl        t0,0(t1)
                    lwr        t0,3(t1)
```

Little Endian

```
lwl t0,3(t1) lwr t0,0(t1)
                    lwl        t0,3(t1)
                    lwr        t0,0(t1)
```

lwr   LOAD WORD RIGHT

Syntax
lwr DestGpr,Src{Imm|Imm(Gpr)|Label}

Description
Loads a number of bytes from memory to the destination register starting at
the specified address. The transfer involves decrementing the address until a
word boundary is reached. The bytes are copied into the destination register
starting with the least significant byte of the register.

   ulw should be used instead of this instruction to avoid Endian-specific
code.

Exceptions
Bus error
Address error

Examples
```
lwr t0,0x4
                  lwr         t0,4(zero)
                  nop
lwr t0,0x1234
                  lwr         t0,4660(zero)
                  nop
lwr t0,0x12340000
                  lui         at,0x1234
                  lwr         t0,0(at)
                  nop
lwr t0,0x12345678
                  lui         at,0x1234
                  lwr         t0,22136(at)
                  nop
lwr t0,0x1234(t2)
                  lwr         t0,4660(t2)
                  nop
lwr t0,0x12340000(t2)
                  lui         at,0x1234
                  addu        at,at,t2
                  lwr         t0,0(at)
                  nop
```

```
lwr t0,0x12345678(t2)
                lui        at,0x1234
                addu       at,at,t2
                lwr        t0,22136(at)
                nop
lwr t0,main
                lui        at,0x40
                lwr        t0,432(at)
                nop
lwr t0,dat1
                lwr        t0,-30692(gp)
                nop
```

mfc0   MOVE FROM COPROCESSOR 0

Syntax
```
mfc0 DestGpr,SrcCpr
```

Description
Moves the contents of the coprocessor register to the destination general register.

Exceptions
Coprocessor unusable

Example
```
mfc0    t0,CO_SR
            mfc0    t0,CO_SR
```

mfc1   MOVE FROM COPROCESSOR 1
mfc2   MOVE FROM COPROCESSOR 2
mfc3   MOVE FROM COPROCESSOR 3

Syntax
```
mfc1 DestGpr,SrcFpr
mfc2 DestGpr,SrcCpr
mfc3 DestGpr,SrcCpr
```

Description
Moves the contents of the coprocessor register to the destination general register.

Exceptions
Coprocessor unusable

Examples
```
mfc1 t0,$f4
                mfc1        t0,$f4
mfc1 t1,$f5
                mfc1        t1,$f5
```

mfhi

MOVE FROM HI

Syntax

```
mfhi DestGpr
```

Description

Moves the contents of the HI register to the destination register.

Exceptions

None

Example

```
mfhi t2
            mfhi        t2
            nop
            nop
```

mflo   MOVE FROM LO

Syntax
```
mflo DestGpr
```

Description
Moves the contents of the LO register to the destination register.

To ensure proper operation when an interrupt occurs, the two instructions that follow an `mflo` instruction may not be an instruction that modifies the LO register (i.e., `mult`, `multu`, `div`, `divu`, or `mtlo`).

To avoid an interlock or stall, this instruction must follow a `mult` or `multu` instruction by a minimum of 12 cycles, and a `div` or `divu` instruction by a minimum of 35 cycles.

Exceptions
None

Example
```
mflo t2
                mflo        t2
                nop
                nop
```

mov.s
mov.d

FLOATING-POINT MOVE SINGLE
FLOATING-POINT MOVE DOUBLE

Syntax

```
mov.s DestFpre,SrcFpre
mov.d DestFpre,SrcFpre
```

Description

Moves the contents of the source floating-point register(s) to the destination floating-point register(s).

Exceptions

Coprocessor unusable
Coprocessor exception trap

Floating-point exceptions

Unimplemented operation

Examples

```
mov.s $f4,$f8
                mov.s      $f4,$f8
mov.d $f4,$f8
                mov.d      $f4,$f8
```

move   MOVE

Syntax
```
move DestGpr,SrcGpr
```

Description
Moves the contents of the source register to the destination register.

Exceptions
None

Example
```
move t0,t2
          add        t0,t2,zero
```

mtc0   MOVE TO COPROCESSOR 0

Syntax
```
mtc0 SrcGpr,DestCpr
```

Description
Moves the contents of the general register into the specified coprocessor 0
general register.

Exceptions
Coprocessor unusable

Example
```
mtc0 t0,CO_SR
                mtc0        t0,CO_SR
```

mtc1   MOVE TO COPROCESSOR 1

Syntax
```
mtc1 SrcGpr,DestFpr
```

Description
Moves the contents of the general register into the specified floating-point
register.

Exceptions
Coprocessor unusable

Examples
```
mtc1 t0,$f4
                mtc1        t0,$f4
mtc1 t1,$f5
                mtc1        t1,$f5
```

mtc2
mtc3

MOVE TO COPROCESSOR 2
MOVE TO COPROCESSOR 3

Syntax

```
mtc2 SrcGpr,DestCpr
mtc3 SrcGpr,DestCpr
```

Description

Moves the contents of the general register into the specified coprocessor register.

Exceptions

Coprocessor unusable

mthi   MOVE TO HI

Syntax
```
mthi DestGpr
```

Description
Moves the contents of the general register to the HI register.

Exceptions
None

Example
```
mthi t2
                mthi        t2
```

mtlo MOVE TO LO

Syntax

mtlo DestGpr

Description

Moves the contents of the general register to the LO register.

Exceptions

None

Example

mtlo t2

```
        mtlo        t2
```

mul   MULTIPLY

Syntax

```
mul DestGpr,Src1Gpr,Src2(Gpr|Imm)
```

Description

Multiplies Src1 by Src2 and puts the product in the destination register. The operands are treated as signed 32-bit values.

Exceptions

None

Examples

```
mul t0,t1,t2
                    multu       t1,t2
                    mflo        t0
                    nop
                    nop
mul t0,t1,0x4
                    sll         t0,t1,2
mul t0,t1,0x1234
                    sll         t0,t1,3
                    addu        t0,t0,t1
                    sll         t0,t0,3
                    addu        t0,t0,t1
                    sll         t0,t0,2
                    subu        t0,t0,t1
                    sll         t0,t0,2
                    addu        t0,t0,t1
                    sll         t0,t0,2
mul t0,t1,0x12340000
                    sll         t0,t1,3
                    addu        t0,t0,t1
                    sll         t0,t0,3
                    addu        t0,t0,t1
                    sll         t0,t0,2
                    subu        t0,t0,t1
                    sll         t0,t0,2
                    addu        t0,t0,t1
                    sll         t0,t0,18
```

```
mul t0,t1,0x12345678
                lui         at,0x1234
                ori         at,at,0x5678
                multu       t1,at
                mflo        t0
                nop
                nop
```

mul.s
mul.d

Syntax

```
mul.s DestFpre,Src1Fpre,Src2Fpre
mul.d DestFpre,Src1Fpre,Src2Fpre
```

Description

Multiplies Src1 by Src2 and puts the product in the floating-point destination register(s).

Exceptions

Coprocessor unusable
Coprocessor exception trap

Floating-point exceptions

Unimplemented operation
Invalid operation
Inexact
Overflow
Underflow

Examples

```
mul.s $f4,$f6,$f8
                    mul.s       $f4,$f6,$f8
mul.d $f4,$f6,$f8
                    mul.d       $f4,$f6,$f8
```

mulo   MULTIPLY WITH OVERFLOW

Syntax
```
mulo DestGpr,Src1Gpr,Src2(Gpr|Imm)
```

Description
Multiplies Src1 by Src2 and puts the product in the destination register. The
operands are treated as signed 32-bit values. A breakpoint exception is generated by overflow.

Exceptions
Break 6 (overflow)

Examples
```
mulo t0,t1,t2
                mult        t1,t2
                mflo        t0
                sra         t0,t0,31
                mfhi        at
                beq         t0,at,1f
                nop
                break       6
           1:   mflo        t0
                nop
                nop
mulo t0,t1,0x4
                add         t0,t1,t1
                add         t0,t0,t0
mulo t0,t1,0x1234
                add         t0,t1,t1
                add         t0,t0,t0
                add         t0,t0,t0
                add         t0,t0,t1
                add         t0,t0,t0
                add         t0,t0,t0
                add         t0,t0,t0
                add         t0,t0,t0
                add         t0,t0,t1
                add         t0,t0,t0
                add         t0,t0,t1
                add         t0,t0,t0
                add         t0,t0,t0
```

```
                    add          t0,t0,t1
                    add          t0,t0,t0
                    add          t0,t0,t0
mulo t0,t1,0x12340000
                    lui          at,0x1234
                    mult         t1,at
                    mflo         t0
                    sra          t0,t0,31
                    mfhi         at
                    beq          t0,at,1f
                    nop
                    break        6
            1:      mflo         t0
                    nop
                    nop

mulo t0,t1,0x12345678
                    lui          at,0x1234
                    ori          at,at,0x5678
                    mult         t1,at
                    mflo         t0
                    sra          t0,t0,31
                    mfhi         at
                    beq          t0,at,1f
                    nop
                    break        6
            1:      mflo         t0
                    nop
                    nop
```

mulou   MULTIPLY WITH OVERFLOW UNSIGNED

Syntax
```
mulou DestGpr,Src1Gpr,Src2(Gpr|Imm)
```

Description
Multiplies Src1 by Src2 and puts the product in the destination register. The operands are treated as unsigned 32-bit values. A breakpoint exception is generated by overflow.

Exceptions
Break 6 (overflow)

Examples
```
mulou t0,t1,t2
                    multu       t1,t2
                    mfhi        at
                    mflo        t0
                    beq         at,zero,1f
                    nop
                    break       6
            1:
mulou t0,t1,0x4
                    addiu       at,zero,4
                    multu       t1,at
                    mfhi        at
                    mflo        t0
                    beq         at,zero,1f
                    nop
                    break       6
            1:
mulou t0,t1,0x1234
                    addiu       at,zero,4660
                    multu       t1,at
                    mfhi        at
                    mflo        t0
                    beq         at,zero,1f
                    nop
                    break       6
            1:
mulou t0,t1,0x12340000
                    lui         at,0x1234
                    multu       t1,at
                    mfhi        at
```

```
                    mflo       t0
                    beq        at,zero,1f
                    nop
                    break      6
            1:
mulou t0,t1,0x12345678
                    lui        at,0x1234
                    ori        at,at,0x5678
                    multu      t1,at
                    mfhi       at
                    mflo       t0
                    beq        at,zero,1f
                    nop
                    break      6
            1:
```

mult MULTIPLY

Syntax

```
mult Src1Gpr,Src2Gpr
```

Description

Multiplies Src1 by Src2 and puts the 64-bit product in the HI/LO register pair (HI contains the most significant word). The source operands are treated as signed 32-bit values.

To avoid an interlock or stall, there must be a minimum of 12 cycles between this instruction and a subsequent mfhi or mflo instruction. Also, there must be at least two instructions between the mult instruction and any preceding mflo or mfhi instruction.

Exceptions

None

Example

```
mult t0,t2
            mult        t0,t2
```

multu   MULTIPLY UNSIGNED

Syntax
```
multu Src1Gpr,Src2Gpr
```

Description
Multiplies Src1 by Src2 and puts the 64-bit product in the HI/LO register pair
(HI contains the most significant word). The source operands are treated as
unsigned 32-bit values.

    To avoid an interlock or stall, there must be a minimum of 12 cycles
between this instruction and a subsequent `mfhi` or `mflo` instruction. Also,
there must be at least two instructions between the `mult` instruction and any
preceding `mflo` or `mfhi` instruction.

Exceptions
None

Example
```
multu t0,t2
             multu      t0,t2
```

neg   NEGATE (WITH OVERFLOW)

Syntax
```
neg DestGpr
neg DestGpr,SrcGpr
```

Description
Negates (changes the sign of) the contents of the source register, treated as a signed 32-bit value, and puts the result in the destination register.

Exceptions
Break 6 (overflow)

Example
```
neg t0,t2
          sub        t0,zero,t2
```

neg.s
neg.d

Syntax
```
neg.s DestFpre,SrcFpre
neg.d DestFpre,SrcFpre
```

Description
Negates (changes the sign of) the contents of the source floating-point register(s) and puts the result in the destination floating-point register(s).

Exceptions
Coprocessor unusable
Coprocessor exception trap

Floating-point exceptions
Unimplemented operation
Invalid operation

Examples
```
neg.s $f4,$f8
                neg.s       $f4,$f8,$f0
neg.d $f4,$f8
                neg.d       $f4,$f8,$f0
```

negu   NEGATE (WITHOUT OVERFLOW)

Syntax
```
negu DestGpr
negu DestGpr,SrcGpr
```

Description
Negates (changes the sign of) the contents of the source register, treated as a signed 32-bit value, and puts the result in the destination register.

Exceptions
None

Example
```
negu t0,t2
            subu        t0,zero,t2
```

nop   NO OPERATION

Syntax
nop

Description
This instruction does not change the state of the machine and takes one cycle
to execute. This instruction must be enclosed by the .set noreorder and
.set reorder assembler directives.

Exceptions
None

Example
nop
```
        sll        zero,zero,0
```

nor   NOT OR

Syntax
```
nor DestGpr,Src1Gpr,Src2(Gpr|Imm)
```

Description
Computes the logical NOR of the corresponding bits of Src1 and Src2 and
puts the result in the destination register. An immediate value is zero-
extended.

Exceptions
None

Examples
```
nor t0,t1,t2
                    nor         t0,t1,t2
nor t0,t1,0x4
                    ori         t0,t1,0x4
                    nor         t0,t0,zero
nor t0,t1,0x1234
                    ori         t0,t1,0x1234
                    nor         t0,t0,zero
nor t0,t1,0x12340000
                    lui         at,0x1234
                    nor         t0,t1,at
nor t0,t1,0x12345678
                    lui         at,0x1234
                    ori         at,at,0x5678
                    nor         t0,t1,at
```

not   NOT

Syntax
```
not DestGpr
not DestGpr,SrcGpr
```

Description
Inverts each of the bits of the source and puts the result in the destination register.

Exceptions
None

Example
```
not t0,t2
            nor        t0,t2,zero
```

or   OR

Syntax
```
or DestGpr,Src1Gpr,Src2(Gpr|Imm)
```

Description
Computes the logical OR of the corresponding bits of Src1 and Src2 and puts the result in the destination register. An immediate value is zero-extended.

Exceptions
None

Examples
```
or t0,t1,t2
                or         t0,t1,t2
or t0,t1,0x4
                ori        t0,t1,0x4
or t0,t1,0x1234
                ori        t0,t1,0x1234
or t0,t1,0x12340000
                lui        at,0x1234
                or         t0,t1,at
or t0,t1,0x12345678
                lui        at,0x1234
                ori        at,at,0x5678
                or         t0,t1,at
```

rem   REMAINDER

Syntax
```
rem DestGpr,Src1Gpr,Src2(Gpr|Imm)
```

Description
Divides Src1 by Src2 and puts the remainder in the destination register. The operands are treated as signed, 32-bit values. A breakpoint exception is generated by divide-by-zero or overflow conditions.

Exceptions
Break 6 (overflow)
Break 7 (divide-by-zero)

Examples
```
rem t0,t1,t2
                div         t1,t2
                mfhi        t0
                bne         t2,zero,1f
                nop
                break       7
        1:      addiu       at,zero,-1
                bne         t2,at,1f
                lui         at,0x8000
                bne         t1,at,1f
                nop
                break       6
            1:
rem t0,t1,0x4
                bgez        t1,1f
                andi        t0,t1,0x3
                beq         t0,zero,1f
                nop
                addiu       t0,t0,-4
            1:
rem t0,t1,0x1234
                addiu       at,zero,4660
                div         t1,at
                mfhi        t0
                nop
                nop
```

```
rem t0,t1,0x12340000
                lui         at,0x1234
                div         t1,at
                mfhi        t0
                nop
                nop
rem t0,t1,0x12345678
                lui         at,0x1234
                ori         at,at,0x5678
                div         t1,at
                mfhi        t0
                nop
                nop
```

remu   REMAINDER UNSIGNED

Syntax
```
remu DestGpr,Src1Gpr,Src2(Gpr|Imm)
```

Description
Divides Src1 by Src2 and puts the remainder in the destination register. The operands are treated as unsigned, 32-bit values. A breakpoint exception is generated by divide-by-zero.

Exceptions
Break 7 (divide-by-zero)

Examples
```
remu t0,t1,t2
                    divu        t1,t2
                    mfhi        t0
                    bne         t2,zero,1f
                    nop
                    break       7
            1:
remu t0,t1,0x4
                    andi        t0,t1,0x3
remu t0,t1,0x1234
                    addiu       at,zero,4660
                    divu        t1,at
                    mfhi        t0
                    nop
                    nop
remu t0,t1,0x12340000
                    lui         at,0x1234
                    divu        t1,at
                    mfhi        t0
                    nop
                    nop
remu t0,t1,0x12345678
                    lui         at,0x1234
                    ori         at,at,0x5678
                    divu        t1,at
                    mfhi        t0
                    nop
                    nop
```

rfe   RESTORE FROM EXCEPTION

Syntax
```
rfe
```

Description
Restores the Current and Previous Mode and Interrupt Enable bits (KUc, KUp, IEc, and IEp) in the Status Register to their contents prior to the interrupt. This instruction is normally placed in the delay slot of the jump instruction that restores the PC.

This instruction must be enclosed by the .set noreorder and .set reorder assembler directives.

Exceptions
Coprocessor Unusable

Example
To return to the interrupted program, we read the value from the EPC Register into k0, insert the required nop (the mfc0 instruction requires two cycles), and then do a jump indirect on k0. The rfe in the delay slot restores the Status Register.

```
.set noreorder
mfc0    k0,CO_EPC
nop
j       k0
rfe
.set reorder
```

rol   ROTATE LEFT

Syntax
```
rol DestGpr,Src1Gpr,Src2(Gpr|Imm)
```

Description
Rotates Src1 to the left by the amount specified by Src2, shifts any bit that
was shifted out of the most significant bit into the least significant bit, and
puts the result in the destination register. When Src2 is a register, only the
five least significant bits are considered.

Exceptions
None

Examples
```
rol t0,t1,t2
                subu        at,zero,t2
                srlv        at,t1,at
                sllv        t0,t1,t2
                or          t0,t0,at
rol t0,t1,0x4
                sll         at,t1,4
                srl         t0,t1,28
                or          t0,t0,at
```

ror ROTATE RIGHT

Syntax

```
ror DestGpr,Src1Gpr,Src2(Gpr|Imm)
```

Description

Rotates Src1 to the right by the amount specified by Src2, shifts any bit that was shifted out of the least significant bit into the most significant bit, and puts the result in the destination register. When Src2 is a register, only the five least significant bits are considered.

Exceptions

None

Examples

```
ror t0,t1,t2
                subu        at,zero,t2
                sllv        at,t1,at
                srlv        t0,t1,t2
                or          t0,t0,at
ror t0,t1,0x4
                srl         at,t1,4
                sll         t0,t1,28
                or          t0,t0,at
```

round.w.s
round.w.d

FLOATING-POINT ROUND SINGLE
FLOATING-POINT ROUND DOUBLE

Syntax
```
round.w.s DestFpre,SrcFpre,Gpr
round.w.d DestFpre,SrcFpre,Gpr
```

Description
Rounds the contents of the source floating-point register(s) and puts the resulting 32-bit signed integer in the destination floating-point register, using a third, general register to hold a temporary value.

Exceptions
Coprocessor unusable
Coprocessor exception trap

Floating-point exceptions
Invalid operation
Unimplemented operation

Examples
```
round.w.s $f4,$f6,t2
                cfc1        t2,$31
                cfc1        t2,$31
                addiu       at,zero,-4
                and         at,at,t2
                ctc1        at,$31
                nop
                cvt.w.s     $f4,$f6
                ctc1        t2,$31
                nop
                nop
round.w.d $f4,$f6,t2
                cfc1        t2,$31
                cfc1        t2,$31
                addiu       at,zero,-4
                and         at,at,t2
                ctc1        at,$31
                nop
```

```
cvt.w.d    $f4,$f6
ctc1       t2,$31
nop
nop
```

roundu.w.s   FLOATING-POINT ROUND UNSIGNED SINGLE
roundu.w.d   FLOATING-POINT ROUND UNSIGNED DOUBLE

Syntax
```
roundu.w.s DestFpre,SrcFpre,Gpr
roundu.w.d DestFpre,SrcFpre,Gpr
```

Description
Rounds the contents of the source floating-point register(s) and puts the
resulting 32-bit unsigned integer in the destination floating-point register,
using a third, general register to hold a temporary value.

Exceptions
Coprocessor unusable
Coprocessor exception trap

Floating-point exceptions
Unimplemented operation
Invalid operation

Example
```
roundu.w.d $f4,$f6,t2
                cfc1        t2,$31
                cfc1        t2,$31
                addiu       at,zero,-3972
                and         at,at,t2
                ctc1        at,$31
                nop
                cvt.w.d     $f4,$f6
                ctc1        t2,$31
                nop
                nop
```

s.s
s.d

FLOATING-POINT STORE SINGLE
FLOATING-POINT STORE DOUBLE

Syntax

```
s.s SrcFpre,Dest{Imm|Imm(Gpr)|Label}
s.d SrcFpre,Dest{Imm|Imm(Gpr)|Label}
```

Description

Stores the contents of the floating-point register(s) in the memory location specified by the address. For double-precision, this instruction should be used instead of two swc1 instructions to avoid Endian-specific code.

Exceptions

Coprocessor unusable

Examples

```
s.s $f4,0x4
                swc1        $f4,4(zero)
s.s $f4,0x1234
                swc1        $f4,4660(zero)
s.s $f4,0x12340000
                lui         at,0x1234
                swc1        $f4,0(at)
s.s $f4,0x12345678
                lui         at,0x1234
                swc1        $f4,22136(at)
s.s $f4,0x1234(t2)
                swc1        $f4,4660(t2)
s.s $f4,0x12340000(t2)
                lui         at,0x1234
                addu        at,at,t2
                swc1        $f4,0(at)
s.s $f4,0x12345678(t2)
                lui         at,0x1234
                addu        at,at,t2
                swc1        $f4,22136(at)
s.s $f4,main
                lui         at,0x40
                swc1        $f4,432(at)
s.s $f4,dat1
                swc1        $f4,-30692(gp)
```

```
s.d $f4,0x4
                    swc1            $f5,4(zero)
                    swc1            $f4,8(zero)
s.d $f4,0x1234
                    swc1            $f5,4660(zero)
                    swc1            $f4,4664(zero)
s.d $f4,0x12340000
                    lui             at,0x1234
                    swc1            $f5,0(at)
                    swc1            $f4,4(at)
s.d $f4,0x12345678
                    lui             at,0x1234
                    swc1            $f5,22136(at)
                    swc1            $f4,22140(at)
s.d $f4,0x1234(t2)
                    swc1            $f5,4660(t2)
                    swc1            $f4,4664(t2)
s.d $f4,0x12340000(t2)
                    lui             at,0x1234
                    addu            at,at,t2
                    swc1            $f5,0(at)
                    swc1            $f4,4(at)
s.d $f4,0x12345678(t2)
                    lui             at,0x1234
                    addu            at,at,t2
                    swc1            $f5,22136(at)
                    swc1            $f4,22140(at)
s.d $f4,main
                    lui             at,0x40
                    swc1            $f5,432(at)
                    swc1            $f4,436(at)
s.d $f4,dat1
                    swc1            $f5,-30692(gp)
                    swc1            $f4,-30688(gp)
```

sb   STORE BYTE

Syntax
```
sb SrcGpr,Dest{Imm|Imm(Gpr)|Label}
```

Description
Stores the contents of the least significant byte of the source register in the memory location specified by the address.

Exceptions
Bus error
Address error

Examples
```
sb t0,0x4
                sb         t0,4(zero)
sb t0,0x1234
                sb         t0,4660(zero)
sb t0,0x12340000
                lui        at,0x1234
                sb         t0,0(at)
sb t0,0x12345678
                lui        at,0x1234
                sb         t0,22136(at)
sb t0,0x1234(t2)
                sb         t0,4660(t2)
sb t0,0x12340000(t2)
                lui        at,0x1234
                addu       at,at,t2
                sb         t0,0(at)
sb t0,0x12345678(t2)
                lui        at,0x1234
                addu       at,at,t2
                sb         t0,22136(at)
sb t0,main
                lui        at,0x40
                sb         t0,432(at)
sb t0,dat1
                sb         t0,-30692(gp)
```

sd   STORE DOUBLE

Syntax
```
sd SrcGpre,Dest{Imm|Imm(Gpr)|Label}
```

Description
Stores the contents of the even/odd source register pair in the memory location specified by the address. Generates an address-error exception if the address is not word-aligned. For compatibility with future machines, addresses should be doubleword-aligned. sd should be used instead of a pair of sw (store word) instructions to avoid Endian-specific code.

Exceptions
Bus error
Address error

Examples
```
sd t0,0x4
                sw          t0,4(zero)
                sw          t1,8(zero)
sd t0,0x1234
                sw          t0,4660(zero)
                sw          t1,4664(zero)
sd t0,0x12340000
                lui         at,0x1234
                sw          t0,0(at)
                sw          t1,4(at)
sd t0,0x12345678
                lui         at,0x1234
                sw          t0,22136(at)
                sw          t1,22140(at)
sd t0,0x1234(t2)
                sw          t0,4660(t2)
                sw          t1,4664(t2)
sd t0,0x12340000(t2)
                lui         at,0x1234
                addu        at,at,t2
                sw          t0,0(at)
                sw          t1,4(at)
```

```
sd t0,0x12345678(t2)
                lui         at,0x1234
                addu        at,at,t2
                sw          t0,22136(at)
                sw          t1,22140(at)
sd t0,main
                lui         at,0x40
                sw          t0,432(at)
                sw          t1,436(at)
sd t0,dat1
                sw          t0,-30692(gp)
                sw          t1,-30688(gp)
```

seq

SET ON EQUAL

Syntax

```
seq DestGpr,Src1Gpr,Src2(Gpr|Imm)
```

Description

Sets the destination register to 0x00000001 if Src1 is equal to Src2; otherwise, the destination register is set to zero.

Exceptions

None

Examples

```
seq t0,t1,t2
                xor         t0,t1,t2
                sltiu       t0,t0,1
seq t0,t1,0x4
                xori        t0,t1,0x4
                sltiu       t0,t0,1
seq t0,t1,0x1234
                xori        t0,t1,0x1234
                sltiu       t0,t0,1
seq t0,t1,0x12340000
                lui         at,0x1234
                xor         t0,t1,at
                sltiu       t0,t0,1
seq t0,t1,0x12345678
                lui         at,0x1234
                ori         at,at,0x5678
                xor         t0,t1,at
                sltiu       t0,t0,1
```

sge   SET ON GREATER-THAN OR EQUAL

Syntax
```
sge DestGpr,Src1Gpr,Src2(Gpr|Imm)
```

Description
Sets the destination register to 0x00000001 if Src1 is greater-than or equal to
Src2; otherwise, the destination register is set to zero. The operands are
treated as signed 32-bit values.

Exceptions
None

Examples
```
sge t0,t1,t2
                slt         t0,t1,t2
                xori        t0,t0,0x1
sge t0,t1,0x4
                slti        t0,t1,4
                xori        t0,t0,0x1
sge t0,t1,0x1234
                slti        t0,t1,4660
                xori        t0,t0,0x1
sge t0,t1,0x12340000
                lui         at,0x1234
                slt         t0,t1,at
                xori        t0,t0,0x1
sge t0,t1,0x12345678
                lui         at,0x1234
                ori         at,at,0x5678
                slt         t0,t1,at
                xori        t0,t0,0x1
```

sgeu   SET ON GREATER-THAN OR EQUAL UNSIGNED

Syntax
```
sgeu DestGpr,Src1Gpr,Src2(Gpr|Imm)
```

Description
Sets the destination register to 0x00000001 if Src1 is greater-than or equal to
Src2; otherwise, the destination register is set to zero. The operands are
treated as unsigned 32-bit values.

Exceptions
None

Examples
```
sgeu t0,t1,t2
                sltu        t0,t1,t2
                xori        t0,t0,0x1
sgeu t0,t1,0x4
                sltiu       t0,t1,4
                xori        t0,t0,0x1
sgeu t0,t1,0x1234
                sltiu       t0,t1,4660
                xori        t0,t0,0x1
sgeu t0,t1,0x12340000
                lui         at,0x1234
                sltu        t0,t1,at
                xori        t0,t0,0x1
sgeu t0,t1,0x12345678
                lui         at,0x1234
                ori         at,at,0x5678
                sltu        t0,t1,at
                xori        t0,t0,0x1
```

sgt   SET ON GREATER-THAN

Syntax

sgt DestGpr,Src1Gpr,Src2(Gpr|Imm)

Description

Sets the destination register to 0x00000001 if Src1 is greater-than Src2; otherwise, the destination register is set to zero. The operands are treated as
signed 32-bit values.

Exceptions

None

Examples

```
sgt t0,t1,t2
                slt         t0,t2,t1
sgt t0,t1,0x4
                addiu       at,zero,4
                slt         t0,at,t1
sgt t0,t1,0x1234
                addiu       at,zero,4660
                slt         t0,at,t1
sgt t0,t1,0x12340000
                lui         at,0x1234
                slt         t0,at,t1
sgt t0,t1,0x12345678
                lui         at,0x1234
                ori         at,at,0x5678
                slt         t0,at,t1
```

sgtu   SET ON GREATER-THAN UNSIGNED

Syntax

```
sgtu DestGpr,Src1Gpr,Src2(Gpr|Imm)
```

Description

Sets the destination register to 0x00000001 if Src1 is greater-than Src2; otherwise, the destination register is set to zero. The operands are treated as
unsigned 32-bit values.

Exceptions

None

Examples

```
sgtu t0,t1,t2
                sltu        t0,t2,t1
sgtu t0,t1,0x4
                addiu       at,zero,4
                sltu        t0,at,t1
sgtu t0,t1,0x1234
                addiu       at,zero,4660
                sltu        t0,at,t1
sgtu t0,t1,0x12340000
                lui         at,0x1234
                sltu        t0,at,t1
sgtu t0,t1,0x12345678
                lui         at,0x1234
                ori         at,at,0x5678
                sltu        t0,at,t1
```

sh   STORE HALFWORD

Syntax
```
sh SrcGpr,Dest{Imm|Imm(Gpr)|Label}
```

Description
Stores the contents of the least significant halfword of the source register in the memory location specified by the address.

Exceptions
Bus error
Address error

Examples
```
sh t0,0x4
                sh            t0,4(zero)
sh t0,0x1234
                sh            t0,4660(zero)
sh t0,0x12340000
                lui           at,0x1234
                sh            t0,0(at)
sh t0,0x12345678
                lui           at,0x1234
                sh            t0,22136(at)
sh t0,0x1234(t2)
                sh            t0,4660(t2)
sh t0,0x12340000(t2)
                lui           at,0x1234
                addu          at,at,t2
                sh            t0,0(at)
sh t0,0x12345678(t2)
                lui           at,0x1234
                addu          at,at,t2
                sh            t0,22136(at)
sh t0,main
                lui           at,0x40
                sh            t0,432(at)
sh t0,dat1
                sh            t0,-30692(gp)
```

sle   SET ON LESS-THAN OR EQUAL

Syntax
```
sle DestGpr,Src1Gpr,Src2(Gpr|Imm)
```

Description
Sets the destination register to 0x00000001 if Src1 is less-than or equal to Src2; otherwise, the destination register is set to zero. The operands are treated as signed 32-bit values.

Exceptions
None

Examples
```
sle t0,t1,t2
                slt        t0,t2,t1
                xori       t0,t0,0x1
sle t0,t1,0x4
                slti       t0,t1,5
sle t0,t1,0x1234
                slti       t0,t1,4661
sle t0,t1,0x12340000
                lui        at,0x1234
                ori        at,at,0x1
                slt        t0,t1,at
sle t0,t1,0x12345678
                lui        at,0x1234
                ori        at,at,0x5679
                slt        t0,t1,at
```

sleu   SET ON LESS-THAN OR EQUAL UNSIGNED

Syntax
```
sleu DestGpr,Src1Gpr,Src2(Gpr|Imm)
```

Description
Sets the destination register to 0x00000001 if Src1 is less-than or equal to Src2; otherwise, the destination register is set to zero. The operands are treated as unsigned 32-bit values.

Exceptions
None

Examples
```
sleu t0,t1,t2
                sltu        t0,t2,t1
                xori        t0,t0,0x1
sleu t0,t1,0x4
                sltiu       t0,t1,5
sleu t0,t1,0x1234
                sltiu       t0,t1,4661
sleu t0,t1,0x12340000
                lui         at,0x1234
                ori         at,at,0x1
                sltu        t0,t1,at
sleu t0,t1,0x12345678
                lui         at,0x1234
                ori         at,at,0x5679
                sltu        t0,t1,at
```

sll   SHIFT LEFT LOGICAL

Syntax
```
sll DestGpr,Src1Gpr,Src2(Gpr|Imm)
```

Description
Left-shifts Src1 by the amount specified by Src2, shifts zeroes into the least significant bit, and puts the result in the destination register. When Src2 is a register, only the five least significant bits are considered.

Exceptions
None

Examples
```
sll t0,t1,t2
                sllv        t0,t1,t2
sll t0,t1,0x4
                sll         t0,t1,4
```

slt   SET ON LESS-THAN

Syntax
```
slt DestGpr,Src1Gpr,Src2(Gpr|Imm)
```

Description
Sets the destination register to 0x00000001 if Src1 is less-than Src2; otherwise, the destination register is set to zero. The operands are treated as signed 32-bit values.

Exceptions
None

Examples
```
slt t0,t1,t2
                slt         t0,t1,t2
slt t0,t1,0x4
                slti        t0,t1,4
slt t0,t1,0x1234
                slti        t0,t1,4660
slt t0,t1,0x12340000
                lui         at,0x1234
                slt         t0,t1,at
slt t0,t1,0x12345678
                lui         at,0x1234
                ori         at,at,0x5678
                slt         t0,t1,at
```

sltu SET ON LESS-THAN UNSIGNED

Syntax
```
sltu DestGpr,Src1Gpr,Src2(Gpr|Imm)
```

Description
Sets the destination register to 0x00000001 if Src1 is less-than Src2; otherwise, the destination register is set to zero. The operands are treated as unsigned 32-bit values.

Exceptions
None

Examples
```
sltu t0,t1,t2
                sltu        t0,t1,t2
sltu t0,t1,0x4
                sltiu       t0,t1,4
sltu t0,t1,0x1234
                sltiu       t0,t1,4660
sltu t0,t1,0x12340000
                lui         at,0x1234
                sltu        t0,t1,at
sltu t0,t1,0x12345678
                lui         at,0x1234
                ori         at,at,0x5678
                sltu        t0,t1,at
```

sne   SET ON NOT EQUAL

Syntax
```
sne DestGpr,Src1Gpr,Src2(Gpr|Imm)
```

Description
Sets the destination register to 0x00000001 if Src1 is not equal to Src2; otherwise, the destination register is set to zero. The operands are treated as signed 32-bit values.

Exceptions
None

Examples
```
sne t0,t1,t2
                xor        t0,t1,t2
                sltu       t0,zero,t0
sne t0,t1,0x4
                xori       t0,t1,0x4
                sltu       t0,zero,t0
sne t0,t1,0x1234
                xori       t0,t1,0x1234
                sltu       t0,zero,t0
sne t0,t1,0x12340000
                lui        at,0x1234
                xor        t0,t1,at
                sltu       t0,zero,t0
sne t0,t1,0x12345678
                lui        at,0x1234
                ori        at,at,0x5678
                xor        t0,t1,at
                sltu       t0,zero,t0
```

sra   SHIFT-RIGHT ARITHMETIC

Syntax
sra DestGpr,Src1Gpr,Src2(Gpr|Imm)

Description
Right-shifts Src1 by the amount specified by Src2, replicates the sign bit in the most significant position, and puts the result in the destination register.

Exceptions
None

Examples
```
sra t0,t1,t2
                srav        t0,t1,t2
sra t0,t1,0x4
                sra         t0,t1,4
```

srl   SHIFT-RIGHT LOGICAL

Syntax
```
srl DestGpr,Src1Gpr,Src2(Gpr|Imm)
```

Description
Right-shifts Src1 by the amount specified by Src2, shifts zeroes into the most significant bit, and puts the result in the destination register. When Src2 is a register, only the five least significant bits are considered.

Exceptions
None

Examples
```
srl t0,t1,t2
                srlv        t0,t1,t2
srl t0,t1,0x4
                srl         t0,t1,4
```

sub   SUBTRACT

Syntax
```
sub DestGpr,Src1Gpr,Src2(Gpr|Imm)
```

Description
Subtracts Src2 from Src1 and puts the result in the destination register. All operands are treated as signed values. An overflow exception is generated if the addition results in a two's-complement overflow.

Exceptions
Break 6 (overflow)

Examples
```
sub t0,t1,t2
                sub        t0,t1,t2
sub t0,t1,0x4
                addi       t0,t1,-4
sub t0,t1,0x1234
                addi       t0,t1,-4660
sub t0,t1,0x12340000
                lui        at,0x1234
                sub        t0,t1,at
sub t0,t1,0x12345678
                lui        at,0x1234
                ori        at,at,0x5678
                sub        t0,t1,at
```

| **sub.s** | FLOATING-POINT SUBTRACT SINGLE |
| **sub.d** | FLOATING-POINT SUBTRACT DOUBLE |

Syntax

```
sub.s DestFpre,Src1Fpre,Src2Fpre
sub.d DestFpre,Src1Fpre,Src2Fpre
```

Description

Subtracts Src2Fpre from Src1Fpre and puts the result in the destination floating-point register(s).

Exceptions

Coprocessor unusable
Coprocessor exception trap

Floating-point exceptions

Unimplemented operation
Invalid operation
Inexact
Overflow
Underflow

Examples

```
sub.s $f4,$f6,$f8
                sub.s        $f4,$f6,$f8
sub.d $f4,$f6,$f8
                sub.d        $f4,$f6,$f8
```

subu   SUBTRACT UNSIGNED

Syntax
```
subu DestGpr,Src1Gpr,Src2(Gpr|Imm)
```

Description
Subtracts Src2 from Src1 and puts the result in the destination register. All operands are treated as unsigned values. It does not check for overflow.

Exceptions
None

Examples
```
subu t0,t1,t2
                    subu        t0,t1,t2
subu t0,t1,0x4
                    addiu       t0,t1,-4
subu t0,t1,0x1234
                    addiu       t0,t1,-4660
subu t0,t1,0x12340000
                    lui         at,0x1234
                    subu        t0,t1,at
subu t0,t1,0x12345678
                    lui         at,0x1234
                    ori         at,at,0x5678
                    subu        t0,t1,at
```

sw   STORE WORD

Syntax

```
sw SrcGpr,Dest{Imm|Imm(Gpr)|Label}
```

Description

Stores the contents of the source register in the memory location specified by the address.

Exceptions

Bus error
Address error

Examples

```
sw t0,0x4
                sw              t0,4(zero)
sw t0,0x1234
                sw              t0,4660(zero)
sw t0,0x12340000
                lui             at,0x1234
                sw              t0,0(at)
sw t0,0x12345678
                lui             at,0x1234
                sw              t0,22136(at)
sw t0,0x1234(t2)
                sw              t0,4660(t2)
sw t0,0x12340000(t2)
                lui             at,0x1234
                addu            at,at,t2
                sw              t0,0(at)
sw t0,0x12345678(t2)
                lui             at,0x1234
                addu            at,at,t2
                sw              t0,22136(at)
sw t0,main
                lui             at,0x40
                sw              t0,432(at)
sw t0,dat1
                sw              t0,-30692(gp)
```

swc1   STORE WORD FROM COPROCESSOR 1

Syntax
swc1 SrcFpr,Dest{Imm|Imm(Gpr)|Label}

Description
Stores the contents of the source floating-point register in the memory location specified by the address.

Exceptions
Bus error
Address error
Coprocessor unusable

Examples
```
swc1 $f4,0x4
                 swc1        $f4,4(zero)
swc1 $f4,0x1234
                 swc1        $f4,4660(zero)
swc1 $f4,0x12340000
                 lui         at,0x1234
                 swc1        $f4,0(at)
swc1 $f4,0x12345678
                 lui         at,0x1234
                 swc1        $f4,22136(at)
swc1 $f4,0x1234(t2)
                 swc1        $f4,4660(t2)
swc1 $f4,0x12340000(t2)
                 lui         at,0x1234
                 addu        at,at,t2
                 swc1        $f4,0(at)
swc1 $f4,0x12345678(t2)
                 lui         at,0x1234
                 addu        at,at,t2
                 swc1        $f4,22136(at)
swc1 $f4,main
                 lui         at,0x40
                 swc1        $f4,432(at)
swc1 $f4,dat1
                 swc1        $f4,-30692(gp)
```

swc2
swc3

STORE WORD FROM COPROCESSOR 2
STORE WORD FROM COPROCESSOR 3

Syntax
```
swc2 SrcCpr,{Imm|Imm(Gpr)|Label}
swc3 SrcCpr,{Imm|Imm(Gpr)|Label}
```

Description
Stores the contents of the source coprocessor register in the memory location specified by the address.

Exceptions
Bus error
Address error
Coprocessor unusable

swl STORE WORD LEFT

Syntax
```
swl SrcGpr,Dest{Imm|Imm(Gpr)|Label}
```

Description
Stores a number of bytes from the source register to memory starting at the specified address. The transfer involves incrementing the address until a word boundary is reached. The bytes are copied to memory starting with the most significant byte of the register.

To avoid Endian-specific code, usw should be used instead of this instruction.

Exceptions
Bus error
Address error

Examples
```
swl t0,0x4
                swl         t0,4(zero)
swl t0,0x1234
                swl         t0,4660(zero)
swl t0,0x12340000
                lui         at,0x1234
                swl         t0,0(at)
swl t0,0x12345678
                lui         at,0x1234
                swl         t0,22136(at)
swl t0,0x1234(t2)
                swl         t0,4660(t2)
swl t0,0x12340000(t2)
                lui         at,0x1234
                addu        at,at,t2
                swl         t0,0(at)
swl t0,0x12345678(t2)
                lui         at,0x1234
                addu        at,at,t2
                swl         t0,22136(at)
swl t0,main
                lui         at,0x40
                swl         t0,432(at)
swl t0,dat1
                swl         t0,-30692(gp)
```

Big Endian

```
swl t0,0(t1) swr t0,3(t1)
            swl           t0,0(t1)
            swr           t0,3(t1)
```

Little Endian

```
swl t0,3(t1) swr t0,0(t1)
            swl           t0,3(t1)
            swr           t0,0(t1)
```

swr   STORE WORD RIGHT

Syntax
```
swr SrcGpr,Dest{Imm|Imm(Gpr)|Label}
```

Description
Stores a number of bytes from the source register to memory starting at the specified address. The transfer involves decrementing the address until a word boundary is reached. The bytes are copied to memory starting with the least significant byte of the register.

To avoid Endian-specific code, usw should be used instead of this instruction.

Exceptions
Bus error
Address error

Examples
```
swr t0,0x4
                swr         t0,4(zero)
swr t0,0x1234
                swr         t0,4660(zero)
swr t0,0x12340000
                lui         at,0x1234
                swr         t0,0(at)
swr t0,0x12345678
                lui         at,0x1234
                swr         t0,22136(at)
swr t0,0x1234(t2)
                swr         t0,4660(t2)
swr t0,0x12340000(t2)
                lui         at,0x1234
                addu        at,at,t2
                swr         t0,0(at)
swr t0,0x12345678(t2)
                lui         at,0x1234
                addu        at,at,t2
                swr         t0,22136(at)
swr t0,main
                lui         at,0x40
                swr         t0,432(at)
swr t0,dat1
                swr         t0,-30692(gp)
```

Big Endian

```
swl t0,0(t1) swr t0,3(t1)
            swl        t0,0(t1)
            swr        t0,3(t1)
```

Little Endian

```
swl t0,3(t1) swr t0,0(t1)
            swl        t0,3(t1)
            swr        t0,0(t1)
```

syscall   SYSTEM CALL

Syntax
```
syscall
```

Description
Generates a syscall exception. By convention, a function code can be passed in v0 ($2).

Exceptions
System call

Example
```
syscall
            syscall
```

teq　　　　　　　　　　　　　　　　　　　　　　　　　TRAP IF EQUAL

Syntax
```
teq Src1Gpr,Src2{Gpr|Imm}
```

Description
Generates a trap (break 8 exception) if Src1 is equal to Src2.

Exceptions
Break 8 (trap on condition)

Examples
```
teq t0,t2
                bne         t0,t2,1f
                nop
                break       8
        1:
teq t0,0x4
                addiu       at,zero,4
                bne         t0,at,1f
                nop
                break       8
        1:
teq t0,0x1234
                addiu       at,zero,4660
                bne         t0,at,1f
                nop
                break       8
        1:
teq t0,0x12340000
                lui         at,0x1234
                bne         t0,at,1f
                nop
                break       8
        1:
teq t0,0x12345678
                lui         at,0x1234
                ori         at,at,0x5678
                bne         t0,at,1f
                nop
                break       8
        1:
```

tge   TRAP IF GREATER-THAN OR EQUAL

Syntax
tge Src1Gpr,Src2{Gpr|Imm}

Description
Generates a trap (break 8 exception) if Src1 is greater than or equal to Src2.
Both operands are treated as signed values.

Exceptions
Break 8 (trap on condition)

Examples
```
tge t0,t2
                slt       at,t0,t2
                bne       at,zero,1f
                nop
                break     8
        1:
tge t0,0x4
                slti      at,t0,4
                bne       at,zero,1f
                nop
                break     8
        1:
tge t0,0x1234
                slti      at,t0,4660
                bne       at,zero,1f
                nop
                break     8
        1:
tge t0,0x12340000
                lui       at,0x1234
                slt       at,t0,at
                bne       at,zero,1f
                nop
                break     8
        1:
```

```
tge t0,0x12345678
                lui         at,0x1234
                ori         at,at,0x5678
                slt         at,t0,at
                bne         at,zero,1f
                nop
                break       8
        1:
```

tgeu   TRAP IF GREATER-THAN OR EQUAL UNSIGNED

Syntax
```
tgeu Src1Gpr,Src2{Gpr|Imm}
```

Description
Generates a trap (break 8 exception) if Src1 is greater-than or equal to Src2.
Both operands are treated as unsigned values.

Exceptions
Break 8 (trap on condition)

Examples
```
tgeu t0,t2
                sltu      at,t0,t2
                bne       at,zero,1f
                nop
                break     8
         1:
tgeu t0,0x4
                sltiu     at,t0,4
                bne       at,zero,1f
                nop
                break     8
         1:
tgeu t0,0x1234
                sltiu     at,t0,4660
                bne       at,zero,1f
                nop
                break     8
         1:
tgeu t0,0x12340000
                lui       at,0x1234
                sltu      at,t0,at
                bne       at,zero,1f
                nop
                break     8
         1:
```

```
tgeu t0,0x12345678
                lui         at,0x1234
                ori         at,at,0x5678
                sltu        at,t0,at
                bne         at,zero,1f
                nop
                break       8
        1:
```

tlt   TRAP IF LESS-THAN

Syntax
tlt Src1Gpr,Src2{Gpr|Imm}

Description
Generates a trap (break 8 exception) if Src1 is less-than Src2.

Exceptions
Break 8 (trap on condition)

Examples
```
tlt t0,t2
                slt       at,t0,t2
                beq       at,zero,1f
                nop
                break     8
        1:
tlt t0,0x4
                slti      at,t0,4
                beq       at,zero,1f
                nop
                break     8
        1:
tlt t0,0x1234
                slti      at,t0,4660
                beq       at,zero,1f
                nop
                break     8
        1:
tlt t0,0x12340000
                lui       at,0x1234
                slt       at,t0,at
                beq       at,zero,1f
                nop
                break     8
        1:
```

```
tlt t0,0x12345678
                lui         at,0x1234
                ori         at,at,0x5678
                slt         at,t0,at
                beq         at,zero,1f
                nop
                break       8
        1:
```

tltu TRAP IF LESS-THAN UNSIGNED

Syntax
```
tltu Src1Gpr,Src2{Gpr|Imm}
```

Description
Generates a trap (break 8 exception) if Src1 is less-than Src2.

Exceptions
Break 8 (trap on condition)

Examples
```
tltu t0,t2
                sltu        at,t0,t2
                beq         at,zero,1f
                nop
                break       8
          1:
tltu t0,0x4
                sltiu       at,t0,4
                beq         at,zero,1f
                nop
                break       8
          1:
tltu t0,0x1234
                sltiu       at,t0,4660
                beq         at,zero,1f
                nop
                break       8
          1:
tltu t0,0x12340000
                lui         at,0x1234
                sltu        at,t0,at
                beq         at,zero,1f
                nop
                break       8
          1:
```

```
tltu t0,0x12345678
                lui        at,0x1234
                ori        at,at,0x5678
                sltu       at,t0,at
                beq        at,zero,1f
                nop
                break      8
        1:
```

tne   TRAP IF NOT EQUAL

Syntax
tne Src1Gpr,Src2{Gpr|Imm}

Description
Generates a trap (break 8 exception) if Src2 is not equal to Src1.

Exceptions
Break 8 (trap on condition)

Examples
```
tne t0,t2
                beq         t0,t2,1f
                nop
                break       8
        1:
tne t0,0x4
                addiu       at,zero,4
                beq         t0,at,1f
                nop
                break       8
        1:
tne t0,0x1234
                addiu       at,zero,4660
                beq         t0,at,1f
                nop
                break       8
        1:
tne t0,0x12340000
                lui         at,0x1234
                beq         t0,at,1f
                nop
                break       8
        1:
tne t0,0x12345678
                lui         at,0x1234
                ori         at,at,0x5678
                beq         t0,at,1f
                nop
                break       8
        1:
```

trunc.w.s
trunc.w.d

TRUNCATE FLOATING-POINT SINGLE
TRUNCATE FLOATING-POINT DOUBLE

Syntax
```
trunc.w.s DestFpre,SrcFpre,Gpr
trunc.w.d DestFpre,SrcFpre,Gpr
```

Description
Truncates the contents of the source floating-point register(s) and puts the
resulting 32-bit signed integer in the destination floating-point register, using
a third, general register to hold a temporary value.

Exceptions
Coprocessor unusable
Coprocessor exception trap

Floating-point exceptions
Unimplemented operation
Invalid operation

Examples
```
trunc.w.s $f4,$f6,t2
                cfc1       t2,$31
                cfc1       t2,$31
                nop
                ori        at,t2,0x3
                xori       at,at,0x2
                ctc1       at,$31
                nop
                cvt.w.s    $f4,$f6
                ctc1       t2,$31
                nop
                nop
trunc.w.d $f4,$f6,t2
                cfc1       t2,$31
                cfc1       t2,$31
                nop
```

```
ori      at,t2,0x3
xori     at,at,0x2
ctc1     at,$31
nop
cvt.w.d  $f4,$f6
ctc1     t2,$31
nop
nop
```

truncu.w.s   TRUNCATE FLOATING-POINT UNSIGNED SINGLE
truncu.w.d   TRUNCATE FLOATING-POINT UNSIGNED DOUBLE

Syntax
```
truncu.w.s DestFpre,SrcFpre,Gpr
truncu.w.d DestFpre,SrcFpre,Gpr
```

Description
Truncates the contents of the source floating-point register(s) and puts the resulting 32-bit unsigned integer in the destination floating-point register, using a third, general register to hold a temporary value.

Exceptions
Coprocessor unusable
Coprocessor exception trap

Floating-point exceptions
Unimplemented operation
Invalid operation

Examples
```
truncu.w.s $f4,$f6,t2
                cfc1        t2,$31
                cfc1        t2,$31
                nop
                ori         at,t2,0xf83
                xori        at,at,0xf82
                ctc1        at,$31
                nop
                cvt.w.s     $f4,$f6
                ctc1        t2,$31
                nop
                nop
truncu.w.d $f4,$f6,t2
                cfc1        t2,$31
                cfc1        t2,$31
                nop
```

```
        ori        at,t2,0xf83
        xori       at,at,0xf82
        ctc1       at,$31
        nop
        cvt.w.d    $f4,$f6
        ctc1       t2,$31
        nop
        nop
```

ulh   UNALIGNED LOAD HALFWORD

Syntax
```
ulh DestGpr,Src{Imm|Imm(Gpr)|Label}
```

Description
Sign-extends the contents of the halfword at the memory location specified
by the address and loads it into the destination register, with a delay of one
instruction. This instruction does not signal an address error exception. This
instruction should be used instead of a pair of *load byte* instructions to avoid
Endian-specific code.

Exceptions
Bus error

Examples
```
ulh t0,0x4
                lb          t0,4(zero)
                lbu         at,5(zero)
                sll         t0,t0,8
                or          t0,t0,at
ulh t0,0x1234
                lb          t0,4660(zero)
                lbu         at,4661(zero)
                sll         t0,t0,8
                or          t0,t0,at
ulh t0,0x12340000
                lui         at,0x1234
                lb          t0,0(at)
                addiu       at,at,0
                lbu         at,1(at)
                sll         t0,t0,8
                or          t0,t0,at
ulh t0,0x12345678
                lui         at,0x1234
                lb          t0,22136(at)
                addiu       at,at,22136
                lbu         at,1(at)
                sll         t0,t0,8
                or          t0,t0,at
```

```
ulh t0,0x1234(t2)
                lb          t0,4660(t2)
                lbu         at,4661(t2)
                sll         t0,t0,8
                or          t0,t0,at
ulh t0,0x12340000(t2)
                lui         at,0x1234
                addu        at,at,t2
                lb          t0,0(at)
                addiu       at,at,0
                lbu         at,1(at)
                sll         t0,t0,8
                or          t0,t0,at
ulh t0,0x12345678(t2)
                lui         at,0x1234
                addu        at,at,t2
                lb          t0,22136(at)
                addiu       at,at,22136
                lbu         at,1(at)
                sll         t0,t0,8
                or          t0,t0,at
ulh t0,main
                lui         at,0x40
                addiu       at,at,432
                lb          t0,0(at)
                lbu         at,1(at)
                sll         t0,t0,8
                or          t0,t0,at
ulh t0,dat1
                lb          t0,-30692(gp)
                lbu         at,-30691(gp)
                sll         t0,t0,8
                or          t0,t0,at
```

ulhu   UNALIGNED LOAD HALFWORD UNSIGNED

Syntax
```
ulhu DestGpr,Src{Imm|Imm(Gpr)|Label}
```

Description
Zero-extends the contents of the halfword at the memory location specified
by the address and loads it into the destination register, with a delay of one
instruction. This instruction does not signal an address error exception. This
instruction should be used instead of a pair of *load byte* instructions to avoid
Endian-specific code.

Exceptions
Bus error

Examples
```
ulhu t0,0x4
                 lbu         t0,4(zero)
                 lbu         at,5(zero)
                 sll         t0,t0,8
                 or          t0,t0,at
ulhu t0,0x1234
                 lbu         t0,4660(zero)
                 lbu         at,4661(zero)
                 sll         t0,t0,8
                 or          t0,t0,at
ulhu t0,0x12340000
                 lui         at,0x1234
                 lbu         t0,0(at)
                 addiu       at,at,0
                 lbu         at,1(at)
                 sll         t0,t0,8
                 or          t0,t0,at
ulhu t0,0x12345678
                 lui         at,0x1234
                 lbu         t0,22136(at)
                 addiu       at,at,22136
                 lbu         at,1(at)
                 sll         t0,t0,8
                 or          t0,t0,at
```

```
ulhu t0,0x1234(t2)
                lbu         t0,4660(t2)
                lbu         at,4661(t2)
                sll         t0,t0,8
                or          t0,t0,at
ulhu t0,0x12340000(t2)
                lui         at,0x1234
                addu        at,at,t2
                lbu         t0,0(at)
                addiu       at,at,0
                lbu         at,1(at)
                sll         t0,t0,8
                or          t0,t0,at
ulhu t0,0x12345678(t2)
                lui         at,0x1234
                addu        at,at,t2
                lbu         t0,22136(at)
                addiu       at,at,22136
                lbu         at,1(at)
                sll         t0,t0,8
                or          t0,t0,at
ulhu t0,main
                lui         at,0x40
                addiu       at,at,432
                lbu         t0,0(at)
                lbu         at,1(at)
                sll         t0,t0,8
                or          t0,t0,at
ulhu t0,dat1
                lbu         t0,-30692(gp)
                lbu         at,-30691(gp)
                sll         t0,t0,8
                or          t0,t0,at
```

ulw   UNALIGNED LOAD WORD

Syntax
```
ulw DestGpr,Src{Imm|Imm(Gpr)|Label}
```

Description
Loads the contents of the word at the memory location specified by the
address into the destination register, with a delay of one instruction. This
instruction does not signal an address error exception. This instruction
should be used instead of a pair of *load word left* and *load word right* instructions to avoid Endian-specific code.

Exceptions
Bus error

Examples
```
ulw t0,0x4
                lwl         t0,4(zero)
                lwr         t0,7(zero)
                nop
ulw t0,0x1234
                lwl         t0,4660(zero)
                lwr         t0,4663(zero)
                nop
ulw t0,0x12340000
                lui         at,0x1234
                lwl         t0,0(at)
                lwr         t0,3(at)
                addiu       at,at,0
ulw t0,0x12345678
                lui         at,0x1234
                lwl         t0,22136(at)
                lwr         t0,22139(at)
                addiu       at,at,22136
ulw t0,0x1234(t2)
                lwl         t0,4660(t2)
                lwr         t0,4663(t2)
                nop
```

```
ulw t0,0x12340000(t2)
                lui         at,0x1234
                addu        at,at,t2
                lwl         t0,0(at)
                lwr         t0,3(at)
                addiu       at,at,0
ulw t0,0x12345678(t2)
                lui         at,0x1234
                addu        at,at,t2
                lwl         t0,22136(at)
                lwr         t0,22139(at)
                addiu       at,at,22136
ulw t0,main
                lui         at,0x40
                addiu       at,at,432
                lwl         t0,0(at)
                lwr         t0,3(at)
                nop
ulw t0,dat1
                lwl         t0,-30692(gp)
                lwr         t0,-30689(gp)
                nop
```

ush UNALIGNED STORE HALFWORD

Syntax

```
ush SrcGpr,Dest{Imm|Imm(Gpr)|Label}
```

Description

Stores the contents of the least significant halfword of the source register in the memory location specified by the address. This instruction does not signal an address error exception for an unaligned access. This instruction should be used instead of a pair of *store byte* instructions in order to avoid Endian-specific code.

Exceptions

Bus error

Examples

```
ush t0,0x4
                srl         at,t0,8
                sb          at,4(zero)
                sb          t0,5(zero)
ush t0,0x1234
                srl         at,t0,8
                sb          at,4660(zero)
                sb          t0,4661(zero)
ush t0,0x12340000
                lui         at,0x1234
                sb          t0,1(at)
                srl         t0,t0,8
                sb          t0,0(at)
                addiu       at,at,0
                lbu         at,1(at)
                sll         t0,t0,8
                or          t0,t0,at
ush t0,0x12345678
                lui         at,0x1234
                sb          t0,22137(at)
                srl         t0,t0,8
                sb          t0,22136(at)
                addiu       at,at,22136
                lbu         at,1(at)
                sll         t0,t0,8
                or          t0,t0,at
```

```
ush t0,0x1234(t2)
                srl        at,t0,8
                sb         at,4660(t2)
                sb         t0,4661(t2)
ush t0,0x12340000(t2)
                lui        at,0x1234
                addu       at,at,t2
                sb         t0,1(at)
                srl        t0,t0,8
                sb         t0,0(at)
                addiu      at,at,0
                lbu        at,1(at)
                sll        t0,t0,8
                or         t0,t0,at
ush t0,0x12345678(t2)
                lui        at,0x1234
                addu       at,at,t2
                sb         t0,22137(at)
                srl        t0,t0,8
                sb         t0,22136(at)
                addiu      at,at,22136
                lbu        at,1(at)
                sll        t0,t0,8
                or         t0,t0,at
ush t0,main
                lui        at,0x40
                addiu      at,at,432
                sb         t0,1(at)
                srl        t0,t0,8
                sb         t0,0(at)
                lbu        at,1(at)
                sll        t0,t0,8
                or         t0,t0,at
ush t0,dat1
                srl        at,t0,8
                sb         at,-30692(gp)
                sb         t0,-30691(gp)
```

usw   UNALIGNED STORE WORD

Syntax
usw SrcGpr,Dest{Imm|Imm(Gpr)|Label}

Description
Stores the contents of the source register in the memory location specified by
the address. This instruction does not signal an address error exception for
an unaligned access. This instruction should be used instead of a pair of *store
word left* and *store word right* instructions to avoid Endian-specific code.

Exceptions
Bus error

Examples
```
usw t0,0x4
                  swl          t0,4(zero)
                  swr          t0,7(zero)
usw t0,0x1234
                  swl          t0,4660(zero)
                  swr          t0,4663(zero)
usw t0,0x12340000
                  lui          at,0x1234
                  swl          t0,0(at)
                  swr          t0,3(at)
                  addiu        at,at,0
usw t0,0x12345678
                  lui          at,0x1234
                  swl          t0,22136(at)
                  swr          t0,22139(at)
                  addiu        at,at,22136
usw t0,0x1234(t2)
                  swl          t0,4660(t2)
                  swr          t0,4663(t2)
usw t0,0x12340000(t2)
                  lui          at,0x1234
                  addu         at,at,t2
                  swl          t0,0(at)
                  swr          t0,3(at)
                  addiu        at,at,0
```

```
usw  t0,0x12345678(t2)
                lui         at,0x1234
                addu        at,at,t2
                swl         t0,22136(at)
                swr         t0,22139(at)
                addiu       at,at,22136
usw  t0,main
                lui         at,0x40
                addiu       at,at,432
                swl         t0,0(at)
                swr         t0,3(at)
usw  t0,dat1
                swl         t0,-30692(gp)
                swr         t0,-30689(gp)
```

xor

EXCLUSIVE OR

Syntax
```
xor DestGpr,Src1Gpr,Src2(Gpr|Imm)
```

Description
Computes the logical XOR of the corresponding bits of Src1 and Src2 and puts the result in the destination register. An immediate value is zero-extended.

Exceptions
None

Examples
```
xor t0,t1,t2
                xor         t0,t1,t2
xor t0,t1,0x4
                xori        t0,t1,0x4
xor t0,t1,0x1234
                xori        t0,t1,0x1234
xor t0,t1,0x12340000
                lui         at,0x1234
                xor         t0,t1,at
xor t0,t1,0x12345678
                lui         at,0x1234
                ori         at,at,0x5678
                xor         t0,t1,at
```

.align

Syntax

`.align expression`

Description

The `.align` directive advances the program counter until the *expression* number of low-order bits is zero.

Example

```
.align 8  # align on a 256-byte boundary
```

.byte
.word
.double

Syntax

```
.byte   expression1 [,expression2]...[,expressionN]
.word   expression1 [,expression2]...[,expressionN]
.double expression1 [,expression2]...[,expressionN]
```

Description

These directives reserve and initialize memory of the specified size with the value named in the *expression*.

Example

```
bcc_table:
        .word 0,bltz,bgez,0,beq,bne,blez,bgtz
```

.comm
.lcomm

Syntax

```
.comm name, expression
.lcomm name, expression
```

Description

Both of these directives allocate a number of bytes, specified by the *expression*, in the uninitialized data section (.bss or .sbss). The bytes can be referred to using an offset from the specified *name*.

Example

```
.comm stack,1024*8  # allocate 8192 bytes
```

.ent
.end

Syntax

```
.ent proc_name
.end [proc_name]
```

Description

The optional .ent/.end directives are used to inform the assembler of the beginning and end of a function. These directives allow the disassembler to produce more informative program listings.

Example

```
        .globl Fred
        .ent Fred
Fred:
        j ra
        .end Fred
```

.frame
.mask

Syntax

```
.frame frame-register offset, return_pc_register
.mask mask, offset
```

Description

The .frame directive specifies the size of the stack context allocated for a
function and the location of the return address. It permits the user to define a
virtual frame pointer, which points to the lowest addressed word location in
the previous activation record (i.e., the previous stack pointer). The frame
pointer is virtual in the sense that it may or may not have a register allocated
for it. The .frame directive is used with two parameters: the location of the
frame pointer relative to the stack pointer (which is equal to the size of the
stack), and the register in which the return address is saved (usually $31). For
example, for a stack size of 24 words and the return address saved in $31:

```
.frame    sp,24,ra
```

The .mask directive declares which registers have been saved, allowing the
debugger to locate variables that have been saved in the stack. For example,
in the statement

```
.mask 0x80000000,-4;
```

the first parameter, 0x80000000, is a 32-bit bit mask that specifies which of the
general-purpose registers have been saved in the stack. Each mask bit represents one general-purpose register, with bit 0 representing $0, bit 1 represent-
ing $1, and so on. Setting the bit means the register is saved in the stack. So
with 0x80000000 only $31 is saved. The second parameter, -4, specifies the
location of the highest addressed saved register relative to the frame pointer,
which is 4 bytes less than fp.

.globl
.extern

Syntax
```
.globl name
.extern name, [expression]
```

Description
The .globl directive changes the scope of a symbol so it can be referred to by other modules.

The .extern directive can be used to "import" global symbols in other modules, but is not required by the assembler. It is also used to permit gp-relative addressing to be used by the assembler for data symbols declared with global scope in another module. When used for this purpose, the declaration must include an *expression*, specifying the size in bytes.

Examples
```
.globl AdEL       # export the symbol AdEL
.extern ticks, 4  # import the symbol ticks
```

.set reorder/noreorder
.set at/noat

Syntax
```
.set option
```

Description
By default, the assembler uses the AT register to implement the macro (synthetic) instructions and issues a warning whenever AT is used explicitly in a program. The `.set noat` directive allows a program to use AT without warnings, and causes the assembler to issue warnings whenever it uses AT. `.set at` restores the default condition.

By default, the assembler reorders code to improve performance. The `.set noreorder` directive prevents the assembler from reordering, and causes it to issue a warning message if an instruction violates the hardware pipeline constraints. The `.set reorder` directive restores the default condition.

Examples
```
        .set noat
isr:

            .

            .

            .
        .set at
        .set noreorder
        mfc0 t0,CO_SR
        nop
        .set reorder
```

.text
.data
.sdata

Syntax
```
.text
.data
.sdata
```

Description
These directives tell the assembler to add subsequent code to the named section. Program sections are described in Chapter 1, Section 1.2. By default the assembler assumes the .text section.

Examples
```
        .data
        /* a table used to get a value from a register */
getreg: .word gr0,gr1,gr2,gr3,gr4,gr5,gr6,gr7,gr8,gr9,
        .text
reset_exception:
        j       init
```

A

Overview of the MIPS1 Architecture

This appendix provides a brief overview of the MIPS1 base architecture. Its purpose is twofold: (1) to provide a quick reference for readers already acquainted with the MIPS architecture and (2) to provide readers who are not so acquainted with enough information to understand the example programs.

A.1 ADDRESSING

The MIPS1 architecture has two address spaces: a virtual address space, consisting of all the addresses that can be used in a program, and a physical address space, consisting of all the addresses that can be sent out on the address bus.

The virtual address space is partitioned into four, fixed-size segments: kuseg, kseg0, kseg1, and kseg2. Thus virtual addresses consist of a segment number (the three most significant bits of the address) and an offset within the segment. In the translation of virtual to physical addresses, the 12 least significant bits of the virtual address are unchanged, so that in implementations using a memory management unit (MMU) and a translation lookaside buffer (TLB), segments can be further partitioned into 4K pages, with addresses consisting of a virtual page number and an offset within the page.

The mapping of virtual addresses to physical addresses is shown in Figure A.1 and Table A.1. The characteristics of the four segments are shown in Table A.2 and described in following sections of this appendix.

The four segments support caching (described in Chapter 3) and the needs of operating systems that implement virtual memory. kuseg, accessible in both user and kernel mode, is designed to be used by user-mode programs (operating modes are described in the following section), while also providing accessibility to this address space in kernel mode. kseg1 is designed for access to peripheral devices and for code that requires noncacheable access, including initialization code that is executed before the caches have been flushed (the processor fetches instructions from this segment following reset, because neither the cache nor the TLB will have been initialized, and this is the only "safe" area from which to execute. kseg2 is designed for those parts of the

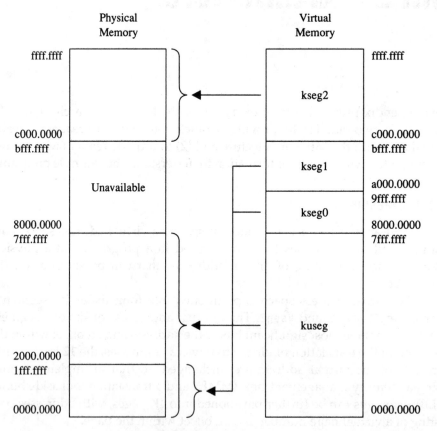

Figure A.1   Virtual to Physical Address Mapping (without TLB)

Table A.1   Segment Addresses

Segment	Address Bits			Virtual Address Range	Physical Address Range
	31	30	29	(Hex)	(Hex)
kseg2	1	1	x	c000.0000–ffff.ffff	c000.0000–ffff.ffff
kseg1	1	0	1	a000.0000–bfff.ffff	0000.0000–1fff.ffff
kseg0	1	0	0	8000.0000–9fff.ffff	0000.0000–1fff.ffff
kuseg	0	x	x	0000.0000–7fff.ffff	0000.0000–7fff.ffff

Table A.2   Segment Characteristics

Segment	Size	Caching	Access
kseg2	1024M*	Cacheable	Kernel
kseg1	512M	Noncacheable	Kernel
kseg0	512M	Cacheable	Kernel
kuseg	2048M	Cacheable	User or kernel

*M=megabyte

operating system that will use virtual memory. kseg0 is for all other parts of the operating system. kseg0 and kseg1 map to the same physical addresses. kuseg and kseg2 are mapped via the TLB (if there is one). When no TLB is present, the mapping of these segments is somewhat vendor-dependent.

A.2 MODES OF OPERATION

The MIPS processor has two modes of operation, *User Mode* and *Kernel Mode*, as selected by the Current Kernel/User Mode bit (KUc) in the Status Register (see Section A.4). The two modes determine the addresses, registers, and instructions that are available to a program.

Kernel-mode programs are permitted to use all addresses, registers, and instructions. User-mode programs, on the other hand, may use only the virtual addresses 0 through 7fff.ffff (2 gigabytes), and an attempt to access any other segment causes an Address Error exception. A user-mode program's use of coprocessor instructions and registers can be restricted by clearing the appropriate Coprocessor Usability bit in the Status Register. (Coprocessors are described in Section A.3.)

The processor enters kernel mode when the system is reset, when an exception occurs, or when the Status Register's Current Kernel/User Mode bit is set by a user-mode program permitted to access coprocessor 0 (an unlikely occurrence).

The processor switches to user mode when the restore from exception instruction is executed and the Status Register's Previous Kernel/User Mode bit is set, or when the Current Kernel/User Mode bit is cleared explicitly by a kernel-mode program (not recommended).

All the examples in this book execute in kernel mode.

A.3 COPROCESSOR UNITS

The MIPS1 architecture defines four *coprocessor units*, Coprocessor 0 through Coprocessor 3. A coprocessor is an auxiliary processing unit that operates in coordination with the MIPS CPU. Each coprocessor may have an instruction set, 32 general-purpose registers, and 32 control registers. Coprocessor 0, called the System Control Processor, provides support for memory-mapping and exception-handling functions. Coprocessor 1 supports floating-point operations. Coprocessors 2 and 3 are undefined and are intended to permit special-purpose engines, such as a graphics accelerator, to be integrated into the architecture.

Execution of coprocessor instructions in user mode is controlled by four Coprocessor Usability (CU) bits in the Status Register, one for each coprocessor (1 = coprocessor usable). Attempts by a user-mode program to access a coprocessor whose Coprocessor Usability bit is zero causes a Coprocessor Unusable exception.

Kernel-mode programs can execute all coprocessor 0 instructions, regardless of the value of the coprocessor's Coprocessor Usability bit, but attempts to execute instructions of other coprocessors whose CU bits are zero will cause a Coprocessor Unusable exception.

Keep in mind when setting the CU bit that a coprocessor is not available for use until the third instruction following the mtc0 instruction that sets the bit. For example,

```
mfc0      t0,CO_SR
nop
and       t0,SR_CU1
mtc0      t0,CO_SR
nop
nop
ctc1      t1,C1_FCR
```

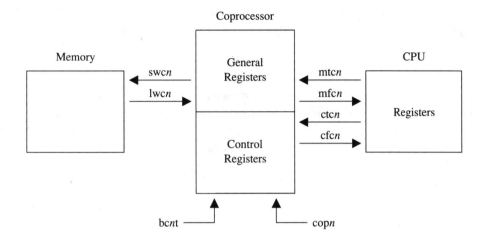

	COP0	COP1	COP2–3
swc*n*—Store word from coprocessor *n*	no	yes	undef
lwc*n*—Load word to coprocessor *n*	no	yes	undef
mtc*n*—Move to coprocessor general register *n*	yes	yes	undef
mfc*n*—Move from coprocessor general register *n*	yes	yes	undef
ctc*n*—Move to coprocessor control register *n*	no	yes	undef
cfc*n*—Move from coprocessor control register *n*	no	yes	undef
bc*n*t—Branch on coprocessor *n* true	yes	yes	undef
bc*n*f—Branch on coprocessor *n* false	yes	yes	undef
cop*n*—Coprocessor operation *n*	yes	yes	undef

Figure A.2   Coprocessor Instructions

The generic coprocessor instructions provided by the MIPS1 architecture are shown in Figure A.2. Not all coprocessors support all coprocessor instructions. For example, Coprocessor 0 supports only the mfc0 and mtc0 instructions for moving data to and from coprocessor registers; it does not permit any memory accesses (loads and stores). Note also that referencing an undefined coprocessor register does not cause an exception, and that the return value is undefined.

The two coprocessor branch instructions, bc*n*t and bc*n*f, test the corresponding Coprocessor Condition input pin if the Coprocessor Usability bit is set (except that bc0t and bc0f always test the input pin, regardless of the setting of CU). The Coprocessor Condition input pin is set or cleared by hardware to reflect the result of a compare instruction. For example,

```
bclt 3f
```

will branch to the next label 3 if the Coprocessor Condition input pin is high.

The mfc0 instruction executes with a delay of one cycle, so its result is not available until the instruction following the instruction in the delay slot. This instruction must appear within a .set noreorder section. For example,

```
.set noreorder
mfc0 t0,C0_SR
nop
or   t0,SR_IEC
.set reorder
```

The mtc0 instruction must also appear within a .set noreorder section but does not require a delay cycle, although the result of setting or clearing bits in C0_SR may require up to three cycles.

```
.set noreorder
mtc0 t0,C0_SR
.set reorder
```

The coprocessor registers are discussed in the next section.

A.4 REGISTERS

The CPU contains 32 general-purpose registers called $0–$31, two Multiply/Divide Registers called HI and LO, and a Program Counter (PC) Register. All registers are 32 bits. The general-purpose registers are summarized in Tables A.3 and A.4.

The general-purpose registers are used to hold instruction operands and results. Two of them, $0 and $31, have uses that are predefined by the hardware: $0 is hardwired to 0, and $31 is used to hold the return address for the jump-and-link and branch-and-link instructions (jalr/balr). HI and LO store the doubleword result of multiply instructions and the quotient and remainder of divide instructions. The PC is not directly accessible by the programmer, but is used by the machine to generate addresses for the branch and jump instructions. Each coprocessor unit can have as many as 32 general-purpose registers and 32 control registers. In the base architecture, the System Control

Table A.3   CPU General Registers

Hardware Name	Software Name	Name in mips.h	Usage
$0	—	zero	Constant zero
$1	$at	AT	Assembler temp
$2–$3	—	v0–v1	Function return
$4–$7	—	a0–a3	Incoming args
$8–$15	—	t0–t7	Temporaries
$16–$23	—	s0–s7	Saved temporaries
$24–$25	—	t8–t9	Temporaries
$26–$27	$kt0–$kt1	k0–k1	Exception handling
$28	$gp	gp	Global data pointer
$29	$sp	sp	Stack pointer
$30	$fp	s8	Saved temporary
$31	—	ra	Return address

Table A.4   CPU Special Registers

Hardware Name	Usage
HI	High-order 32 bits of multiply and remainder of divide
LO	Low-order 32 bits of multiply and quotient of divide

Processor (coprocessor 0) has 5 general-purpose registers that are used for CPU status and control functions and for exception handling. These registers are summarized in Table A.5 and described individually in Figures A.4–A.8.

Coprocessor 1 has 32, 32-bit general-purpose registers and 2, 32-bit control registers (refer to Table A.6 and Table A.7). The general-purpose registers can be used to hold either 16 single-precision (32-bit) values or 16 double-precision (64-bit) values. As shown in Figure A.3, single-precision values are stored in even-numbered registers, whereas double-precision values are stored in register pairs, with the sign, exponent, and the most significant part of the mantissa in the even-numbered register. Coprocessor 1 registers are summarized in Tables A.7 and A.8 and described individually in Figures A.9 and A.10.

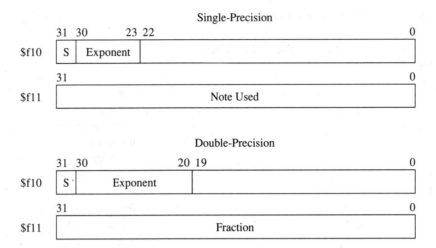

Figure A.3 Coprocessor 1 (Floating-Point) Register Formats

Note that all floating-point instructions except the generic coprocessor data-movement instructions require that the floating-point register number be even. For example,

```
div.d $f4,$f6,$f8
```

which multiplies the contents of $f6 and $f8 and puts the result in $f4, implies the use of the next register: $f4 implies the use of $f5. Conversely,

```
mtc1 t0,$f6
mtc1 t4,$f7
```

loads a double-precision value into the register pair $f6/$f7 from general registers t0 and t4.

Coprocessor 1 has two control registers: a Control/Status Register and an Implementation/Revision Register. For example, to initialize the Control/Status Register to 0 (the usual default case), you would use

```
ctc1 zero,$31
```

which specifies rounding to nearest representable value and disables all traps. Note that some trap handling is necessary for full compliance with the IEEE Standard because the hardware floating-point unit does not handle all cases, such as denormalized numbers.

Table A.5   Coprocessor 0 (System-Control Processor) Registers

Proper Name	Hardware Name	Name in mips.h	Access
Bad Virtual Address	$8	C0_BADVA	r
Status Register	$12	C0_SR	r/w*
Cause Register	$13	C0_CAUSE	r**
Exception Program Counter Register	$14	C0_EPC	r
Processor Revision Identification Register	$15	C0_PRID	r

*All bits are read/write except the Ts bit, which is read-only.
**All bits are read-only except the Sw bits, which are read/write.

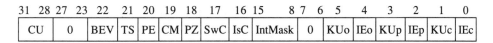

Figure A.4   Status Register (C0_SR)

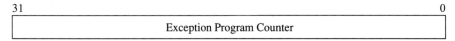

Reset state = Undefined

Figure A.5   Cause Register (C0_CAUSE)

Reset state = Undefined

Figure A.6   EPC: Exception Program Counter Register (C0_EPC)

31	0
Bad Virtual Address	

Reset state = Undefined

Figure A.7   BadVAddr: Bad Virtual Address Register

31	16	15	8	7	0
0		IMP		REV	

Figure A.8   PRId: Processor Revision Identifier Register (C0_PRID)

Table A.6   Coprocessor 1 (Floating-Point) General Registers

Hardware Name	Name in mips.h	Usage
$f0–$f3	—	Function return
$f4–$f14	—	Temporaries
$f12–$f15	—	Incoming arguments
$f16–$f19	—	Temporaries
$f20–$f31	—	Saved temporaries

Table A.7   Coprocessor 1 (Floating-Point) Control Registers

Proper Name	Hardware Name	Usage
Implementation/Revision	FCR0	Revision information
Control/Status Register	FCR31	Status and control functions

31	24	23	22	18	17	12	11	7	6	2	1	0
0		C	0		Exceptions E V Z O U I		TrapEnable V Z O U I		Sticky Bits V Z O U I		RM	

Reset state = Undefined

Figure A.9   Coprocessor 1 Control/Status Register (FPA_CSR)

31	16	15	8	7	0
0		IMP		REV	

Figure A.10   Coprocessor 1 Implementation/Revision Register

CU: Coprocessor Usable (SR_CU0–SR_CU3)   These 4 bits are used by software to control accesses to coprocessor 0–3 (corresponding to bits 28–31). Attempted execution of a coprocessor instruction will cause a Coprocessor Unusable exception when its CU bit is clear, with the exception that kernel-mode programs can execute any Coprocessor 0 instruction, regardless of the setting of bit 28.

BEV: Bootstrap-Exception Vectors (SR_BEV)   This bit is set by hardware when the processor is reset and can be set or cleared by software. When this bit is set, the General Exception Vector is mapped to a noncacheable kseg1 address; when this bit is clear, the General-Exception Vector is mapped to a cacheable kseg0 address (refer to Table 4.1 in Chapter 4).

TS: TLB Shutdown (SR_TS)   This read-only bit is set by hardware when an address matches more than one TLB entry. Some implementations (such as the R3051 from IDT) use this bit to indicate the presence (TS = 1) or absence (TS = 0) of a TLB.

PE: Parity Error (SR_PE)   This bit is set by hardware when there is a cache parity error. Because the processor recovers transparently from parity errors (by taking a cache miss and accessing main memory), this bit is helpful in diagnostics. To clear this bit, write a 1 to PE; writing a zero to this bit does not affect its value.

CM: Cache Miss (SR_CM)   This bit is set by hardware when there is a cache miss on a load instruction and the Isolate Cache bit is also set.

PZ: Parity Zero (SR_PZ)   This bit is set by software to clear outgoing parity bits (both cache data and tags) on store instructions.

SwC: Swap Caches (SR_SWC)   This bit is set by software to enable swapping the two caches' control signals (1 = swapped). When the caches are swapped, loads and stores access the I-cache.

IsC: Isolate Cache (SR_ISC)   This bit is set by software to isolate the cache from main memory (1 = isolated).

IntMask: Interrupt Mask (SR_IBIT8–SR_IBIT0)   These bits are used by software to individually enable/disable hardware and software interrupts. Setting the IntMask bit enables the corresponding interrupt if the Interrupt

Enable bit is also set. When an interrupt's corresponding IntMask bit is cleared, the interrupt is disabled.

KUo/KUp/KUc: Kernal/User Mode–Old/Previous/Current
(SR_KUO, SR_KUP, SR_KUC)   The KUc bit indicates the processor's current mode of operation, as described in Section A.2 (0 = kernel mode, 1 = user mode). The KUc bit is cleared by hardware on reset and when an exception occurs (exceptions are described in Chapter 3). After the exception is taken, the contents of KUc is copied into the KUp bit, and the KUp bit is copied into the KUo bit. When a return-from-exception instruction is executed, KUp and KUc are restored, leaving the KUo bit unchanged.

IEo/IEp/IEc: Interrupt Enable–Old/Previous/Current
(SR_IEO, SR_IEP, SR_IEC)   The IEc bit indicates whether or not interrupts are currently enabled (1 = interrupts enabled). The IEc bit is cleared by hardware on reset and when an exception occurs. It is cleared by software to disable all interrupts and set by software to enable those interrupts whose IntMask bit is also set. When an exception occurs, the IEc bit is copied into the IEp bit, and the IEp bit is copied into the IEo bit. When a return-from-exception instruction is executed, IEp and IEc are restored, leaving the IEo bit unchanged.

BD: Branch Delay (CAUSE_BD)   This bit is set by hardware if the instruction executing when an exception occurred is in the delay slot of a branch. The state of this bit is relevant only to exceptions other than hardware and software interrupts (i.e., when the ExcCode field does not equal zero).

CE: Coprocessor Error (CAUSE_CEMASK)   When a Coprocessor Unusable Exception occurs, these bits are set by hardware to indicate which coprocessor was referenced, with 00 indicating coprocessor 0 and so on. CAUSE_CESHIFT can be used to shift the value of CE into the least significant position in a register.

IP: Interrupts Pending (CAUSE_IP8–CAUSE_IP3)   These bits are set by hardware to indicate which hardware interrupt is currently pending, as described in Chapter 3. CAUSE_IPMASK and CAUSE_IPSHIFT can be used to mask and shift the IP field (including the Sw field).

Sw: Software Interrupts (CAUSE_SW2–CAUSE_SW1)   These bits are set by software to generate a software interrupt and are the only writable bits in this register.

Table A.8 Exception Codes

ExcCode Value	Assembler Mnemonic	Exception Type
0	EXC_INT	External interrupt
1	DDD	Reserved
2	DDD	Reserved
3	DDD	Reserved
4	EXC_ADEL	Address error (load or instruction fetch)
5	EXC_ADES	Address error (data store)
6	EXC_IBE	Bus error (instruction fetch)
7	EXC_DBE	Bus error (data load or store)
8	EXC_SYS	Syscall instruction
9	EXC_BP	Breakpoint
10	EXC_RI	Reserved instruction
11	EXC_CPU	Coprocessor unusable
12	EXC_OVF	Arithmetic overflow
13–15	DDD	Not used

ExcCode: Exception Code Field (CAUSE_EXCMASK) This field is written by hardware with a number, between 0 and 15, that indicates the cause of an exception, as shown in Table A.8. CAUSE_EXCMASK and CAUSE_EXCSHIFT can be used to mask and shift the ExcCode field.

When an exception occurs, this read-only register is written by hardware with the address at which the program can be correctly restarted. If the instruction causing the exception is in the delay slot of a branch (BD = 1), the EPC is written with the virtual address of the preceding branch or jump instruction. Otherwise, it is written with the virtual address of the instruction that caused the exception or, in the case of an interrupt, with the address of the next instruction to be executed.

This read-only register is written by hardware with the virtual address associated with an Address Error exception. This register saves only addressing errors (AdEL or AdES), not bus errors.

Imp: Implementation Identifier This field identifies the implementation of the processor and the System Control Coprocessor.

Rev: Revision Identifier This field identifies the revision level of the processor and the System Control Coprocessor.

C: Condition　　This bit is set or cleared by hardware to reflect the result of a compare instruction and drives the CpCond output signal (refer to Section A.3).

Exceptions　　These bits are set by hardware when an exception occurs.

TrapEnable　　These bits are set to enable the assertion of the CpInt signal if the corresponding Exception bit is set during a floating-point operation.

Sticky Bits　　These bits are set by hardware if an exception occurs and are reset by software.

RM: Rounding Mode　　These bits specify which of the four rounding modes will be used.

Imp: Implementation Identifier　　This field identifies the implementation of the processor and coprocessor 1.

Rev: Revision Identifier　　This field identifies the revision level of coprocessor 1.

A.5 DATA TYPES

There are nine basic data types: signed and unsigned bytes, signed and unsigned halfwords (16 bits), signed and unsigned words (32 bits), doublewords (64 bits), single-precision floating-point (32 bits), and double-precision floating-point (64 bits).

Bytes and halfwords are sign- or zero-extended to 32 bits before they are put in registers. The significance of register bits increases from right to left. Doubleword values are stored in register pairs, with the most significant word in the even-numbered register.

A.6 INSTRUCTIONS

The MIPS instruction set consists of both *machine* instructions and *macro* (also called *synthetic*) instructions. The machine instructions are hardwired; macro instructions are expanded into sequences of machine instructions by the assembler.

All machine instructions are singleword-aligned (32 bits) on a word boundary. An instruction consists of an opcode (the 6 most significant bits) and from zero to three operands. The operands may be the contents of a register (a 5 bit field), an immediate value (contained in a 16-bit instruction field), or an address of either code or data (contained in a 24-bit instruction field).

A.6.1 Delay Instructions

Because of the processor's pipelined architecture and the data dependencies among pipeline stages, some instructions require an extra instruction cycle in which to complete execution. For this reason they must be followed by an instruction, called the *delay instruction*, that does not depend on the completion of the preceding instruction.

Four categories of instructions require delay instructions: jumps, branches, loads, and the mfc0 (move from coprocessor 0) instruction. The load and move-from-coprocessor instructions require an additional instruction cycle for data to be fetched from the D-cache or coprocessor. Jump and branch instructions require an extra cycle for the target to be fetched from the I-cache.

In the case of the load instructions and move from coprocessor 0, the delay instruction must be one that does not use the results of the preceding instruction. For jump and branch instructions, the delay instruction must be an instruction that logically precedes the jump or branch (because it is always executed, regardless of the outcome of the branch). If there is no useful delay instruction, nop is used. For example,

```
lw t0,(t1)
nop    # delay instruction
addu t2,t0

beq t0,t1,fred
nop    # delay instruction
addu t1,3
```

Delay slots are filled by either the programmer or the assembler. If the instruction is within a reorder section (the default), only the assembler can fill the delay slot, and nop instructions cannot be used. Within a noreorder section, the delay slot must be explicitly filled by the programmer, and the assembler issues a warning if there is an attempt to use the result before it is available. Note that because the mfc0 instruction must be in a noreorder section, its delay slot must always be explicitly filled by the programmer. Also note that when you are filling the delay slot of a branch, be careful not to use a synthetic instruction that will expand to more than one machine instruction, because only the first instruction of the expansion will be in the delay slot and if the branch is taken, the complete instruction will not be executed.

In the case of a conditional branch instruction, the branch condition is evaluated before the instruction in the delay slot is executed, so the instruction in the delay slot can use a register that was used as one of the branch's source registers. For example,

```
        .set noreorder
        beq t0,t1,label
        add t0,t4,6                    .set reorder
```

A.6.2 Computational Instructions

Computational instructions perform arithmetic, logical, and shift operations. The source operand can be either an immediate value or the contents of a general register (memory operands must be first loaded from memory into a register); the destination is always a general register.

Most arithmetic and logical instructions use three register operands—two sources and a destination. The assembler syntax specifies the first operand as the destination followed by one or more sources. For example,

```
        sub t0,t1,t2
```

means that t0 is assigned the value t1 minus t2.

Three-operand instructions can also be written with two operands, where the destination is the same as the first source in the three-operand version. For example,

```
        sub t0,t1
```

is expanded by the assembler to

```
        sub t0,t0,t1
```

If the immediate value in an instruction can be represented in 16 bits, the assembler will generate a single instruction. If the immediate value is greater than 16 bits, the assembler generates multiple instructions, using the register AT to hold the immediate value. For example, the instruction

```
        add t0,t1,0x12340000
```

is implemented as

```
lui at,0x1234
add t0,t1,at
```

The processor's machine-level multiply and divide instructions place their results in the HI and LO registers (after the required number of cycles have elapsed). However, to make these instructions easier to use, macro instructions are provided that place results in a general-purpose register. For example,

```
mult t1,t2
mflo t0
```

is equivalent to

```
mul t0,t1,t2
```

An advantage of using the macro instruction is that the assembler will attempt to place the two instructions so as to minimize the possibility of a stall. If you use the machine instructions, the processor will stall if you attempt to use the result before it is available.

For the multiply instruction, the macro instructions and the machine macro instruction have different names: mult and multu are machine instructions; mul, mulo, and mulou are macro instructions. For the divide instruction, the machine instruction is generated if a zero is specified as the destination register; otherwise, the assembler generates a macro instruction.

Shift instructions can shift from 0 to 31 places in a single cycle. The shift amount can be specified as an immediate value or the contents of a register. For example, to shift the contents of a register six places to the left:

```
sll t0,6
```

or

```
li  t1,6
sll t0,t1
```

Some computational instructions generate an exception when a two's-complement overflow occurs (add, subtract, etc.). Unless signalling of a two's-complement overflow is required, be sure to use the unsigned version of the instruction (addu, subu, etc.).

The li (load immediate) instruction is used to load an immediate value into a register. Depending on the size of the immediate value, the assembler will automatically generate the most efficient instruction(s). For example,

```
li t0,0x12345678
```

is implemented by the assembler using an lui instruction that loads the upper 16 bits of the register with 0x1234 and sets the lower 16 bits to 0x0000, and an ori that loads 0x5678 into the lower 16 bits.

```
lui t0,0x1234
ori t0,t0,0x5678
```

The li instruction used with an immediate value of 1

```
li t0,1
```

is implemented as

```
addu t0,zero,1
```

If an immediate value cannot be determined at assembly time, the la (load address) instruction must be used.

A.6.3 Branches and Jumps

The MIPS1 architecture provides two types of control transfer instructions—branches and jumps. Jumps transfer control to a target address using an absolute address; branches transfer control using a PC-relatve address.

Referring to Figure A.11, the target address for a branch instruction is computed using the 16-bit immediate field of the instruction as a word offset from the address of the instruction following the branch. Thus the maximum addressing range of a branch is ±128K from the current PC value. Jumps use an absolute address that is merged with the 4 most significant bits of the PC, so they can jump anywhere within the current 256M region of memory.

Subroutine calls are made using either jal (jump and link), bltzal (branch on less-than zero and link), or bgezal (branch on greater-than or equal to zero and link), all of which save the return address in a register. ra is used for this purpose, except that jal can specify another register.

In conditional branch instructions that compare two values, the values can either be the contents of two registers or the contents of a register and an

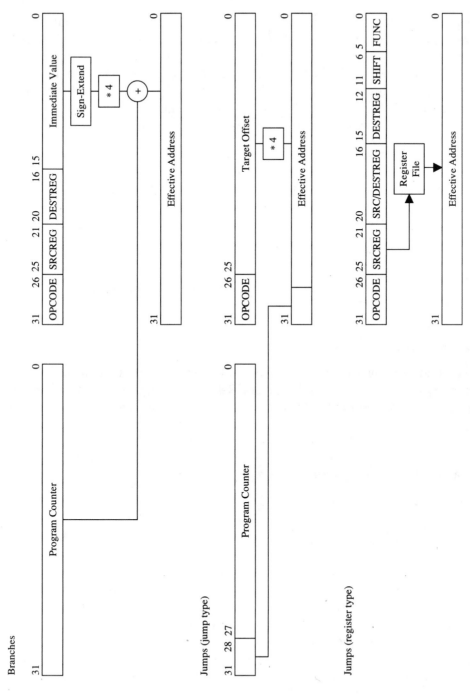

Figure A.11   Address Calculation for Branches and Jumps

immediate value. Branch instructions that test for equality of the contents of two registers and those that compare the contents of a register with zero are performed in a single instruction, such as `beq t0,t1,1f` and `bltz t0,1f`.

For all other branch instructions, including those that specify an immediate value, multiple instructions will be generated. For example, branch instructions that compare the magnitude of two registers are implemented by the assembler as two instructions. For example,

```
bge t0,t1,1f
```

is implemented by the assembler as

```
slt AT,t0,t1
beq AT,zero,1f
nop
```

where `slt` tests the two registers and places the Boolean result in AT, where it can be tested by `beq`.

A.6.4 Loads and Stores

Load and store instructions are the only instructions that move data between memory and the CPU general registers. Referring to Figure A.12, the memory address may be specified as the contents of a register, such as

```
lw t0,(t1)
```

or as an offset from an address in a register, such as

```
lw t0,0x1234(t1)
```

or as a label, such as

```
lw t0,main
```

The assembler generates a single instruction for loads and stores when the address is specified in a register, as a 16-bit offset from an address in a register, or as a gp-relative label (described in Chapter 1, Section 1.2). For offsets greater than 16 bits, the assembler generates two instructions—one that loads the most significant 16 bits of the address into a temporary register, and a sub-

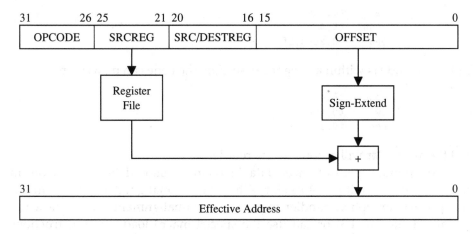

Figure A.12   Address Calculation for Loads and Stores

sequent instruction that loads the value from the effective address generated by adding the offset to the temporary register. For example,

```
lw      t0,0x12345678
```

is implemented as

```
lui     AT,0x1234
lw      t0,0x5678(AT)
```

Note that the offset is sign-extended before it is added to the temporary register. Note also that expressions containing parentheses can be distinguished by prepending a plus sign, +. When the source operand is a label, as in

```
lw      t0,main
```

the assembler generates

```
lui     AT,0x8002
lw      t0,538(AT)
```

The macro instruction la (load address) is used to load a relocatable address into a register. If the value can be determined at assembly time, the more efficient li instruction should be used.

As previously explained, the result of a load instruction is available after a delay of one instruction. In the example below, the value of t0 cannot be tested until after the delay slot instruction, addu t6,4:

```
lw      t0,(t4)
addu    t6,4
beq     t0,zero,1f
```

Unless the code is within a noreorder section, the code can be written

```
addu    t6,4
lw      t0,(t4)
beq     t0,zero,1f
```

and the assembler will automatically reorder it.

To optimize performance, data in memory should be aligned on an address that is a multiple of its size. When data is unaligned, the program can either use an exception handler to manage the unalignment (this is shown in Chapter 4, Section 4.3) or can use the special macro load/store instructions that accept unaligned data without causing an exception. These instructions are summarized in Figure A.13.

Load Instructions

	Unaligned		Aligned	
	Unsigned	Sign-extended	Unsigned	Sign-extended
Byte	—	—	lbu	lb
Halfword	ulhu	ulh	lhu	lh
Word	ulw	—	lw	—
Doubleword	—	—	ld	—
Partial word	lwl , lwr	—	—	—

Store Instructions

	Unaligned		Aligned	
	Unsigned	Sign-extended	Unsigned	Sign-extended
Byte	—	—	sb	—
Halfword	ush	—	sh	—
Word	usw	—	sw	—
Doubleword	—	—	sd	—
Partial word	swl , swr	—	—	—

Figure A.13   Load and Store Instructions

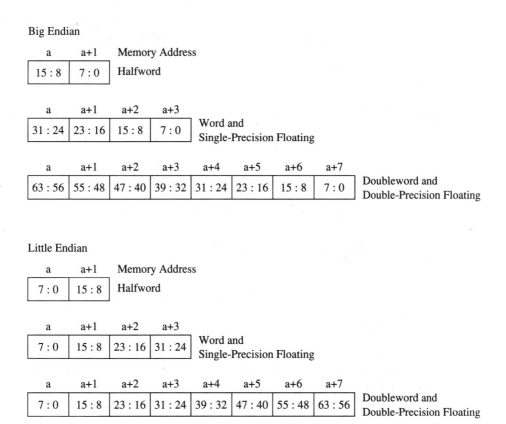

Big Endian

a	a+1	Memory Address
15 : 8	7 : 0	Halfword

a	a+1	a+2	a+3	
31 : 24	23 : 16	15 : 8	7 : 0	Word and Single-Precision Floating

a	a+1	a+2	a+3	a+4	a+5	a+6	a+7	
63 : 56	55 : 48	47 : 40	39 : 32	31 : 24	23 : 16	15 : 8	7 : 0	Doubleword and Double-Precision Floating

Little Endian

a	a+1	Memory Address
7 : 0	15 : 8	Halfword

a	a+1	a+2	a+3	
7 : 0	15 : 8	23 : 16	31 : 24	Word and Single-Precision Floating

a	a+1	a+2	a+3	a+4	a+5	a+6	a+7	
7 : 0	15 : 8	23 : 16	31 : 24	39 : 32	47 : 40	55 : 48	63 : 56	Doubleword and Double-Precision Floating

Figure A.14 Big and Little Endian Byte Ordering and Addressing

A.6.4.1 Big and Little Endian Byte Orderings

The MIPS processor and compilers support both the Big Endian and Little Endian byte-ordering conventions. The names Big Endian and Little Endian are used because of the apt analogy to the bloody feud in the classic children's book *Gulliver's Travels* (*quod vide*). The feud was between the two mythical islands, Lilliput and Blefescu, over the correct end (big or little) at which to crack an egg.[1] In our case, the issue has to do with the "end" (most significant or least significant) of a multiple-byte data type.

With Big Endian ordering, the address of a multiple-byte data type is of its most significant byte (its "big end"), whereas with Little Endian ordering, the address is of its least significant byte (its "little end"). This is shown in Figure A.14. For structures declared in a high-level language, the order of bytes in

---

1 Danny Cohen, "On Holy Wars and a Plea for Peace," *IEEE Computer*, Oct. 1981, pp. 48–54.

Code	Big Endian Memory Contents		Little Endian Memory Contents	
struct {				
long a;				
short b[2];				
char c[4];				
} S1 = {	/*	Big Endian	Little Endian	*/
0x12345678,	/*	12345678	78563412	*/
0x1234,0x5678,	/*	1234 5678	3412 7856	*/
"ABC"	/*	41 42 43 00	41 42 43 00	*/

Figure A.15 Big and Little Endian Byte-Ordering Example

memory will differ depending on the byte ordering and the particular data type, as shown for a C structure in Figure A.15.

Note that Endianness only affects the operation of the load and store instructions, which means when data is moved between memory or peripheral devices and registers.

Except in cases where the host and target have the same byte-ordering convention, you must explicitly define the required Endianness of the target code using the appropriate command-line option (EB or EL). This will override the host's default byte ordering. For example,

```
cc -EB -o prog prog.c
cc -EL -o prog prog.c
```

To write code that can be compiled/assembled to execute correctly in either a Big or a Little Endian target environment, the user must follow one basic rule: either eliminate Endian-specific code or enclose it with #ifdef/else statements, using the appropriate preprocessor flag (MIPSEB or MIPSEL). Endian-specific code is produced whenever the data type implicit in the instruction (e.g., "byte" in load byte) differs from the data type of the accessed data, such as using four load-byte instructions to read a single word or using a store-word instruction to store 4 bytes. I/O addresses are also Endian-specific, because a peripheral device is hardwired to a specific part of the data bus (typically D0–D7).

The example programs main.c and asm.s print Endian-sensitive values returned from the functions end1 and end2 and the contents of two Endian-sensitive I/O locations, SIOCNTL and SIODATA. For purposes of illustration, the functions return correct results when passed the value 0 and incorrect results when passed the value 1. The programs are shown in their entirety in the final section of this appendix and are discussed below.

The C program defines two base addresses for the peripheral device (SIOBASE) and uses the preprocessor variable MIPSEB (Big Endian) to select between the two byte-ordering conventions.

```
1  #ifdef MIPSEB
2  #define SIOBASE     0xbe000003 /* Big Endian base address */
3  #else
4  #define SIOBASE     0xbe000000 /* Little Endian base address */
5  #endif
6  #define SIOCNTL     *((volatile unsigned char *)SIOBASE+4)
7  #define SIODATA     *((volatile unsigned char *)SIOBASE+12)
```

The function main prints the results of the functions end1 and end2. Incorrect results are produced by end1 because when the function is passed a 1, it reads the word as a series of 4 bytes, rather than as a single word. Starting at the word address, each byte is read into the variable v, such that the lowest addressed byte ends up in the most significant byte of the variable. This is the correct byte ordering for Big Endian but incorrect for Little Endian:

```
19              for (i=0;i<4;i++) {
20                  v <<= 8;
21                  v |= p[i];
22                  }
23          }
```

Incorrect results are produced by end2 because the lwl and lwr instructions are used to access unaligned data; the non-Endian-sensitive solution uses the ulw instruction:

```
8  end2:    la      t0,dat2
9           beq     a0,zero,1f
10          nop
11          lwl     v0,0(t0)
12          lwr     v0,3(t0)
13          b       2f
14          nop
15  1:      ulw     v0,(t0)
16  2:      jr      ra
```

For Big Endian the program prints:

```
12345678 12345678
12345678 12345678
00 3b
```

and for Little Endian it prints:

```
12345678 78563412
12345678 78345612
00 3b
```

Keep in mind that a program's binary cannot be converted from one byte-ordering convention to another by simply swapping all the bytes. This would produce correct results only if all of the program's data were of the same type (size) and the same size as the instructions. To change the byte ordering, programs must be recompiled using the appropriate compiler option.

A.7 PROGRAM LISTINGS

main.c:

```
 1  #ifdef MIPSEB
 2  #define SIOBASE     0xbe000003 /* Big Endian base address */
 3  #else
 4  #define SIOBASE     0xbe000000 /* Little Endian base address */
 5  #endif

 6  #define SIOCNTL    *((volatile unsigned char *)SIOBASE+4)
 7  #define SIODATA    *((volatile unsigned char *)SIOBASE+12)

 8  int dat1 = 0x12345678;
 9  end1(n)
10  int n;
11  {
12  int i,v;
13  unsigned char *p;

14  /* set up a pointer into the data */
15  p = (unsigned char *)&dat1;

16  if (n==0) v = dat1;
17  else {
18          v = 0;
19          for (i=0;i<4;i++) {
20                  v <<= 8;
21                  v |= p[i];
22                  }
23          }
24  return(v);
25  }
```

```
26   main()
27   {

28   printf("%08x %08x\n",end1(0),end1(1));
29   printf("%08x %08x\n",end2(0),end2(1));
30   printf("%02x %02x\n",SIOCNTL,SIODATA);
31   }
```

asm.s:

```
 1   #include "mips.h"

 2          .data
 3   dat2:  .word   0x12345678
 4          .text
 5          .globl end2
 6          .ent end2
 7          .set noreorder
 8   end2:  la      t0,dat2
 9          beq     a0,zero,1f
10          nop
11          lwl     v0,0(t0)
12          lwr     v0,3(t0)
13          b       2f
14          nop

15   1:     ulw     v0,(t0)
16   2:     jr      ra
17          nop
18          .end end2
```

B

Instruction Summary

This appendix contains a summary of the MIPS instruction set. Tables B.2 and B.3 contain listings of all MIPS1 instructions, their addressing modes (the various combinations of operands), and the number of instructions required for each addressing mode. The column headings, designating operand types, are substituted for the "X" in the corresponding instruction. When the number of instructions is expressed as a range from n through m, this means the assembler will insert up to $m-n$ nops when no useful instructions can be found to fill the delay slot(s). Table B.1 describes the operand types.

Table B.1   Operand Types for Tables B.2 and B.3

Operand	Meaning
Gpr	CPU general register
Fpre	Floating-point general register, even
Cpr	Coprocessor general register
I2	Immediate value, power of 2
I16	16-bit immediate value
I16r	16-bit immediate value relative to Gpr
I32z	32-bit immediate value, lower 16 bits = 0
I32	32-bit immediate value
Ifp	Floating-point immediate value
Tlabel	Text (code) label, address in .text section
Dlabel	Data label, address in .data section
Slabel	Short data label, address in .sdata section, gp-relative

Table B.2 MIPS Instruction Quick Reference

	Gpr	Fpre	Cpr	Imm2	Imm16	Imm32z	Imm32	Immfp	Imm16r	Imm32zr	Imm32r	Tlabel	Slabel	Dlabel
abs t0.X	3	—	—	—	—	—	—	—	—	—	—	—	—	—
abs.d $f4.X	—	1	—	—	—	—	—	—	—	—	—	—	—	—
abs.s $f4.X	—	1	—	—	—	—	—	—	—	—	—	—	—	—
add t0.t1.X	1	—	—	1	1	2*	3*	—	—	—	—	—	—	—
add.d $f4.$f6.X	—	1	—	—	—	—	—	—	—	—	—	—	—	—
add.s $f4.$f6.X	—	1	—	—	—	—	—	—	—	—	—	—	—	—
addu t0.t1.X	1	—	—	1	1	2*	3*	—	—	—	—	—	—	—
and t0.t1.X	1	—	—	1	1	2*	3*	—	—	—	—	—	—	—
b X	—	—	—	—	—	—	—	—	—	—	—	1-2	—	1-2
bal X	—	—	—	—	—	—	—	—	—	—	—	1-2	—	1-2
bc0f X	—	—	—	—	—	—	—	—	—	—	—	1-2	—	1-2
bc0t X	—	—	—	—	—	—	—	—	—	—	—	1-2	—	1-2
beq t0.X.main	1-2	—	—	2-3*	2-3*	2-3*	3-4*	—	—	—	—	—	—	—
beqz t0.X	—	—	—	—	—	—	—	—	—	—	—	1-2	—	1-2
bge t0.X.main	2-3*	—	—	2-3*	2-3*	3-4*	4-5*	—	—	—	—	—	—	—
bgeu t0.X.main	2-3*	—	—	2-3*	2-3*	3-4*	4-5*	—	—	—	—	—	—	—
bgez t0.X	—	—	—	—	—	—	—	—	—	—	—	1-2	—	1-2
bgezal t0.X	—	—	—	—	—	—	—	—	—	—	—	1-2	—	1-2
bgt t0.X.main	2-3*	—	—	2-3*	2-3*	4-5*	4-5*	—	—	—	—	—	—	—
bgtu t0.X.main	2-3*	—	—	2-3*	2-3*	4-5*	4-5*	—	—	—	—	—	—	—
bgtz t0.X	—	—	—	—	—	—	—	—	—	—	—	1-2	—	1-2
ble t0.X.main	2-3*	—	—	2-3*	2-3*	4-5*	4-5*	—	—	—	—	—	—	—
bleu t0.X.main	2-3*	—	—	2-3*	2-3*	4-5*	4-5*	—	—	—	—	—	—	—
blez t0.X	—	—	—	—	—	—	—	—	—	—	—	1-2	—	1-2
blt t0.X.main	2-3*	—	—	2-3*	2-3*	3-4*	4-5*	—	—	—	—	—	—	—
bltu t0.X.main	2-3*	—	—	2-3*	2-3*	3-4*	4-5*	—	—	—	—	—	—	—
bltz t0.X	—	—	—	—	—	—	—	—	—	—	—	1-2	—	1-2
bltzal t0.X	—	—	—	—	—	—	—	—	—	—	—	1-2	—	1-2
bne t0.X.main	1-2	—	—	2-3*	2-3*	2-3*	3-4*	—	—	—	—	—	—	—
bnez t0.X	—	—	—	—	—	—	—	—	—	—	—	1-2	—	1-2
break X	—	—	—	—	1	—	—	—	—	—	—	—	—	—
c.cond.d $f4.X	—	1-2	—	—	—	—	—	—	—	—	—	—	—	—

Table B.2 MIPS Instruction Quick Reference *(continued)*

	Gpr	Fpre	Cpr	Imm2	Imm16	Imm32z	Imm32	Immfp	Imm16r	Imm32zr	Imm32r	Tlabel	Slabel	Dlabel
ceil.w.d $f4,$f6,X	7-11*	—	—	—	—	—	—	—	—	—	—	—	—	—
ceil.w.s $f4,$f6,X	7-11*	—	—	—	—	—	—	—	—	—	—	—	—	—
ceil.w.s $f4,$f6,X	7-11*	—	—	—	—	—	—	—	—	—	—	—	—	—
ceilu.w.d $f4,$f6,X	7-11*	—	—	—	—	—	—	—	—	—	—	—	—	—
cfc1 t0,X	—	—	2-3	—	—	—	—	—	—	—	—	—	—	—
ctc1 t0,X	—	—	1-3	—	—	—	—	—	—	—	—	—	—	—
cvt.d.s $f4,X	—	1	—	—	—	—	—	—	—	—	—	—	—	—
cvt.d.w $f4,X	—	1	—	—	—	—	—	—	—	—	—	—	—	—
cvt.s.d $f4,X	—	1	—	—	—	—	—	—	—	—	—	—	—	—
cvt.s.w $f4,X	—	1	—	—	—	—	—	—	—	—	—	—	—	—
cvt.w.d $f4,X	—	1	—	—	—	—	—	—	—	—	—	—	—	—
cvt.w.s $f4,X	—	1	—	—	—	—	—	—	—	—	—	—	—	—
div t0,t1,X	9-11*	—	—	4*	3-5*	3-5*	4-6*	—	—	—	—	—	—	—
div zero,t0,X	1	—	—	4*	2*	2*	3*	—	—	—	—	—	—	—
div.d $f4,$f6,X	—	1-2	—	—	—	—	—	—	—	—	—	—	—	—
div.s $f4,$f6,X	—	1-2	—	—	—	—	—	—	—	—	—	—	—	—
divu t0,t1,X	4-5	—	—	1	3-5*	3-5*	4-6*	—	—	—	—	—	—	—
divu zero,t0,X	1	—	—	1	2*	2*	3*	—	—	—	—	—	—	—
floor.w.d $f4,$f6,X	7-11*	—	—	—	—	—	—	—	—	—	—	—	—	—
floor.w.s $f4,$f6,X	7-11*	—	—	—	—	—	—	—	—	—	—	—	—	—
flooru.w.d $f4,$f6,X	7-11*	—	—	—	—	—	—	—	—	—	—	—	—	—
flooru.w.s $f4,$f6,X	7-11*	—	—	—	—	—	—	—	—	—	—	—	—	—
j X	1-2	—	—	1-2	1-2	—	—	—	—	—	—	1-2	1-2	1-2
jal X	1-2	—	—	1-2	1-2	—	—	—	—	—	—	1-2	1-2	1-2
l.d $f4,X	—	—	—	2-3	2-3	3-4*	3-4*	—	2-3	4-5*	4-5*	3-4*	2-3	3-4*
l.s $f4,X	—	—	—	1-2	1-2	2-3*	2-3*	—	1-2	3-4*	3-4*	2-3*	1-2	2-3*
la t0,X	—	—	—	1	1	2	2	—	1	3	3	2	1	2
lb t0,X	—	—	—	1-2	1-2	2-3	2-3	—	1-2	3-4	3-4	2-3	1-2	2-3
lbu t0,X	—	—	—	1-2	1-2	2-3	2-3	—	1-2	3-4	3-4	2-3	1-2	2-3
ld t0,X	—	—	—	2-3	2-3	3-4*	3-4*	—	2-3	4-5*	4-5*	3-4*	2-3	3-4*
lh t0,X	—	—	—	1-2	1-2	2-3	2-3	—	1-2	3-4	3-4	2-3	1-2	2-3
lhu t0,X	—	—	—	1-2	1-2	2-3	2-3	—	1-2	3-4	3-4	2-3	1-2	2-3
li t0,X	—	—	—	1	1	1	2	—	—	—	—	—	—	—

Table B.2 MIPS Instruction Quick Reference (continued)

	Gpr	Fpre	Cpr	Imm2	Imm16	Imm32z	Imm32	Immfp	Imm16r	Imm32zr	Imm32r	Tlabel	Slabel	Dlabel
li.d $f4,X	—	—	—	—	—	—	—	2-3	—	—	—	—	—	—
li.s $f4,X	—	—	—	—	—	—	—	1-2	—	—	—	—	—	—
lui t0,X	—	—	—	1	1	—	—	—	—	—	—	—	—	—
lw t0,X	—	—	—	1-2	1-2	2-3	2-3	—	1-2	3-4	3-4	2-3	1-2	2-3
lwc1 $f4,X	—	—	—	1-2	1-2	2-3*	2-3*	—	1-2	3-4*	3-4*	2-3*	1-2	2-3*
lwl t0,X	—	—	—	1-2	1-2	2-3*	2-3*	—	1-2	3-4*	3-4*	2-3*	1-2	2-3*
lwr t0,X	—	—	—	1-2	1-2	2-3*	2-3*	—	1-2	3-4*	3-4*	2-3*	1-2	2-3*
mfc0 t0,X	—	—	1	—	—	—	—	—	—	—	—	—	—	—
mfhi X	1-3	—	—	—	—	—	—	—	—	—	—	—	—	—
mflo X	1-3	—	—	—	—	—	—	—	—	—	—	—	—	—
mov.d $f4,X	—	1	—	—	—	—	—	—	—	—	—	—	—	—
mov.s $f4,X	—	1	—	—	—	—	—	—	—	—	—	—	—	—
move t0,X	1	—	—	—	—	—	—	—	—	—	—	—	—	—
mtc0 t0,X	—	—	1	—	—	—	—	—	—	—	—	—	—	—
mthi X	1	—	—	—	—	—	—	—	—	—	—	—	—	—
mtlo X	1	—	—	—	—	—	—	—	—	—	—	—	—	—
mul t0,t1,X	2-4	—	—	1	9	9	4-6*	—	—	—	—	—	—	—
mul.d $f4,$f6,X	—	1	—	—	—	—	—	—	—	—	—	—	—	—
mul.s $f4,$f6,X	—	1	—	—	—	—	—	—	—	—	—	—	—	—
mulo t0,t1,X	7-10*	—	—	2	16	8-11*	9-12*	—	—	—	—	—	—	—
mulou t0,t1,X	5-6*	—	—	6-7*	6-7*	6-7*	7-8*	—	—	—	—	—	—	—
mult t0,X	1	—	—	—	—	—	—	—	—	—	—	—	—	—
multu t0,X	1	—	—	—	—	—	—	—	—	—	—	—	—	—
neg t0,X	1	—	—	—	—	—	—	—	—	—	—	—	—	—
neg.d $f4,X	—	1	—	—	—	—	—	—	—	—	—	—	—	—
neg.s $f4,X	—	1	—	—	—	—	—	—	—	—	—	—	—	—
negu t0,X	1	—	—	—	—	—	—	—	—	—	—	—	—	—
nor t0,t1,X	1	—	—	2	2	2*	3*	—	—	—	—	—	—	—
not t0,X	1	—	—	1	1	2*	3*	—	—	—	—	—	—	—
or t0,t1,X	1	—	—	1	1	2*	3*	—	—	—	—	—	—	—
rem t0,t1,X	9-11*	—	—	4-5	3-5*	3-5*	4-6*	—	—	—	—	—	—	—
remu t0,t1,X	4-5	—	—	1	3-5*	3-5*	4-6*	—	—	—	—	—	—	—
rfe	—	—	—	—	—	—	—	—	—	—	—	—	—	—

Table B.2 MIPS Instruction Quick Reference (*continued*)

	Gpr	Fpre	Cpr	Imm2	Imm16	Imm32z	Imm32	Immfp	Imm16r	Imm32r	Imm32zr	Tlabel	Slabel	Dlabel
rol t0,t1,X	4*	—	—	3*	—	—	—	—	—	—	—	—	—	—
ror t0,t1,X	4*	—	—	3*	—	—	—	—	—	—	—	—	—	—
round.w.d $f4,$f6,X	7–10*	—	—	—	—	—	—	—	—	—	—	—	—	—
round.w.s $f4,$f6,X	7–10*	—	—	—	—	—	—	—	—	—	—	—	—	—
roundu.w.d $f4,$f6,X	7–10*	—	—	—	—	—	—	—	—	—	—	—	—	—
roundu.w.s $f4,$f6,X	7–10*	—	—	—	—	—	—	—	—	—	—	—	—	—
s.d $f4,X	—	—	—	2	2	3*	3*	—	2	4*	4*	3*	2	3*
s.s $f4,X	—	—	—	1	1	2*	2*	—	1	3*	3*	2*	1	2*
sb t0,X	—	—	—	1	1	2*	2*	—	1	3*	3*	2*	1	2*
sd t0,X	—	—	—	2	2	3*	3*	—	2	4*	4*	3*	2	3*
seq t0,t1,X	2	—	—	2	2	3*	4*	—	—	—	—	—	—	—
sge t0,t1,X	2	—	—	2	2	3*	4*	—	—	—	—	—	—	—
sgeu t0,t1,X	2	—	—	2	2	3*	4*	—	—	—	—	—	—	—
sgt t0,t1,X	1	—	—	2*	2*	2*	3*	—	—	—	—	—	—	—
sgtu t0,t1,X	1	—	—	2*	2*	2*	3*	—	—	—	—	—	—	—
sh t0,X	—	—	—	1	1	2*	2*	—	1	3*	3*	2*	1	2*
sle t0,t1,X	2	—	—	1	1	3*	3*	—	—	—	—	—	—	—
sleu t0,t1,X	2	—	—	1	1	3*	3*	—	—	—	—	—	—	—
sll t0,t1,X	1	—	—	1	1	2*	3*	—	—	—	—	—	—	—
slt t0,t1,X	1	—	—	1	1	2*	3*	—	—	—	—	—	—	—
sltu t0,t1,X	1	—	—	1	1	2*	4*	—	—	—	—	—	—	—
sne t0,t1,X	2	—	—	2	2	3*	—	—	—	—	—	—	—	—
sra t0,t1,X	1	—	—	1	—	—	—	—	—	—	—	—	—	—
srl t0,t1,X	1	—	—	1	—	—	—	—	—	—	—	—	—	—
sub t0,t1,X	1	—	—	1	1	2*	3*	—	—	—	—	—	—	—
sub.d $f4,$f6,X	—	1	—	—	—	—	—	—	—	—	—	—	—	—
sub.s $f4,$f6,X	—	1	—	—	—	—	—	—	—	—	—	—	—	—
subu t0,t1,X	1	—	—	1	1	2*	2*	—	—	—	—	—	—	—
sw t0,X	—	—	—	1	1	2*	2*	—	1	3*	3*	2*	1	2*
swc1 $f4,X	—	—	—	1	1	2*	2*	—	1	3*	3*	2*	1	2*
swl t0,X	—	—	—	1	1	2*	2*	—	1	3*	3*	2*	1	2*
swr t0,X	—	—	—	1	1	2*	2*	—	1	3*	3*	2*	1	2*
syscall	—	—	—	—	—	—	—	—	—	—	—	—	—	—

Table B.2 MIPS Instruction Quick Reference (*continued*)

	Gpr	Fpre	Cpr	Imm2	Imm16	Imm32z	Imm32	Immfp	Imm16r	Imm32zr	Imm32r	Tlabel	Slabel	Dlabel
teq t0,X	2–3	—	—	3–4*	3–4*	3–4*	4–5*	—	—	—	—	—	—	—
tge t0,X	3–4*	—	—	3–4*	3–4*	4–5*	5–6*	—	—	—	—	—	—	—
tgeu t0,X	3–4*	—	—	3–4*	3–4*	4–5*	5–6*	—	—	—	—	—	—	—
tlt t0,X	3–4*	—	—	3–4*	3–4*	4–5*	5–6*	—	—	—	—	—	—	—
tltu t0,X	3–4*	—	—	3–4*	3–4*	4–5*	5–6*	—	—	—	—	—	—	—
tne t0,X	2–3	—	—	3–4*	3–4*	3–4*	4–5*	—	—	—	—	—	—	—
trunc.w.d $f4,$f6,X	7–11*	—	—	—	—	—	—	—	—	—	—	—	—	—
trunc.w.s $f4,$f6,X	7–11*	—	—	—	—	—	—	—	—	—	—	—	—	—
truncu.w.d $f4,$f6,X	7–11*	—	—	—	—	—	—	—	—	—	—	—	—	—
truncu.w.s $f4,$f6,X	7–11*	—	—	—	—	—	—	—	—	—	—	—	—	—
ulh t0,X	—	—	—	4*	4*	6*	6*	—	4*	7*	7*	6*	4*	6*
ulhu t0,X	—	—	—	4*	4*	6*	6*	—	4*	7*	7*	6*	4*	6*
ulw t0,X	—	—	—	2–3	2–3	4*	4*	—	2–3	5*	5*	4–5*	2–3	4–5*
ush t0,X	—	—	—	3*	3*	8*	8*	—	3*	9*	9*	8*	3*	8*
usw t0,X	—	—	—	2	2	4*	4*	—	2	5*	5*	4*	2	4*
xor t0,t1,X	1	—	—	1	1	2*	3*	—	—	—	—	—	—	—

X Placeholder for selected addressing mode.
* Instruction requires use of the AT register.
n–m Number of instructions in a range from *n* through *m*.

Table B.3   MIPS Instruction Quick Reference by Type

Arithmetic

	Gpr	Imm2	Imm16	Imm32z	Imm32
add t0,t1,X	1	1	1	2*	3*
addu t0,t1,X	1	1	1	2*	3*
sub t0,t1,X	1	1	1	2*	3*
subu t0,t1,X	1	1	1	2*	3*
mul t0,t1,X	2–4	1	9	9	4–6*
mulo t0,t1,X	7–10*	2	16	8–11*	9–12*
mulou t0,t1,X	5–6*	7*	6–7*	6–7*	7–8*
mult t0,X	1	—	—	—	—
multu t0,X	1	—	—	—	—
div t0,t1,X	9–11*	4*	3–5*	3–5*	4–6*
div zero,t0,X	1	4*	2*	2*	3*
divu t0,t1,X	4–5	1	3–5*	3–5*	4–6*
divu zero,t0,X	1	1	2*	2*	3*
rem t0,t1,X	9–11*	5	3–5*	3–5*	4–6*
remu t0,t1,X	4–5	1	3–5*	3–5*	4–6*
abs t0,X	3	—	—	—	—
neg t0,X	1	—	—	—	—
negu t0,X	1	—	—	—	—

Logical

	Gpr	Imm2	Imm16	Imm32z	Imm32
and t0,t1,X	1	1	1	2*	3*
nor t0,t1,X	1	2	2	2*	3*
not t0,X	1	—	—	—	—
or t0,t1,X	1	1	1	2*	3*
xor t0,t1,X	1	1	1	2*	3*

Rotates and Shifts

	Gpr	Imm2	Imm16	Imm32z	Imm32
rol t0,t1,X	4*	3*	—	—	—
ror t0,t1,X	4*	3*	—	—	—
sll t0,t1,X	1	1	—	—	—
sra t0,t1,X	1	1	—	—	—
srl t0,t1,X	1	1	—	—	—

Table B.3   MIPS Instruction Quick Reference by Type (*continued*)

Data Movement (between registers)

mfhi X	1–3	—	—	—	—
mflo X	1–3	—	—	—	—
move t0,X	1	—	—	—	—
mthi X	1	—	—	—	—
mtlo X	1	—	—	—	—

Set Register on Condition

	Gpr	Imm2	Imm16	Imm32z	Imm32
seq t0,t1,X	2	2	2	3*	4*
sge t0,t1,X	2	2	2	3*	4*
sgeu t0,t1,X	2	2	2	3*	4*
sgt t0,t1,X	1	2*	2*	2*	3*
sgtu t0,t1,X	1	2*	2*	2*	3*
sle t0,t1,X	2	1	1	3*	3*
sleu t0,t1,X	2	1	1	3*	3*
slt t0,t1,X	1	1	1	2*	3*
sltu t0,t1,X	1	1	1	2*	3*
sne t0,t1,X	2	2	2	3*	4*

Trap on Condition

	Gpr	Imm2	Imm16	Imm32z	Imm32
teq t0,X	2–3	3–4*	3–4*	3–4*	4–5*
tge t0,X	3–4*	3–4*	3–4*	4–5*	5–6*
tgeu t0,X	3–4*	3–4*	3–4*	4–5*	5–6*
tlt t0,X	3–4*	3–4*	3–4*	4–5*	5–6*
tltu t0,X	3–4*	3–4*	3–4*	4–5*	5–6*
tne t0,X	2–3	3–4*	3–4*	3–4*	4–5*

Branches and Jumps

	Gpr	Imm2	Imm16	Imm32z	Imm32	TDlabel	Slabel
b X	—	—	—	—	—	1–2	—
j X	1–2	2	1–2	—	—	1–2	1–2
beqz t0,X	—	—	—	—	—	1–2	—
bgez t0,X	—	—	—	—	—	1–2	—
bgtz t0,X	—	—	—	—	—	1–2	—

Table B.3 MIPS Instruction Quick Reference by Type (*continued*)

blez t0,X	—	—	—	—	—	1–2	—
bltz t0,X	—	—	—	—	—	1–2	—
bnez t0,X	—	—	—	—	—	1–2	—
beq t0,X,main	1–2	3*	2–3*	2–3*	3–4*	—	—
bge t0,X,main	2–3*	3*	2–3*	3–4*	4–5*	—	—
bgeu t0,X,main	2–3*	3*	2–3*	3–4*	4–5*	—	—
bgt t0,X,main	2–3*	3*	2–3*	4–5*	4–5*	—	—
bgtu t0,X,main	2–3*	3*	2–3*	4–5*	4–5*	—	—
ble t0,X,main	2–3*	3*	2–3*	4–5*	4–5*	—	—
bleu t0,X,main	2–3*	3*	2–3*	4–5*	4–5*	—	—
blt t0,X,main	2–3*	3*	2–3*	3–4*	4–5*	—	—
bltu t0,X,main	2–3*	3*	2–3*	3–4*	4–5*	—	—
bne t0,X,main	1–2	3*	2–3*	2–3*	3–4*	—	—

Subroutine Calls

bal X	—	—	—	—	—	1–2	—
bgezal t0,X	—	—	—	—	—	1–2	—
bltzal t0,X	—	—	—	—	—	1–2	—
jal X	1–2	2	1–2	—	—	1–2	1–2

Loads and Stores

	Imm 2-16	Imm32	Imm16r	Imm32zr	Imm32r	TDlabel	Slabel
lb t0,X	1–2	2–3	1–2	3–4	3–4	2–3	1–2
lbu t0,X	1–2	2–3	1–2	3–4	3–4	2–3	1–2
lh t0,X	1–2	2–3	1–2	3–4	3–4	2–3	1–2
lhu t0,X	1–2	2–3	1–2	3–4	3–4	2–3	1–2
lw t0,X	1–2	2–3	1–2	3–4	3–4	2–3	1–2
ld t0,X	2–3	3–4*	2–3	4–5*	4–5*	3–4*	2–3
lwl t0,X	1–2	2–3*	1–2	3–4*	3–4*	2–3*	1–2
lwr t0,X	1–2	2–3*	1–2	3–4*	3–4*	2–3*	1–2
sb t0,X	1	2*	1	3*	3*	2*	1
sh t0,X	1	2*	1	3*	3*	2*	1
sw t0,X	1	2*	1	3*	3*	2*	1
sd t0,X	2	3*	2	4*	4*	3*	2
swl t0,X	1	2*	1	3*	3*	2*	1
swr t0,X	1	2*	1	3*	3*	2*	1

Table B.3 MIPS Instruction Quick Reference by Type (*continued*)

Unaligned Loads and Stores

ulh t0,X	4*	6*	4*	7*	7*	6*	4*
ulhu t0,X	4*	6*	4*	7*	7*	6*	4*
ulw t0,X	2–3	4*	2–3	5*	5*	4–5*	2–3
ush t0,X	3*	8*	3*	9*	9*	8*	3*
usw t0,X	2	4*	2	5*	5*	4*	2

Coprocessor Zero

	Cpr	TDlabel
bc0f X	—	1–2
bc0t X	—	1–2
mfc0 t0,X	1	—
mtc0 t0,X	1	—
rfe	—	—

Coprocessor 1 Arithmetic

	Gpr	Fpre
abs.d $f4,X	—	1
abs.s $f4,X	—	1
add.d $f4,$f6,X	—	1
add.s $f4,$f6,X	—	1
ceil.w.d $f4,$f6,X	7–11*	—
ceil.w.s $f4,$f6,X	7–11*	—
ceil.w.s $f4,$f6,X	7–11*	—
ceilu.w.d $f4,$f6,X	7–11*	—
cvt.d.s $f4,X	—	1
cvt.d.w $f4,X	—	1
cvt.s.d $f4,X	—	1
cvt.s.w $f4,X	—	1
cvt.w.d $f4,X	—	1
cvt.w.s $f4,X	—	1
div.d $f4,$f6,X	—	1–2
div.s $f4,$f6,X	—	1–2
floor.w.d $f4,$f6,X	7–11*	—
floor.w.s $f4,$f6,X	7–11*	—
flooru.w.d $f4,$f6,X	7–11*	—

Table B.3   MIPS Instruction Quick Reference by Type (*continued*)

flooru.w.s $f4,$f6,X	7–11*	—	
mul.d $f4,$f6,X	—	1	
mul.s $f4,$f6,X	—	1	
neg.d $f4,X	—	1	
neg.s $f4,X	—	1	
round.w.d $f4,$f6,X	7–10*	—	
round.w.s $f4,$f6,X	7–10*	—	
roundu.w.d $f4,$f6,X	7–10*	—	
roundu.w.s $f4,$f6,X	7–10*	—	
trunc.w.d $f4,$f6,X	7–11*	—	
trunc.w.s $f4,$f6,X	7–11*	—	
truncu.w.d $f4,$f6,X	7–11*	—	
truncu.w.s $f4,$f6,X	7–11*	—	
sub.d $f4,$f6,X	—	1	
sub.s $f4,$f6,X	—	1	

	Fpre	Cpr	Immfp	TDlabel
bc1f X	—	—	—	1–2
bc1t X	—	—	—	1–2
c.cond.d $f4,X	1–2	—	—	—
cfc1 t0,X	—	2–3	—	—
ctc1 t0,X	—	1–3	—	—
li.d $f4,X	—	—	2–3	—
li.s $f4,X	—	—	1–2	—
mov.d $f4,X	1	—	—	—
mov.s $f4,X	1	—	—	—

Coprocessor 1 Loads and Stores

	Imm 2-16	Imm32	Imm16r	Imm32r	TDlabel	Slabel
l.d $f4,X	2–3	3–4*	2–3	4–5*	3–4*	2–3
l.s $f4,X	1–2	2–3*	1–2	3–4*	2–3*	1–2
lwc1 $f4,X	1–2	2–3*	1–2	3–4*	2–3*	1–2
s.d $f4,X	2	3*	2	4*	3*	2
s.s $f4,X	1	2*	1	3*	2*	1
swc1 $f4,X	1	2*	1	3*	2*	1

Table B.3   MIPS Instruction Quick Reference by Type (*continued*)

Miscellaneous

	Imm2	Imm16	Imm32z	Imm32	Imm32r	TDlabel	Slabel
break X	1	—	—	—	—	—	—
la t0,X	1	1	2	2	3	2	1
li t0,X	1	1	1	2	—	—	—
lui t0,X	1	1	—	—	—	—	—
syscall	—	—	—	—	—	—	—

C

Prologue and Epilogue Templates

This appendix contains a C program, genproc, that generates the correct prologue and epilogue for a specified function.

The program accepts three arguments: (1) the number of words of local stack storage required for the function, (2) the number of registers that need to be saved, and (3) the maximum number of outgoing arguments required. For leaf functions, this value will be zero. A nonzero argument indicates a nonleaf function.

For example, the command line

```
genproc func 16 5 7
```

means 16 words of local stack storage are required for the function, 5 registers need to be saved, and there are 7 outgoing arguments. (A nonleaf function is indicated by having a nonzero number of outgoing arguments.) The output is:

```
#include <regdef.h>
        .globl func
        .ent func
```

```
func:
        .mask 0x80f00000,-68
         .frame sp,112,ra
         subu sp,28*4
         sw  ra,11*4(sp)
         sw  s3,10*4(sp)
         sw  s2,9*4(sp)
         sw  s1,8*4(sp)
    sw    s0,7*4(sp)
    # incoming args: a0..a3 32*4(sp)..
    # locals 16 words: 12*4(sp)..
    # 10 temp registers available [t0..t9]
    # 5 saved registers available [ra s0..]
    # max 7 outgoing args: a0..a3 4*4(sp)..
    ##############################
    #         Function Body        #
    ##############################
    # place return values in v0 & v1
    lw    s0,7*4(sp)
    lw    s1,8*4(sp)
    lw    s2,9*4(sp)
    lw    s3,10*4(sp)
    lw    ra,11*4(sp)
    addu  sp,28*4
    j     ra
    .end func
```

C.1 PROGRAM LISTING

```c
#include <stdio.h>
#include <ctype.h>
#include <stdio.h>
#include <ctype.h>

/*
 * This program generates the prologue and epilogue for a function.
 */

char usage[] = "usage: genproc [label locs regs args]";

char *getlab();

/************************************************************
 * main(argc,argv)
 */
main(argc,argv)
int argc;
char *argv[];
```

```
{
int i,alloc,locs,regs,args;
unsigned long mask;
char *label,sbuf[80];

if (argc != 5) {
        label = getlab("Enter label",sbuf);
        locs = getval("Enter local variable space in words");
        regs = getval("Enter number of registers to be saved");
        args = getval("Enter max number of outgoing arguments");
        }
else { /* get args from command line */
        label = argv[1];
        sscanf(argv[2],"%d",&locs);
        sscanf(argv[3],"%d",&regs);
        sscanf(argv[4],"%d",&args);
        }

/* enforce legal combinations */
if (regs && args == 0) args = 4;
if (args > 0 && args < 4) args = 4;
if (args && regs == 0) regs = 1;
/* doubleword align */
if ((locs+regs+args)%2) args++;
alloc = locs+regs+args;

/* include register name definitions */
printf("#include <regdef.h>\n");

/* declare function name */
printf("\t.globl %s\n",label);
printf("\t.ent %s\n",label);
printf("%s:\n",label);

/* generate register save mask */
mask = 0;
for (i=0;i<regs;i++) {
        mask <<= 1;
        mask |= 1;
        if (i == 0) mask <<= 7;
        }
if (mask) while (!(mask&0x80000000)) mask <<= 1;

/* print mask and frame directives */
if (regs) printf("\t.mask\t0x%08x,%d\n",mask,0-(4+(locs*4)));
printf("\t.frame\tsp,%d,ra\n",alloc*4);

/* alloc stack area and save registers */
```

```
if (alloc > 0) printf("\tsubu\tsp,%d*4\n",alloc);
for (i=regs-1;i>=0;i-) {
        if (i == regs-1) printf("\tsw\tra,%d*4(sp)\n",args+i);
        else printf("\tsw\ts%d,%d*4(sp)\n",i,args+i);
        }

/* print helpful comments */
printf("\t# incoming args: a0..a3 %d*4(sp)..\n",alloc+4);
if (locs > 0)
        printf("\t# locals %d words: %d*4(sp)..\n",locs,args+regs);
printf("\t# 10 temp registers available [t0..t9]\n");
if (regs > 2)
        printf("\t# %d saved registers available [ra s0..]\n",regs);
else if (regs == 2) printf("\t# 2 saved registers available [ra s0]\n");
else if (regs == 1) printf("\t# 1 saved register available [ra]\n");
if (args > 4) printf("\t# max %d outgoing args: a0..a3 4*4(sp)..\n",
                                                        args);
else if (args > 0) printf("\t# max %d outgoing args: a0..a3\n",args);
printf("\t##############################\n");
printf("\t#          Function Body          #\n");
printf("\t##############################\n");
printf("\t# place return values in v0 & v1\n");

/* restore registers and dealloc stack area */
for (i=0;i<regs;i++) {
        if (i == regs-1) printf("\tlw\tra,%d*4(sp)\n",args+i);
        else printf("\tlw\ts%d,%d*4(sp)\n",i,args+i);
        }
if (alloc > 0) printf("\taddu\tsp,%d*4\n",alloc);
/* return to caller and close function */
printf("\tj\tra\n");
printf("\t.end %s\n",label);
}


/***************************************************************
 *  getval(p)
 *      get a value from the keyboard
 */
getval(p)
char *p;
{
char buf[80];
int n,val;

for (;;) {
        printf("%s > ",p);
        gets(buf);
        n = sscanf(buf,"%d",&val);
```

```
          if (n == 1) return(val);
          printf("Illegal value\n");
          }
}


/****************************************************************
* char *getlab(p,buf)
*     get a label from the keyboard
*/
char *getlab(p,buf)
char *p,*buf;
{

for (;;) {
        printf("%s > ",p);
        gets(buf);
        if (!isdigit(buf[0])) return(buf);
        printf("Illegal label\n");
        }
}
```

D

Include Files

This appendix contains all the include files that were used in the compilation of the example programs.

D.1 machine.h

```
* This file contains all the hardware dependencies. There are *
* selections for CLOCK, CPU, and SIO type.                     *
****************************************************************/

/* The CPU type is set in make.inc */

/* Select the board type */
#define IDT7RS385 /* enable if you are using the IDT board */
/*#define LSIROCKET /* enable if you are using the LSI board */

/* Select the clock type */
/* #define CLK33000 /* enable if you are using the 33k internal clocks */
/* #define CLK2681 /* enable if you are using the 2681 clock */
#define CLK8254 /* enable if you are using the 8254 clock */

/*======================= CLOCK DEFINITIONS ======================*/
/* The int mask can always be derived from INTNUM */
#define  CLK1_INT (0x100<<CLK1_INTNUM)
```

```
#define  CLK2_INT (0x100<<CLK2_INTNUM)

#ifdef CLK2681
/* clock definitions for the counter/timer within the 2681 DUART */
/* on the Pocket Rocket, it's connected to INT2 */
#ifdef POCKET_ROCKET
#define CLK1_INTNUM 4  /* INT2 */
#else
/* IDT 7RS385 board */
#define CLK1_INTNUM 7  /* INT5 */
#endif

#ifdef LANGUAGE_ASSEMBLY
#define CLK1_INIT(x)                                     \
        /* set clock rate to x millisecs */        \
        li t0,SIOBASE                                ;\
        li t1,(1152*x)/10                            ;\
        sb t1,0x1c(t0)          /* lower */     ;\
        srl t1,8                                     ;\
        sb t1,0x18(t0)          /* upper */     ;\
        li t1,0x08                                   ;\
        sb t1,0x14(t0)          /* int mask */
#define CLK1_ACK                                     \
        /* acknowledge the int request */       \
        li k0,SIOBASE                                ;\
        lbu zero,0x3c(k0)

#define CLK1_ACKT                                    \
        /* acknowledge the int request */       \
        li t0,SIOBASE                                ;\
        lbu zero,0x3c(t0)
#else /* LANGUAGE_C */
#define CLK1_INIT(x)                                  \
        *((char *)SIOBASE+0x1c) = ((1152*x)/10)&0xff, \
        *((char *)SIOBASE+0x18) = ((1152*x)/10)>>8, \
        *((char *)SIOBASE+0x14) = 0x08               \

#define CLK1_ACK  {char t; t = *((char *)SIOBASE+0x3c);}
#endif
#endif

#ifdef CLK8254
/* IDT 7RS385 board */
#define CLK1_INTNUM 2   /* INT0 */
#define CLK2_INTNUM 3   /* INT1 */
#define T8254B 0xbf800000

#ifdef MIPSEB
```

```
        #define T8254BASE T8254B+3
        #else
        #define T8254BASE T8254B+0
        #endif

        #ifdef LANGUAGE_ASSEMBLY
        #define CLK1_INIT(x)                                    \
                /* set clock rate to x millisecs */      \
                li t0,T8254BASE                          ;\
                /* t2 */                                         \
                li t1,0xb4              /* mode          ;\
                sb t1,0xc(t0)             /* ctl wrd */  ;\
                li t1,3680                               ;\
                sb t1,0x8(t0)            /* lower */     ;\
                srl t1,8                                 ;\
                sb t1,0x8(t0)            /* upper */     ;\
                /* t0 */                                         \
                li t1,0x34              /* mode 2 */     ;\
                sb t1,0xc(t0)            /* ctl wrd */   ;\
                li t1,x                                  ;\
                sb t1,0x0(t0)            /* lower */     ;\
                srl t1,8                                 ;\
                sb t1,0x0(t0)            /* upper */

        #define CLK1_ACK                                          \
                /* acknowledge the int request */        \
                li      k0,T8254BASE                     ;\
                lbu     zero,0x10(k0)
        #define CLK1_ACKT                                         \
                /* acknowledge the int request */        \
                li      t0,T8254BASE                     ;\
                lbu     zero,0x10(t0)

        #define CLK2_INIT(x)                                      \
                /* set clock rate to x millisecs */      \
                li      t0,T8254BASE                     ;\
                /* t2 */                                         \
                li      t1,0xb4         /* mode 2 */     ;\
                sb      t1,0xc(t0)      /* ctl wrd */    ;\
                li      t1,3680                          ;\
                sb      t1,0x8(t0)      /* lower */      ;\
                srl     t1,8                             ;\
                sb      t1,0x8(t0)      /* upper */      ;\
                /* t1 */                                         \
                li      t1,0x74         /* mode 2 */     ;\
                sb      t1,0xc(t0)      /* ctl wrd */    ;\
                li      t1,x                             ;\
                sb      t1,0x4(t0)      /* lower */      ;\
```

```
        srl     t1,8                                  ;\
        sb      t1,0x4(t0)          /* upper */

#define CLK2_ACK                                      \
        /* acknowledge the int request */            \
        li      k0,T8254BASE                          ;\
        lbu     zero,0x14(k0)

#define CLK2_ACKT                                     \
        /* acknowledge the int request */            \
        li      t0,T8254BASE                          ;\
        lbu     zero,0x14(t0)
#else /* LANGUAGE_C */
#define CLK1_INIT(x)                                  \
        *((char *)T8254BASE+0xc) = 0xb4, \
        *((char *)T8254BASE+0x8) = 3680&0xff, \
        *((char *)T8254BASE+0x8) = 3680>>8, \
        *((char *)T8254BASE+0xc) = 0x34, \
        *((char *)T8254BASE+0x0) = (x)&0xff, \
        *((char *)T8254BASE+0x0) = (x)>>8

#define CLK1_ACK  {char t; t = *((char *)T8254BASE+0x10);}
#define CLK2_INIT(x)        \
        *((char *)T8254BASE+0xc) = 0xb4, \
        *((char *)T8254BASE+0x8) = 3680&0xff, \
        *((char *)T8254BASE+0x8) = 3680>>8, \
        *((char *)T8254BASE+0xc) = 0x74, \
        *((char *)T8254BASE+0x4) = (x)&0xff, \
        *((char *)T8254BASE+0x4) = (x)>>8

#define CLK2_ACK  {char t; t = *((char *)T8254BASE+0x14);}
#endif
#endif


#ifdef CLK33000
/* clock definitions for the counter/timers within the LR33000 */
#define  CLKRATE 25              /* CPU clock rate in MHz */
#define  CLK1_INTNUM 2           /* INT0 */
#define  CLK2_INTNUM 3           /* INT1 */

#ifdef LANGUAGE_ASSEMBLY
#define CLK1_INIT(x)        \
        /* set clock rate to x millisecs */   \
        /* set clock rate */                  \
        li      t0,M_TIC1                     ;\
        li      t1,CLKRATE*1000*x             ;\
        sw      t1,(t0)                       ;\
        /* start clock */                     \
```

```
            li      t0,M_TC1                        ;\
            li      t1,(TC_IE|TC_CE)                ;\
             sw     t1,(t0)

#define CLK2_INIT(x)                                \
        /* set clock rate to x millisecs */         \
        /* set clock rate */                        \
            li      t0,M_TIC2                        ;\
            li      t1,CLKRATE*1000*x               ;\
            sw      t1,(t0)                         ;\
        /* start clock */                           \
            li      t0,M_TC2                        ;\
            li      t1,(TC_IE|TC_CE)                ;\
             sw     t1,(t0)

#define CLK1_ACK                                    \
        /* acknowledge the int request */           \
            li      k0,M_TC1                        ;\
            lw      k1,(k0)                         ;\
            srl     k1,1                            ;\
            sll     k1,1                            ;\
            sw      k1,(k0)

#define CLK2_ACK                                    \
        /* acknowledge the int request */           \
            li      k0,M_TC2                        ;\
            lw      k1,(k0)                         ;\
            srl     k1,1                            ;\
            sll     k1,1                            ;\
            sw      k1,(k0)
#define CLK1_ACKT                                   \
        /* acknowledge the int request */           \
            li      t0,M_TC1                        ;\
            lw      t1,(t0)                         ;\
            srl     t1,1                            ;\
            sll     t1,1                            ;\
            sw      t1,(t0)

#define CLK2_ACKT                                   \
        /* acknowledge the int request */           \
            li      t0,M_TC2                        ;\
            lw      t1,(t0)                         ;\
            srl     t1,1                            ;\
            sll     t1,1                            ;\
            sw      t1,(t0)
#else
#define CLK1_INIT(x)        TIC1 = CLKRATE*1000*x, TC1 = (TC_IE|TC_CE)
#define CLK1_ACK            TC1 &= TC_INT
```

```
#define CLK2_INIT(x)      TIC2 = CLKRATE*1000*x, TC2 = (TC_IE|TC_CE)
#define CLK2_ACK          TC2 &= TC_INT
#endif


#endif


/*===================== CPU DEFINITIONS =====================*/
#ifdef R3000
#define FLUSH_ICACHE      r3k_iflush
#define FLUSH_DCACHE      r3k_dflush
#define RAMINIT                              \
        li      t0,SR_BEV                  ;\
        .set noreorder                     ;\
        mtc0    t0,C0_SR                   ;\
        .set reorder
#endif


#ifdef LR33000
#define FLUSH_ICACHE      r33k_iflush
#define FLUSH_DCACHE      r33k_dflush
#ifdef LANGUAGE_ASSEMBLY
/*
 * The Pocket Rocket has LEDs connected to the DUART's two aux
 * outputs, these macros can be used to control them.
 */
#define GRNLEDOFF                            \
        li      t0,SIOBASE                 ;\
        li      t1,0x01                    ;\
        sb      t1,0x38(t0)

#define GRNLEDON                             \
        li      t0,SIOBASE                 ;\
        li      t1,0x01                    ;\
        sb      t1,0x3c(t0)

#define REDLEDOFF                            \
        li      t0,SIOBASE                 ;\
        li      t1,0x02                    ;\
        sb      t1,0x38(t0)

#define REDLEDON                             \
        li      t0,SIOBASE                 ;\
        li      t1,0x02                    ;\
        sb      t1,0x3c(t0)

#define RAMINIT                              \
        /* turn on the RAM */              ;\
        li      t1,M_CFGREG                ;\
```

```
        li      t0,0x0028c629                           ;\
        /* CS=CL=RPC=0 PWAIT=6 */                        \
        sw      t0,(t1)                                 ;\
        li      t1,M_RTIC /* refresh */                 ;\
        li      t0,375                                  ;\
        /* 512 rows in 8ms = 15us */                     \
        sw      t0,(t1)
#endif
#else /* LANGUAGE_C */
#define REDLEDON (*((char *)SIOBASE+0x3c)) = 0x02
#define REDLEDOFF (*((char *)SIOBASE+0x38)) = 0x02
#define GRNLEDON (*((char *)SIOBASE+0x3c)) = 0x01
#define GRNLEDOFF (*((char *)SIOBASE+0x38)) = 0x01
#endif


/*===================== SIO DEFINITIONS =====================*/
/* assume that it's a 2681 DUART */
#define INITSIO init2681
#define PUTSIO  put2681

/* base address of the 2681 DUART */
#ifdef LSIROCKET
#define SIOB 0xbe000000
#endif

#ifdef IDT7RS385
#define SIOB 0xbfe00000
#endif

#ifdef LANGUAGE_ASSEMBLY
#ifdef MIPSEB
#define SIOBASE SIOB+3
#else
#define SIOBASE SIOB+0
#endif
#else
#define SIOBASE            ((volatile int *)SIOB)
#endif
```

D.2 mips.h

```
/* mips.h - CPU-dependent definitions for the MIPS architecture
        The contents of this file are not copyrighted in any
 *      way, and may therefore be used without restriction.
 */


/*
 * This file supports both the LR3000 and the LR33000. By default
```

```
 * the LR3000 is assumed. For the LR33000 invoke the compiler with
 * the option -DLR33000.
 *
 */


#ifndef _MIPS_
#define _MIPS_

#define K0BASE        0x80000000
#define K0SIZE        0x20000000
#define K1BASE        0xa0000000
#define K1SIZE        0x20000000
#define K2BASE        0xc0000000
#define IS_K0SEG(x)   ((unsigned)(x)>=K0BASE && (unsigned)(x)<K1BASE)
#define IS_K1SEG(x)   ((unsigned)(x)>=K1BASE && (unsigned)(x)<K2BASE)
#define GEN_VECT      0x80000080
#define UTLB_VECT     0x80000000

#ifdef LANGUAGE_ASSEMBLY

#define jr j
#define jalr jal

/* aliases for general registers */
#define zero       $0
#define AT         $1            /* assembler temporaries */
#define v0         $2            /* value holders */
#define v1         $3
#define a0         $4            /* arguments */
#define a1         $5
#define a2         $6
#define a3         $7
#define t0         $8            /* temporaries */
#define t1         $9
#define t2         $10
#define t3         $11
#define t4         $12
#define t5         $13
#define t6         $14
#define t7         $15
#define s0         $16           /* saved registers */
#define s1         $17
#define s2         $18
#define s3         $19
#define s4         $20
#define s5         $21
#define s6         $22
#define s7         $23
```

```
#define t8              $24              /* temporaries */
#define t9              $25
#define k0              $26              /* kernel registers */
#define k1              $27
#define gp              $28              /* global pointer */
#define sp              $29              /* stack pointer */
#define s8              $30              /* saved register */
#define fp              $30              /* frame pointer (old usage) */
#define ra              $31              /* return address */

/* System-control coprocessor (CP0) registers */
#define CO_SR           $12              /* processor status */
#define CO_CAUSE        $13              /* exception cause */
#define CO_EPC          $14              /* exception PC */
#define CO_BADADDR      $8               /* bad address */
#define CO_BADVADDR     $8               /* bad virtual address */
#define CO_PRID         $15              /* processor rev identifier */


#ifdef LR33000
#include "lr33000.h"
#else
#define CO_CTEXT        $4               /* context */
#define CO_TLBHI        $10              /* TLB EntryHi */
#define CO_TLBLO        $2               /* TLB EntryLo */
#define CO_INX          $0               /* TLB index */
#define CO_RAND         $1               /* TLB Random */
#endif

/* Floating-point control registers */
#define FPA_CSR         $31              /* control/status register */
#define FPA_IRR         $0               /* implementation/rev register */

#else /* LANGUAGE_C */

#define CO_SR           12               /* processor status */
#define CO_CAUSE        13               /* exception cause */
#define CO_EPC          14               /* exception PC */
#define CO_BADADDR      8                /* bad address */
#define CO_BADVADDR     8                /* bad virtual address */
#define CO_PRID         15               /* processor rev identifier */


#ifdef LR33000
#include "lr33000.h"
#else
#define CO_CTEXT        4                /* context */
#define CO_TLBHI        10               /* TLB EntryHi */
#define CO_TLBLO        2                /* TLB EntryLo */
#define CO_INX          0                /* TLB index */
```

```
#define C0_RAND          1                    /* TLB random */
#endif

/* Floating-point control registers */
#define FPA_CSR          31                   /* control/status register */
#define FPA_IRR          0                    /* implementation/rev register */
#endif /* LANGUAGE_C */

/* Floating-point control-register bits */
#define CSR_C            0x00800000
#define CSR_EXC          0x0003f000
#define CSR_EE           0x00020000
#define CSR_EV           0x00010000
#define CSR_EZ           0x00008000
#define CSR_EO           0x00004000
#define CSR_EU           0x00002000
#define CSR_EI           0x00001000
#define CSR_TV           0x00000800
#define CSR_TZ           0x00000400
#define CSR_TO           0x00000200
#define CSR_TU           0x00000100
#define CSR_TI           0x00000080
#define CSR_SV           0x00000040
#define CSR_SZ           0x00000020
#define CSR_SO           0x00000010
#define CSR_SU           0x00000008
#define CSR_SI           0x00000004
#define CSR_RM           0x00000003


/* Status register */
#define SR_CUMASK        0xf0000000           /* coprocessor-usable bits */
#define SR_CU3           0x80000000           /* coprocessor 3 usable */
#define SR_CU2           0x40000000           /* coprocessor 2 usable */
#define SR_CU1           0x20000000           /* coprocessor 1 usable */
#define SR_CU0           0x10000000           /* coprocessor 0 usable */
#define SR_BEV           0x00400000           /* bootstrap-exception vector */
#define SR_TS            0x00200000           /* TLB shutdown */
#define SR_PE            0x00100000           /* parity error */
#define SR_CM            0x00080000           /* cache miss */
#define SR_PZ            0x00040000           /* parity zero */
#define SR_SWC           0x00020000           /* swap caches */
#define SR_ISC           0x00010000           /* isolate cache */

#define SR_IMASK         0x0000ff00           /* interrupt mask */
#define SR_IMASK8        0x00000000           /* interrupt mask level=8 */
#define SR_IMASK7        0x00008000           /* interrupt mask level=7 */
#define SR_IMASK6        0x0000c000           /* interrupt mask level=6 */
#define SR_IMASK5        0x0000e000           /* interrupt mask level=5 */
```

```
#define SR_IMASK4        0x0000f000        /* interrupt mask level=4 */
#define SR_IMASK3        0x0000f800        /* interrupt mask level=3 */
#define SR_IMASK2        0x0000fc00        /* interrupt mask level=2 */
#define SR_IMASK1        0x0000fe00        /* interrupt mask level=1 */
#define SR_IMASK0        0x0000ff00        /* interrupt mask level=0 */

#define SR_IBIT8         0x00008000        /* (Intr5) */
#define SR_IBIT7         0x00004000        /* (Intr4) */
#define SR_IBIT6         0x00002000        /* (Intr3) */
#define SR_IBIT5         0x00001000        /* (Intr2) */
#define SR_IBIT4         0x00000800        /* (Intr1) */
#define SR_IBIT3         0x00000400        /* (Intr0) */
#define SR_IBIT2         0x00000200        /* (software interrupt 1) */
#define SR_IBIT1         0x00000100        /* (software interrupt 0) */

#define SR_KUO           0x00000020        /* kernel/user mode, old */
#define SR_IEO           0x00000010        /* interrupt enable, old */
#define SR_KUP           0x00000008        /* kernel/user mode, previous */
#define SR_IEP           0x00000004        /* interrupt enable, previous */
#define SR_KUC           0x00000002        /* kernel/user mode, current */
#define SR_IEC           0x00000001        /* interrupt enable, current */

/* Cause register */
#define CAUSE_BD             0x80000000    /* branch delay */
#define CAUSE_CEMASK         0x30000000    /* coprocessor error */
#define CAUSE_CESHIFT        28            /* right justify CE  */
#define CAUSE_IPMASK         0x0000ff00    /* interrupt pending */
#define CAUSE_IPSHIFT        8             /* right justify IP  */
#define CAUSE_IP8            0x00008000    /* (Intr5) */
#define CAUSE_IP7            0x00004000    /* (Intr4) */
#define CAUSE_IP6            0x00002000    /* (Intr3) */
#define CAUSE_IP5            0x00001000    /* (Intr2) */
#define CAUSE_IP4            0x00000800    /* (Intr1) */
#define CAUSE_IP3            0x00000400    /* (Intr0) */
#define CAUSE_SW2            0x00000200    /* (software int 1) */
#define CAUSE_SW1            0x00000100    /* (software int 0) */
#define CAUSE_EXCMASK        0x0000003c    /* exception code */
#define CAUSE_EXCSHIFT       2             /* right justify EXC */

/* Exception code */
#define EXC_INT          (0 << 2)          /* external interrupt */
#define EXC_MOD          (1 << 2)          /* TLB modification */
#define EXC_TLBL         (2 << 2)          /* TLB miss (load or Ifetch) */
#define EXC_TLBS         (3 << 2)          /* TLB miss (save) */
#define EXC_ADEL         (4 << 2)          /* addr error (load or Ifetch) */
#define EXC_ADES         (5 << 2)          /* address error (save) */
#define EXC_IBE          (6 << 2)          /* bus error (Ifetch) */
#define EXC_DBE          (7 << 2)          /* bus error (data load/store) */
```

```
#define EXC_SYS        (8 << 2)        /* system call */
#define EXC_BP         (9 << 2)        /* breakpoint */
#define EXC_RI         (10 << 2)       /* reserved instruction */
#define EXC_CPU        (11 << 2)       /* coprocessor unusable */
#define EXC_OVF        (12 << 2)       /* arithmetic overflow */

/* FPU stuff */
#define C1_CSR         $31
#define CSR_EMASK      (0x3f<<12)
#define CSR_TMASK      (0x1f<<7)
#define CSR_SMASK      (0x1f<<2)
#define C1_FRID        $0

#endif /* _MIPS_ */
```

D.3 lr33000.h

```
/* lr33000.h - defines for LSI Logic LR33000 */

#ifndef _LR33000_
#define _LR33000_

#ifdef LANGUAGE_ASSEMBLY

#define CO_DCIC $7                /* cache control */
#define CO_BPC $3                 /* breakpoint on instr */
#define CO_BDA $5                 /* breakpoint on data */

#endif /* LANGUAGE_ASSEMBLY */

#define DEBUG_VECT 0x80000040

/* definitions for DCIC register bits */
#define DCIC_TR 0x80000000        /* trap enable */
#define DCIC_UD 0x40000000        /* user-debug enable */
#define DCIC_KD 0x20000000        /* kernel-debug enable */
#define DCIC_TE 0x10000000        /* trace enable */
#define DCIC_DW 0x08000000        /* enable data breakpoints on write */
#define DCIC_DR 0x04000000        /* enable data breakpoints on read */
#define DCIC_DAE 0x02000000       /* enable data address breakpoints */
#define DCIC_PCE 0x01000000       /* enable instruction breakpoints */
#define DCIC_DE 0x00800000        /* debug enable */
#define DCIC_DL 0x00008000        /* data cache line invalidate */
#define DCIC_IL 0x00004000        /* instruction cache line invalidate */
#define DCIC_D 0x00002000         /* data cache invalidate enable */
#define DCIC_I 0x00001000         /* instruction cache invalidate enable */
#define DCIC_T 0x00000020         /* trace, set by CPU */
#define DCIC_W 0x00000010         /* write reference, set by CPU */
```

```
#define DCIC_R  0x00000008      /* read reference, set by CPU */
#define DCIC_DA 0x00000004      /* data address, set by CPU */
#define DCIC_PC 0x00000002      /* program counter, set by CPU */
#define DCIC_DB 0x00000001      /* debug, set by CPU */


/* Define counter/timer register addresses */
#define M_TIC1  0xfffe0000      /* timer 1 initial count */
#define M_TC1   0xfffe0004      /* timer 1 control        */
#define M_TIC2  0xfffe0008      /* timer 2 initial count */
#define M_TC2   0xfffe000c      /* timer 2 control        */
#define M_RTIC  0xfffe0010      /* refresh timer          */
#define M_CFGREG        0xfffe0020      /* configuration reg      */

#ifdef LANGUAGE_C
#define TIC1   (*((volatile unsigned long *)M_TIC1)) /* timer1 count */
#define TC1    (*((volatile unsigned long *)M_TC1))  /* timer1 cntrl */
#define TIC2   (*((volatile unsigned long *)M_TIC2)) /* timer2 count */
#define TC2    (*((volatile unsigned long *)M_TC2))  /* timer2 cntrl */
#define RTIC   (*((volatile unsigned long *)M_RTIC)) /* refrsh timer */
#define CFGREG (*((volatile unsigned long *)M_CFGREG)) /* config reg */
#endif

/* Definitions for counter/timer control-register bits */
#define TC_CE   0x00000004      /* count enable */
#define TC_IE   0x00000002      /* interrupt enable */
#define TC_INT  0x00000001      /* interrupt request */

/* Definitions for configuration-register bits */
#define CR_WBE        0x80000000      /* write buffer enable */
#define CR_BEN        0x40000000      /* block write enable *
#define CR_PGSZMSK    0x38000000      /* page-size mask */
#define CR_PGSZSHFT   27              /* page-size shift amount */
#define CR_IW8        0x02000000      /* add 8 cycles to IOWAIT */
#define CR_PW8        0x01000000      /* add 8 cycles to PWAIT */
#define CR_ICDISABLE  0x00800000      /* instruction-cache disable */
#define CR_DCDISABLE  0x00400000      /* data-cache disable */
#define CR_IBLK_2     0x00000000      /* instruction-cache block size */
#define CR_IBLK_4     0x00100000      /* instruction-cache block size */
#define CR_IBLK_8     0x00200000      /* instruction-cache block size */
#define CR_IBLK_16    0x00300000      /* instruction-cache block size */
#define CR_IBLKMSK    0x00300000      /* instruction-cache block size */
#define CR_DBLK_2     0x00000000      /* data-cache block size */
#define CR_DBLK_4     0x00040000      /* data-cache block size */
#define CR_DBLK_8     0x00080000      /* data-cache block size */
#define CR_DBLK_16    0x000c0000      /* data-cache block size */
#define CR_DBLKMSK    0x000c0000      /* data-cache block size */
#define CR_IODIS      0x00020000      /* disable DRDY for I/O addr's */
```

```
#define CR_IOWAITSHFT   13              /* I/O wait states */
#define CR_PDIS         0x00001000      /* disable DRDY for PROM addr's */
#define CR_PWAITSHFT    8               /* PROM wait states */
#define CR_DPEN         0x00000040      /* enable parity check for DRAM */
#define CR_RDYGEN       0x00000020      /* disable DRDY for DRAM addr's */
#define CR_BLKFDIS      0x00000010      /* disable DRAM block refill */
#define CR_RFSHEN       0x00000008      /* enable refresh generator */
#define CR_RASPCHG      0x00000004      /* define RAS precharge */
#define CR_CASLNTH      0x00000002      /* define CAS active time */
#define CR_DRAMEN       0x00000001      /* enable DRAM controller */

#endif /* _LR33000_ */
```

E

Libraries

This appendix contains a library of C functions that are used by the example programs in this book.

E.1 stdio.c

```
============ lib/stdio.c ============
#include <machine.h>
#include <varargs.h>

/*************************************************************
*   char *strcpy(dst,src) copy src to dst
*/
char *strcpy(dstp,srcp)
char *dstp,*srcp;
{
char *dp = dstp;

if (!dstp) return(0);
*dp = 0;
if (!srcp) return(dstp);

while ((*dp++ = *srcp++) != 0) ;
return (dstp);
```

```
        }

/****************************************************************
 *   char *strcat(dst,src)
 * concatenate two strings
 */
char *strcat(dst,src)
char *dst,*src;
{
char *d;

d = dst;
for (;*d;d++) ;
for (;*src;src++)
*d++ = *src; *d = 0;
return(dst);
}

/****************************************************************
 *   int strlen(p)
 *         return the length of the string
 */
int strlen(p)
char *p;
{
int n;
for (n=0;*p;p++) n++;
return(n);
}

/****************************************************************
 *   char *btoa(dst,value,base)
 *         convert binary to ascii using specified base
 */
char *btoa(dst,value,base)
char *dst;
int base;
unsigned int value;
{
char buf[34],digit;
int i,j,rem,neg;

if (value == 0) {
        dst[0] = '0';
        dst[1] = 0;
        return(dst);
        }
```

```
neg = 0;
if (base == 10 && (value&(1L<<31))) {
        value = (value)+1;
        neg = 1;
        }

for (i=0;value != 0;i++) {
        rem = value % base;
        value /= base;
        if (rem >= 0 && rem <= 9) digit = rem + '0';
        else if (rem >= 10 && rem <= 36) digit = (rem-10) + 'a';
        buf[i] = digit;
        }
buf[i] = 0;
if (neg) strcat(buf,"-");

/* reverse the string */
for (i=0,j=strlen(buf)-1;j>=0;i++,j--) dst[i] = buf[j];
dst[i] = 0;
return(dst);
}

/*************************************************************
 *  puts(p)
 *       put a string
 */
puts(p)
char *p;
{
for (;*p;p++) putchar(*p);
}

/*************************************************************
 *  putchar(c)
 *        put a character
 */
putchar(c)
int c;
{

if (c == '\n') PUTSIO('\r');
PUTSIO(c);
}

/*************************************************************
 *  printf(fmt,va_alist)
 */
printf(fmt,va_alist)
```

```
char *fmt;
va_dcl
{
va_list ap;
char buf[100];
int n;

va_start(ap);
n = vsprintf(buf,fmt,ap);
puts(buf);
va_end(ap);
return(n);
}


/****************************************************************
 *   int vsprintf(d,s,ap)
 *        A simplified implementation of printf. No support for
 *        field widths.
 */
int vsprintf(d,s,ap)
char *d,*s;
va_list ap;
{
char *p,*dst;
unsigned int n;

dst = d;
for (;*s;) {
        if (*s == '%') {
                s++;
                if (*s == '%') {
                        *d++ = '%';
                        *d = 0;
                        }
                else if (*s == 's') {
                        p = va_arg(ap,char *);
                        if (p) strcpy(d,p);
                        else strcpy(d,"(null)");
                        }
                else if (*s == 'c') {
                        n = va_arg(ap,int);
                        *d = n;
                        d[1] = 0;
                        }
                else if (*s == 'd') btoa(d,va_arg(ap,int),10);
                else if (*s == 'o') btoa(d,va_arg(ap,int),8);
                else if (*s == 'x') btoa(d,va_arg(ap,int),16);
                for (;*d;d++) ;
```

```
                    s++;
                    }
            else *d++ = *s++;
            }
    *d = 0;
    return(d-dst);
    }
```

E.2 put2681.c

============== lib/put2681.c ==============

```
#define SIOBASE          ((volatile int *)0xbe000000)

#define CHA      0
#define CHB      8

/* offsets and bit field definitions for the 2681 duart */
#define SR 1
#define   RXRDY 0x01
#define   TXRDY 0x04
#define CSR 1
#define CMD 2
#define RHR 3
#define THR 3

int inittab[][2] = {
        {5,0x00},               /* mask off all ints */

        /* resets */
        {2,0x0a},               /* disable tx & rx */
        {2,0x10},               /* reset MR ptr */
        {2,0x20},               /* reset rx */
        {2,0x30},               /* reset tx */
        {10,0x0a},              /* disable tx & rx */
        {10,0x10},              /* reset MR ptr */
        {10,0x20},              /* reset rx */
        {10,0x30},              /* reset tx */

        /* MRs */
        {0,0x13},               /* no parity, 8 bits data */
        {0,0x0f},               /* 2 stop bits */
        {8,0x13},               /* no parity, 8 bits data */
        {8,0x0f},               /* 2 stop bits */

        /* timer */
        {4,0xf0},
```

```
        /* enable status outputs */
        {13,0x00},
        {15,0xff},                  /* reset all output bits */
        {14,0x00},                  /* don't set any output bits */

        /* select baud rate */
        {1,0xbb},                   /* 9600 */
        {9,0xbb},                   /* 9600 */

        /* enable rxs & txs */
        {2,0x05},
        {10,0x05},

        {255,0}
        };

init2681()
{
int i;

for (i=0;inittab[i][0] !=255;i++)
        SIOBASE[inittab[i][0]] = inittab[i][1];
}


put2681(c)
int c;
{

while ((SIOBASE[CHA+SR]&TXRDY) == 0) ;
SIOBASE[CHA+THR] = c; }
```

E.3 r3kcflu.s

============== lib/r3kcflu.s ==============

```
#include <mips.h>


        .globl  r3k_iflush
        .ent    r3k_iflush
r3k_iflush:
        subu    sp,24
        sw      ra,20(sp)

        # make me uncacheable
        la      t0,1f
        li      t1,K1BASE
```

```
        or      t0,t1
        j       t0

1:      # get size
        la      t0,icache_size
        li      t1,K1BASE
        or      t0,t1
        lw      v0,(t0)
        # if size == 0, call size_cache
        bne     v0,zero,1f
        li      a0,(SR_ISC|SR_SWC)          # sr bits
        jal     size_cache

        # if size == 0, return
        beq     v0,zero,10f

        # update size
        la      t0,icache_size
        li      t1,K1BASE
        or      t0,t1
        sw      v0,(t0)

1:      li      a0,(SR_ISC|SR_SWC)      # sr bits
        move    a1,v0                   # size

        jal     flush_common

10:     lw      ra,20(sp)
        addu    sp,24
        j       ra
        .end    r3k_iflush
        .globl  r3k_dflush
        .ent    r3k_dflush
r3k_dflush:
        subu    sp,24
        sw      ra,20(sp)

        # get size
        la      t0,dcache_size
        li      t1,K1BASE
        or      t0,t1
        lw      v0,(t0)

        # if size == 0, call size_cache
        bne     v0,zero,1f
        li      a0,SR_ISC # sr bits
        jal     size_cache
```

```
        # if size == 0, return
        beq     v0,zero,10f

        # update size
        la      t0,dcache_size
        li      t1,K1BASE
        or      t0,t1
        sw      v0,(t0)

1:      li a0,SR_ISC              # sr bits
        move a1,v0                # size

        jal     flush_common

10:     lw      ra,20(sp)
        addu    sp,24
        j       ra
        .end    r3k_dflush

        .globl flush_common
        .ent flush_common
flush_common:
        # a0=sr bits a1=size

        # set selected SR bits and disable ints
        .set noreorder
        mfc0    t8,C0_SR
        nop
        or      t0,a0,t8
        and     t0,SR_IEC
        mtc0    t0,C0_SR

        li      v0,K0BASE
        addu    v1,v0,a1
1:      # flush loop
        sb      zero,0x0(v0)
        sb      zero,0x4(v0)
        sb      zero,0x8(v0)
        sb      zero,0xc(v0)
        addiu   v0,v0,0x10
        bltu    v0,v1,1b
        nop

        mtc0    t8,C0_SR          # restore sr
        .set reorder
        j       ra
        .end flush_common
```

```
        .globl size_cache
        .ent size_cache
size_cache:
        # a0=sr bits rtn=size

        # set selected SR bits and disable ints
        .set noreorder
        mfc0    t8,C0_SR
        nop
        or      t0,a0,t8
        and     t0,SR_IEC
        mtc0    t0,C0_SR

        /* clear possible cache boundaries */
        lui     v0,0x8000
        sw      zero,0x1000(v0)         /* clear KSEG0 (+  4K) */
        sw      zero,0x2000(v0)         /*            (+  8K) */
        sw      zero,0x4000(v0)         /*            (+ 16K) */
        ori     v0,0x8000
        sw      zero,0(v0)              /*            (+ 32K) */
        lui     v0,0x8001
        sw      zero,0(v0)              /*            (+ 64K) */
        lui     v0,0x8002
        sw      zero,0(v0)              /*            (+128K) */

        lui     a0,0x8000               /* set marker */
        li      a1,0x6d61726b           /* "mark" */
        sw      a1,0(a0)

        li      t0,SR_CM                /* cache-miss bit */

        li      v0,0            /* no cache if we fail the next tests */
        lw      a2,0(a0)
        mfc0    a3,C0_SR
        nop
        and     a3,t0
        bne     a3,zero,2f              # bra if cache miss
        nop
        bne     a1,a2,2f
        nop

        li      v0,0x1000               /* min cache size */
1:      addu    t1,a0,v0
        lw      a2,0(t1)
        mfc0    a3,C0_SR
        nop
        and     a3,t0
        bne     a3,zero,2f              # bra if cache miss
```

```
        nop
        beq     a1,a2,2f                /* check data */
        sll     v0,1
        j       1b
        nop

2:      mtc0    t8,CO_SR
        .set reorder
        j       ra
        .end size_cache
```

E.4 r33kcflu.s

```
============== lib/r33kcflu.s ==============

#include <mips.h>

        .globl r33k_iflush
        .ent r33k_iflush
r33k_iflush:
        # disable ints
        .set noreorder
        mfc0    t7,CO_SR
        nop
        and     t0,t7,SR_IEC
        mtc0    t0,CO_SR
        .set reorder

        # switch to kseg1
        la      t0,1f
        li      t1,K1BASE
        or      t0,t1
        j       t0

1:      li      t0,K0BASE
        addu    t4,t0,511*16
        li      t2,DCIC_I

        .set noreorder
        mfc0    t8,CO_DCIC
        nop
        mtc0    t2,CO_DCIC
        nop
        nop
 .set reorder

1:       sw     zero,(t0)
        addu    t0,16
```

```
            bne       t4,t0,1b

            .set noreorder
            nop
            nop
            nop
            mtc0      t8,C0_DCIC          # restore DCIC
            mtc0      t7,C0_SR            # restore SR
            .set reorder
            j         ra
            .end r33k_iflush
            .globl r33k_dflush
            .ent r33k_dflush
r33k_dflush:
            # disable ints
            .set noreorder
            mfc0      t7,C0_SR
            nop
            and       t0,t7,SR_IEC
            mtc0      t0,C0_SR
            .set reorder

            # switch to kseg1
            la        t0,1f
            li        t1,K1BASE
            or        t0,t1
            j         t0

1:          li        t0,K0BASE
            addu      t4,t0,63*16
            li        t2,DCIC_D

            .set noreorder
            mfc0      t8,C0_DCIC
            nop
            mtc0      t2,C0_DCIC
            nop
            nop
            .set reorder

1:          sw        zero,(t0)
            addu      t0,16
            bne       t4,t0,1b

            .set noreorder
            nop
            nop
            nop
```

```
        mtc0    t8,C0_DCIC
        mtc0    t7,C0_SR              # restore SR
        .set reorder
        j       ra
        .end r33k_dflush
```

E.5 putsable.c

============ lib/putsable.c ============

```c
#define SABLE_TX        *((volatile int *)0xbf00000c)

initsable()
{
}

putsable(c)
{
SABLE_TX = c;
}
```

F

Vendors of MIPS Products

Algorithmics Ltd.
3 Drayton Park
London N5 1NU
United Kingdom
44-71-700-3301

BSO/Tasking
333 Elm Street
Dedham, MA 02026-4530
(617) 320-9400

Digital Equipment Corporation
Corporate Headquarters
Maynard, MA 07154
(617) 897-5111

Embedded Performance, Inc.
3385 Scott Boulevard
Santa Clara, CA 95054
(408) 980-8833

Green Hills Software, Inc.
510 Castillo Street
Santa Barbara, CA 93101
(805) 965-6044

Integrated Device Technology
3236 Scott Boulevard
Santa Clara, CA 95054-3090
(408) 726-6116

LSI Logic Corporation
1551 McCarthy Boulevard
Milpitas, CA 95035
(408) 433-8000

MIPS Technology, Inc.
2011 North Shoreline Boulevard
P.O. Box 7311
Mountain View, CA 94039-7311
(415) 960-1980

NEC Electronics, Inc.
401 Ellis Street
P.O. Box 7241
Mountain View, CA 94043
(415) 960-6000

Performance Semiconductor Corporation
610 East Weddell Drive
Sunnyvale, CA 94086-3650
(408) 734-9000

Siemens Components, Inc.
2191 Laurelwood Road
Santa Clara, CA 95054
(408) 980-4500

Silicon Graphics, Inc.
2011 North Shoreline Boulevard
Mountain View, CA 94043
(415) 960-1980

Index